"*Hungry for Hope* is a rich and nourishing feast, thoughtfully crafted through the collaboration of emerging adults and leading experts to address the most pressing questions of young adulthood. For young adults, this book is a trusted guide—written by peers who offer wisdom, clarity, and language to navigate the complexities of life and faith. For mentors and adults, it is an open invitation to a table set for meaningful, authentic conversations—conversations that young people are eager to have and that our communities desperately need."

—**STEVEN ARGUE**
associate professor of Youth, Family, and Culture at Fuller Theological Seminary and applied research strategist at the Fuller Youth Institute

"This powerful book invites readers to embrace the wisdom of young adults confronting the complex realities of climate change, grief, and injustice. It guides us beyond anxiety toward a courageous, hopeful path of authentic connection. With inspiring clarity, it reminds us that courage can transform our world and churches through collective action rooted in love and belonging."

—**REGGIE BLOUNT**
director of Holy Partnerships Young Adult Initiative at Garrett-Evangelical Theological Seminary

"A veritable feast around a lively table, *Hungry for Hope* is honest, wise, deeply courageous, and an open-hearted call to what the church can become. Thank you for bringing together these beloved voices in this season."

—**JEN NAGEL**
bishop of the Minneapolis Area Synod of the Evangelical Lutheran Church in America

"For those of us who care deeply about the future of our faith communities, *Hungry for Hope* is a remarkable gift. With its chapters cowritten by young adults and their mentors, these reflections invite all of us into a conversation about our most pressing challenges as people of faith committed to being God's hands and fee

future. We must pay attention to these prophetic voices, whose faith and hope for the church offer a compelling path forward."

—PAUL C. PRIBBENOW
president of Augsburg University

"*Hungry for Hope* is a sacred invitation to listen with our whole hearts to the voices of young adults who are longing, grieving, resisting, and imagining. As someone who has journeyed alongside young adults for decades—in ministry, in community, and in the movement for justice—I know the power their stories carry to transform the church and the world. This book is not just a collection of letters; it is a prophetic call for the church to love big, to relinquish control, and to co-create a future with young people at the center. Read it. Be moved. Be changed."

—ROZELLA HAYDÉE WHITE
author of *Love Big: The Power of Revolutionary Relationships to Heal the World*

"A remarkable holy conversation that calls us to challenge assumptions, dismantle injustice, confess complicity, lament trauma, release imagination, embolden courage, and renew hope for the church and the world."

—MARK S. HANSON
presiding bishop emeritus,
Evangelical Lutheran Church in America

HUNGRY FOR HOPE

Letters to the Church from Young Adults

edited by

Jeremy Paul Myers

Kristina Frugé

WILLIAM B. EERDMANS PUBLISHING COMPANY
GRAND RAPIDS, MICHIGAN

Wm. B. Eerdmans Publishing Co.
2006 44th Street SE, Grand Rapids, MI 49508
www.eerdmans.com

© 2025 Jeremy Paul Myers and Kristina Frugé
All rights reserved
Published 2025
Printed in the United States of America

Illustrations by Lindsay Fertig-Johnson

31 30 29 28 27 26 25   1 2 3 4 5 6 7

ISBN 978-0-8028-8552-4

Library of Congress Cataloging-in-Publication Data

A catalog record for this book is available from the Library of Congress.

CONTENTS

Preface — xi

Introduction — 1
Amanda Vetsch and Kristina Frugé
    Our Invitation — 3
    Setting the Table — 5
    Who's at the Table? — 6
    Welcome to the Table — 9

1. What Else Could It Be? Courageous Curiosity and the Postures That Get Us There — 11
Rev. Amber Kalina and Reesheda N. Graham Washington
    Our Invitation — 13
    Defining Courageous Curiosity — 15
    The Gift of Courageous Curiosity — 16
    The Killers of Courageous Curiosity — 17
    Postures for Practicing Courageous Curiosity — 22
    Applying the Postures — 30
    Encouragement for What's Next — 31

Contents

2. Tokenism of Young Adults: Moving from Anxious Relationships Toward Cocreative Communities — 33
Baird Linke and Rev. Kristen Glass Perez

- Our Invitation — 35
- Baird's Journey — 36
- Kristen's Journey — 37
- Transformation Promises Disruption — 39
- Tokenism Is Amplified by a "Hyperarchy" — 40
- Exhausted — 42
- Accompaniment Leads to Authentic Relationships Instead of Tokenism — 44
- Tokenism Soothes Institutional Anxiety — 47
- The Seven Grandfather Teachings Return Us to the Collective — 51
- Holding Hope in Tandem with Reality — 53

3. Destruction and Re-Creation: Wayfinding in a Climate Apocalypse — 55
JD Mechelke and Rev. Talitha Amadea Aho

- Our Invitation — 57
- A Rolling Catastrophe — 58
- Progress Will End Us — 63
- God in the Ruins — 71
- Packing a Spiritual Go-Bag — 75

4. Lament Embodied in Community: Accompanying Grief Toward Genuine Healing — 81
Shaya Aguilar and Rev. Dr. Soong-Chan Rah

- Our Invitation — 83
- Generational Grief — 88
- Theology of Lament — 90

Contents

    An Embodied Psychology of Lament   95
    Untangling Trauma Today   98
    Epilogue   100

5. **Health and Wholeness: Trauma, Anxiety, and Our Call to Mental Health**   103

    Sarah Brock Iverson and Jia Johnson

    Our Invitation   105
    Unpacking Mental Health and Trauma   106
    Unpacking Mental Health and Anxiety   111
    Our Call to Mental Health   117
    Mental Wellness in Community   122
    Conclusion   126

6. **Why Are You So Angry? Power, Fear, and Anger Among Historically Powerful and Historically Powerless Communities**   129

    Rev. Drew Stever and Rev. Dr. Eric H. F. Law

    Our Invitation   131
    Rev. Drew Stever (Pronouns: They/He)   133
    Rev. Dr. Eric H. F. Law (Pronouns: He/Him)   135
    An Exercise in Power   137
    What Jesus's Anger Is and What Jesus's Anger Is Not   148
    Final Thoughts   151

7. **Liberating the Sanctuary: Beyond Marginalization, Intersectionality, and Inclusion to Reach Liberation**   153

    Abby Grifno and Dr. Jimmy Hoke

    Our Invitation   155
    Imagining Liberation   156

Contents

Understanding Marginalization	158
The Journey from Marginalization to Liberation	163
Liberation Means Decentering	170
Imagining Sanctuary to Foster Liberation	171
Taking Steps Toward Liberation	173

8. Sex Is a Gift: The Bigger Gift Is Talking About It — 177
Rev. Madeline Burbank and Kara Haug

Our Invitation	179
Why Is This Hard? A Sex Educator's Perspective	180
Why Is This Hard? A Pastor's Perspective	183
What Needs to Change?	188
Where Do We Go from Here?	196
Made for Radical Intimacy	199

9. Gather at the Table: A Call for Communities Marked by Love and Belonging — 201
Amar D. Peterman and Nicholas Tangen

Our Invitation	203
Diagnosing the Problem	205
Church as a Community Joined Together and Marked by the Centrality of Jesus Christ	208
Turning to Today	212
What Does Christian Community Look Like?	214
Faith Formation Toward a Common Good	222
Creating Communities Marked by Love and Belonging	225

10. Beyond the Walls: The Church's Call to Be in the World — 227
Kayla Zopfi and Dr. Jeremy Paul Myers

Our Invitation	229

Contents

Our Call Beyond the Walls	231
God Is a Public God	234
Young Adults Live Public Lives	237
The Church Is Called to Be Public	240
Holy Trinity and Exodus Lending	241
Where Do We Go from Here?	243
Your Sending	248

11. Reclaiming "Enough": Away from Scarcity Toward True Abundance — 251
Catalina Morales Bahena and Dr. Cherice Bock

Our Invitation	253
Settler Colonialism: Abundance to Scarcity	254
Worth and Value	261
Made in God's Image, from the Soil	264
Moving Toward "Enough"	268
Returning to the Soil	271

Acknowledgments	275
List of Contributors	277
Bibliography	285

PREFACE

In 2018 my colleague Kristina Frugé and I had the pleasure of hiring eight young adults in their late twenties to help us create and lead a project called the Riverside Innovation Hub at Augsburg University in Minneapolis. These are eight of the most tenderhearted and beautiful people I have ever had the opportunity to be around, and this book is dedicated to them. One day we were speaking to an audience of professional ministry leaders when Amanda, one of these young adults, dropped the truthiest of truth bombs. She said, "I don't want people or institutions to know *about* me. I want them to know *me*." And since then, that has been my motivation for this work.

It's not uncommon for congregations and ministry leaders to invest their time and money in noble attempts to learn more about young adults. Unfortunately, it is rare to see the same effort put toward coming to know actual young adults. Thirty years ago, as college students involved with Lutheran Campus Ministry, my peers and I were regularly speaking at congregations about "who Generation X is and how we keep them involved in church." Thirty years before that my parents were running a coffee house ministry on the boardwalk in Ocean City, Maryland, reaching out to the hippies who were living there. Congregations have always been anxious about the next generation. This book is not a book about young adults. It is a book of wisdom from young adults about issues that are incredibly important to them. It is a book in which young adults call the church to look these issues square in the eye, even if we find them haunting and daunting, until we are able to see the hope.

Preface

Much ink has been spilled on how or if the church is dying and how or if it can be saved. This book is not about the church. This book is about the world. Over many years of doing this work, we have not encountered many young adults who spend their days worrying about the future of the church. Instead, they spend their days worrying about human rights, our climate, and safe communities. I have read many books and articles making the case that transcendence is the most urgent thing lacking in the lives of our young adults. This is often lifted up as the reason why the church must work to reengage young adults, because they need the church as a mediator of the transcendent. Yet, in our work with young adults we have seen a growing desire and ability to seek and encounter the transcendent in the immanent. The physical reality of this life, this cosmos, this planet, and all the living things that call it home, is where young people encounter and come to know the love of God. Our young adults are calling us to turn our eyes from the heavens to our neighborhoods.

The Riverside Innovation Hub at Augsburg University is one of twelve innovation hubs created in 2017 by Lilly Endowment, Inc., to engage congregations in innovative ministry with young adults between the ages of twenty-three and twenty-nine. Lilly's Young Adult Initiative made an original investment of $19.4 million in these hubs, and their faithful stewardship of this network has generated incredible insights into the good work congregations are doing with young adults. Our hub is unique in that we are not teaching congregations how to attract young adults. We are helping congregations become more connected to their neighbors, and one of the most effective ways to do this is by allowing young adults to lead us. We are seeking to know young adults and to be led by them, not just know about them. This book is another step into this learning process. Each time we stop and listen to young adults, we learn more about ourselves, our world, and God. We hope this book will amplify their voices and their wisdom, that you might be transformed.

Rather than putting finite resources toward trying to attract young adults, may we be transformed into allowing young adults to lead us into cocreating the world God desires for all living things. May we listen to their constructive and creative theology as they make meaning of a world that no longer makes sense. May we chase after truth with them

Preface

as they embrace the multiplicity of truth claims with an admiration for pluralism that believes truth is relational rather than authoritarian. May we wander and wonder into despair with them, where they will show us what resurrection looks like. May we allow them to pull back the curtains hiding all that haunts us so they might lead us with hope.

Jeremy Paul Myers
June 2024

INTRODUCTION

Amanda Vetsch
Kristina Frugé

OUR INVITATION

My name is Amanda Vetsch, and I have been involved as a young adult leader since the launching of the Riverside Innovation Hub (RIH); this has included coordinating many of the tasks involved in the creation of this book. My voice of invitation joins with a growing body of voices of my peers daring to hope for a better way forward—for the church, but especially for the world we live in. The wisdom shared in this book comes from a deep love of the church, and with deep love come heartbreak and grief, gratitude and joy. We, young adults, have a vision and a hope that a better world, and a better church, are possible. We dare to hope for a church that embodies God's promises of love, grace, and liberation in all aspects of life—from the tangible and mundane to the dreaming of and creation of communities we long to belong to. We lament the ways that the church has created, sustained, and continues to participate in harm, sometimes by action and often by inaction. This book will touch on all of this through the particular focus of each chapter. One thing that makes this book special is that it's a work of love from over a hundred people. The twenty-two authors whose voices are echoed across these pages are joined by many others whose wisdom, love, and grief shaped this book.

In 2022, we had the opportunity to share what RIH was learning from our work with young adults and congregations, and because we continued to emphasize the commitment to being led by young adults, we took up the task of creating this book. What would young adults most want the church to hear about their hopes and laments, their dreams and fears? To answer this question and distill the direction of the book, we gathered fifty young adults from across the United States at Augsburg

Introduction

University in Minneapolis. Over a weekend, the group generously shared stories, and as they did, themes began to emerge. The most common theme by far: grief. Young adults are holding so much grief in our experiences in the church. Many are grieving harm at the hands of church leaders, or harm in the teachings and policies of the larger church. Some are grieving inaction or apathy, as we grieve the hurts and heartaches of our neighborhoods and our planet while longing for the church to show up with us in response. The voices of those gathered echoed my own deep longing for the church to embody the values and commitments I've been taught from a young age, and to apply them in our daily lives, in the face of injustice, harm, and scarcity. As this compelling pattern of grief was named, those gathered for our listening event found themselves on common holy ground—not only the young adults but the forty-somethings, fifty-somethings, sixty-somethings, and seventy-somethings in the room. Grief touches all of us. Some also shared stories in which they experienced their faith community show up and grieve together. The church has in its DNA, in the God story that animates the church's very existence, the know-how and call to lament. In a time of so much grief, the church just may be discovering our next chapter: to accompany the heartache surrounding us, to grieve and heal, together.

This gathering gave birth to eleven themes that have become the chapters of the book. Each chapter is coauthored by a young adult and a thought leader with particular experiences or expertise on the theme of the chapter. Over the course of eighteen months, twenty-two authors (and our RIH team) worked diligently through two writing retreats, crafting multiple drafts of each chapter, consumed innumerable cups of coffee, and logged long hours at the laptop, to bring this book to life. The authors that wrote this book have so much wisdom to share, and I'm so glad you get to meet them here.

The many voices behind this book are inviting *you* to join us in the conversation. We are inviting you to grab your own warm beverage and sit with our voices at the table to wonder about what's possible for the church and for this beautiful, grieving world we share. We are inviting you to trust the wisdom of young adults and to reimagine (or remember!) what might be possible if we truly trust in God's promises for our mutual well-being.

Introduction

SETTING THE TABLE

This book is a third space, a table to meet at and to have conversations that deeply matter. My name is Kristina Frugé, and I've had the privilege and responsibility of stewarding the writing process and compiling and editing this book. All of those involved in its creation have been setting this table with deep care, a sense of urgency, and a prayer that folks will welcome the book's invitation. Young adults are pleading with the church: Don't sidestep the hard stuff in your rush to the resurrection. Sit together on Holy Saturday as we face the heartaches and possibilities of this uncertain time. Sit together and wrestle with complex but important questions that hold the well-being of our siblings, neighbors, and the planet in their grasp. Sit together as we acknowledge the anxiety about an unknown future and take the risks together in hoping for better ways forward.

Each chapter provides an invitation to a table. Chapter 1 describes what courageous curiosity looks like and proposes this posture as necessary for the church and young adults to embody as we approach the present-day challenges lifted up in this book. Chapter 2 orients us to the young adult experience, too often shaped by tokenization. It offers an alternative approach rooted in relationship, one where young adults are valued cocreators for our shared future.

Chapter 3 (on our climate crisis), chapter 4 (on grief and lament), and chapter 5 (on mental health) work together to paint the bigger picture of our times. Our planet and the worlds we have constructed in this place are dying, and the stories of progress we've believed in will not carry us into the uncertainties of the future. On every level of the human experience, grief looms large, often without places to grieve at or people to grieve with. Because of this, from the global to deeply personal fears and sorrows, collectively our mental health is struggling. Together these three chapters name the very hard realities that shape our human experience, while also offering guidance for finding our way in the ruins.

Chapters 6 (on abuse of power), 7 (on marginalization, inclusion, and liberation), and 8 (on sex, shame, and intimacy) reveal some of the particular ways young adults have been grieving as our churches have contributed to harm and avoided confronting the ways change is needed. The themes of these chapters are inherently intertwined.

Chapter 9 brings us back to the importance of community, and how the church can, with insights gained from the preceding chapters, more fully embody a community defined by the centrality of Jesus. Chapter 10 ("Beyond the Walls") further fleshes out the faithful next steps for our church communities. Being centered on Jesus, in fact, means our churches are called to be decentered toward our neighbors, becoming trustworthy partners in God's mending work in the world. Finally, chapter 11 (on scarcity and abundance) lifts up a more adequate and faithful narrative from which we can enter into the challenges before us. A narrative rooted in fear has created scarcity and pursuits of false abundance, but the true abundance found in trusting God makes room for us to reclaim "enough" and root ourselves in relationship, with God, with each other, and with the earth.

WHO'S AT THE TABLE?

The writers of this book carry a wide variety of identities with them. This includes different races, ethnicities, gender identities and sexual orientations, abilities, socioeconomic backgrounds, and ages. This writing community hails from different parts of the country, works across a variety of professions in both secular and ministry contexts, and has been shaped by an eclectic mix of religious expressions. We believe the diverse perspectives and identities held by those authoring this book are an asset. Yet each author is only speaking from their own individual experience and not being asked to represent all people that share their identities or experiences. This also means there are voices and perspectives missing from the author team, and there are therefore insights and wisdom missing on each theme this book tackles. You will also hear distinct approaches to each theme among coauthors, even some disagreement at times. As different human beings, the contributors bring unique perspectives to these topics that deeply impact our lives. This is yet another illustration of how this book is intended to be a conversation partner. It does not say everything there is to say, because the challenges on these

Introduction

pages require ongoing conversation and faithful responses unique to our particular contexts.

The two main characters of this book are given some fairly ambiguous titles—young adults and the church. These labels can mean very different things to different people. These labels can also carry some baggage. When authors of this book use the term "young adults," they are referring to persons roughly in their twenties and thirties, or folks who might fall into the millennial or Generation Z categories. The label "young adults" describes people who are coming of age and engaging the world as independent adults during a particular time in history. The term says much more about the realities and challenges of the wider world context than it does about any particular individual. Their voices have been amplified in this work because of the particular experience this population of fellow humans has had navigating our ever-changing and complex landscape. Additionally, they share a stage in life where the horizon of their collective future is long and what happens on this planet will shape the majority of their lives. The stakes are high.

The church is an equally ambiguous character with many expressions theologically, geographically, historically, and pragmatically. The context in which this book is written is primarily focused on the Christian church in the United States of America. The ecumenical perspectives shaping authors' understanding of the church include mainline Protestantism, Catholicism, the Quaker faith, evangelicalisms, and an understanding of spirituality outside of organized religion. While some themes in this book resonate across the globe and within various faith traditions, the particularities of how these things play out in distinct cultures and places may look, sound, and feel different than what is described here.

The church can also be thought of on the spectrum of the individual humans that make up this body of Christ, our quirky and beloved local congregations, and also as an institution—the universal church. This book is written to "all of the above," although some chapters may emphasize one aspect of the church more than others.

As a reader, you likely identify with one or several of the descriptions of church above. You may be a church member or a college campus pas-

Introduction

tor. You may hold a position of great influence in the church or be a young adult experiencing little power in the church communities you've been a part of. Perhaps you volunteer with young people in your congregation or sit on a committee at your church tasked with discerning what is next for your congregation. You also come from your own social location and with your own lived experiences. Inevitably you will bring those realities and stories with you to this table. Some of these are very much shaped by your access to privilege or identities you hold that afford or deny you power in the contexts that are part of your daily lives. Jia Johnson, a co-author of the chapter on mental health, offers some guidance to consider as you approach the hard but important conversations in this book:

> Depending on your social location, social identity based on race, gender, class, nationality, etc., and lived experiences, your responses to the stories shared will be filtered through those lenses. You may resonate deeply with some of the stories, and others may invoke resistance. You may be confronted with new concepts and realities that are foreign to you or deeply familiar. Your resistance and resonance are opportunities to explore how the Holy Spirit speaks to you through these stories and invites you into a deeper awareness of self, your neighbor, and the broader world around you for your spiritual formation. In those moments of resistance, I invite you to lean in and get curious. Ask the Holy Spirit to reveal to you what you are being invited to see more clearly about yourself and those around you.

As you read this book, periodically pause, breathe, and check in with yourself. These breath breaks are moments that allow for spaciousness between the text and your present experience while reading. What we share in the book may be heavy and activate your nervous system. When those moments occur, it's important for you to tend to your well-being by pausing to settle your nervous system with your breath and attention.

Here is a simple breath prayer to help center and ground you from Christine Valters Paintner's book *Breath Prayer: An Ancient Practice for the Everyday Sacred*.[1] This breath prayer is used when learning some-

---

1. Christine Valters Paintner, *Breath Prayer: An Ancient Practice for the Everyday Sacred* (Broadleaf, 2021).

Introduction

thing new. It is inspired by the prophet Isaiah's words, "Now I am revealing new things to you, things hidden and unknown to you, created just now, this very moment, of these things you have heard nothing until now, so you cannot say, 'Oh yes, I knew this.'" Breathe in and say now, "I am revealing," breathe out and say, "new things to you." For Paintner, this prayer invites her "into a deep trust that there are actions or unfoldings at work beneath the surface." Allow these contemplative practices to be a reminder the Spirit is at work in and through you and your community as you read this book.

WELCOME TO THE TABLE

Whether you are a church leader, church member, young adult, someone who has young adults in your life you care about, or are just a curious reader who finds this book in their hands—welcome! The challenges before us require curiosity, humility, imagination, and trust. Most importantly, these challenges require relationships—people coming together in their own context to wrestle with what it looks like to respond faithfully today. Your experience of this book will be enhanced if you find ways to wrestle with the questions of each chapter in community. *We urge you to find a friend or two who will join you in your reading.* As you read together, we hope what you hear instigates more conversation, taking the implications of each chapter's theme beyond the words on these pages and into your congregation, neighborhood, and context.

There is also a companion website with additional resources to help further the reflection, conversation, and action we hope this book inspires. At our website, www.hungryforhopebook.com, you will find discussion questions to accompany each chapter, some suggested activities, and additional resources recommended by our authors on each chapter theme.

We (Amanda and Kristina) imagine, if you picked this book up, you too have a love for the church that is full of heartbreak and grief, gratitude and joy. Thank you for picking it up. Thank you for your curiosity. Thank you for caring about the intersection of young adults and the church. Let's be abundantly clear from the beginning—this book is not about young adults. It is not a book about how to attract young adults to the church or how to save the church from dying. This book shares the

Introduction

wisdom of young adults for the church, as the church continues to discern how to be God's people in an ever-changing world. Our hope is that you handle this book, and yourself, with care, and that the stories and wisdom shared in these pages compel you to embody God's promises.

1

WHAT ELSE COULD IT BE?

Courageous Curiosity and the Postures That Get Us There

Rev. Amber Kalina
Reesheda N. Graham Washington

OUR INVITATION

Imagine a simple square. Picture the parameters—four even sides, four right angles, two pairs of parallel lines. But consider this question: What else could it be? This simple question has a multitude of answers. Take a moment to consider some answers before reading on.

Welcome back. What did you think of? What else could it be? Perhaps you thought the image could be a window or a door or a photograph. If you took an aerial view, perhaps you found the image was just a line. Or perhaps you found the image has sides and dimensions, meaning it could be a house or a present. Such discovery may have led to more questions: What's in the house? What's in the present? Suddenly, the simple square you imagined is much more than a square; it is something brimming with possibility, because you dared to get a little curious.

Now, what would happen if we told you the square you imagined is a church? Did your mind snap to a church you know, the one you call home or one near your home? Or did it launch a thousand miles high to survey the universal church across numerous lands and languages? Did you see a building? Did you see a collection of people? Now, one more question: What else could the church be?

Like the simple square that can be so much more than a square, we (Amber and Reesheda) are convinced that the church is brimming with possibility. This comes from our own experiences in churches and communities and a deep belief in both the Holy Spirit and the human spirit. I (Amber) am a young adult pastor of the Evangelical Lutheran Church in America (ELCA) in rural Minnesota, where I work to create room in ministry for playfulness and pondering what the Holy Spirit is up to in churches and communities. I (Reesheda) am a Womxnist who leads and consults in the development of human-centered experiences toward inclusivity and authentic curiosity.

This church of possibility comprises people from across the spectrum of ages and races. It is a beautiful melding of varied life and faith experiences. There is so much more that churches could be with their communities, in their communities, and for their communities by becoming a little curious—being willing to think beyond the box.

And yet, the difficult truth is that sometimes churches prefer to stay in their box. They like to rely on the ways of being that have gotten them through in the past, looking to tradition or "the way things used to be" for guidance. This is particularly true for churches that arose in a time when church membership was expected and encouraged by the dominant society, when social cohesion was very pronounced (particularly around the time of World War II), and when trust of institutions was relatively high. In this time, sameness was a social good, and churches found strength and stability in it. However, this convergence of social circumstances, according to Gil Rendle, was "an aberration—a confluence of conditions that prompted growth and strength that later could not be sustained or repeated, not only by the church but by myriad other organizations and institutions."[1]

This confluence of conditions no longer exists. Churches now need ways of being that open them up to more vast possibilities. Churches need postures that liberate them from limited, narrow boxes. Postures that bear the image of their divinely creative Creator, help them discern the movement of the Spirit, and evoke togetherness as the beloved community of Christ in discipleship, ministries, and relationships. For this, the church is going to need a little more curiosity and a lot more courage.

Younger generations—those who did not grow up in the days of aberration Rendel mentions—have been yearning for a renaissance in the church. I (Amber) was a participant in the envisioning process for this book. My young adult peers who put forward the theme of this chapter said some of their most powerful experiences of God's consolation came when the faith community was courageously curious. When faith communities were willing to play and experiment. When they were in-

---

1. Gil Rendle, *Quietly Courageous: Leading the Church in a Changing World* (Rowman & Littlefield, 2019), 23.

terested in knowing who people really were, inside and outside of the church community. When they became more open to the movement of the Spirit. These young adults acknowledged the difficulties that can come with confinement and narrow understandings of what it means to be church—marginalization, minimization, and isolation, to name a few. However, they experienced the freedom found in curiosity and discovered deeper relationships through becoming earnestly curious about others in and around the faith community.

Courageous curiosity is an entrée into discovering how to better engage in the life of the church, and perhaps more importantly, to engage the church in the life and times of humanity. In practicing courageous curiosity, the church will become equipped to hear the yearnings of younger generations and actively listen to what these generations are imparting to it. With these pages we encourage you to get courageously curious, recognize the roadblocks, and explore postures that transform how you connect with yourself, with God, and with others as an individual and as a church community. We hope courageous curiosity will shape your approach to all the other important themes shared by our writing community throughout the rest of this book.

DEFINING COURAGEOUS CURIOSITY

Courageous curiosity is not a new concept invented for this moment—it is something humanity inherently possesses as children made in the image of our creative Creator.

To be curious means to be open to wonderment: about the world, about people, about God, about ourselves. We might think of the often-repeated "Why?" that comes from the lips of children, or the inquisitive "How?" that comes from the mouths of scientists, or the daily "What?" that emerges as people communicate about what is happening in their lives. When we get curious, we acknowledge that there are things we do not yet know. For instance, there may be things we do not know about the person with whom we're engaging; or there may be truths about God that we are not yet aware of; or there may be opportunities that we have not explored yet as the body of Christ. Rather than operating on assumption or autopilot (staying inside the box), curiosity humbly coaxes humanity to engage with the world, one another, and God with more questions than answers. We may not know what the outcome will be, but curiosity opens us to wonder, search, and discover anyway.

While the process of getting curious can feel invigorating, it can also be intimidating, like wading in the ocean, with no certainty about whether your next step will land you on soft sand, a sharp shell, or a wiggling creature. Curiosity brings us into the unknown. Therefore, in addition to curiosity, courage is necessary. To be clear, this does not mean waiting for fear to subside before proceeding—it means being willing to get curious even while being afraid. With racing hearts and squinting eyes, churches must wade forward, asking risky questions, trying out different patterns. To act courageously is to acknowledge that with change comes risk. Yet, we write this chapter with full conviction that the learning, experience, and discovery that lie on the other side of courageous curiosity will always be worth it, for all of humanity, both in and out of the church, recognizing that even what might be considered failure can yield fruit.

At the outset, we wish to clarify that while courageous curiosity considers what is beyond our current understandings and ways of operating in order to consider new horizons, it does not inherently require a complete departure from well-known and cherished traditions. The witness of the Bible illustrates that traditions can be worth treasuring, as they invite us into the rhythms of our faith's ancestry. However, clenching traditions too tightly can become idolatrous and isolating. This behavior can tempt us to place trust in the tradition rather than in the living God. It can cause people to push aside new ideas, especially those posed by people who embody differences, as sometimes experienced by young adults. In these situations, courageous curiosity invites a fresh take on beloved traditions so that the traditions may breathe life into our communities of faith and beyond.

THE GIFT OF COURAGEOUS CURIOSITY

Courageous curiosity is a gift and a practice that has been shared with humanity, especially from a Christian faith perspective. Generatively speaking, consider the reality that God could easily have created humanity without the capacity or desire to be curious. Yet, knowing that creating humanity as curious beings would also mean bestowing the capacity to be disobedient, even unto God, the Lord still opted to make people curious. Why? A curious question, indeed! The Christian faith tradition espouses that human beings are made, every single one, in the *imago Dei*, the image of God. This belief asserts that God's very essence and ways of being are inherent within humanity. Furthermore, Christian faith and doctrine describe a God who was curious to *know* humans and become more intimately entwined with humanity. God put on flesh as Jesus Christ to come and be with humanity, embodying and sharing our human experiences. This was a *courageous* curiosity. God had never before become flesh in the manner that God did when God put on the body of Christ to come and experience life, death, and everything in between. In Luke 22:42, Jesus says, "Father, if you are willing, remove this cup from me; yet, not my will but yours be done."[2] Undoubtedly, this was a courageous decision on behalf of God and Jesus. As is often the case with curiosity, the beauty of the discovery and redemption was tantamount to the trepidation of the invitation—an invitation to be in greater relationship with humanity as ones who bear the image of God.

So, because God is a *courageously curious* God, and humanity is made in God's image, as people, we literally *get to* be courageously and wildly curious, just as God is and has gifted people to be! This is God's beautiful invitation: that the embodiment of becoming courageously curious is acting in accordance with how God and the Holy Spirit move.

THE KILLERS OF COURAGEOUS CURIOSITY

"We can't do that."

Did you feel that—the jolt backward prompted by that statement? If you want to destroy the encouraging energy of courageous curiosity, just speak this statement and watch the bubble burst. "We can't do that" is one of the main killers of courageous curiosity, as it insists on the presence of something permanent that no manner of hope, faith, or courage can

---

2. Unless otherwise indicated, Scripture references in the book come from the New Revised Standard Version.

change, alter, or edit. There are very few things in this world that are actually *that* permanent, but there are many things that are treated as such.

Think of times when these sentiments have stymied vision in a church: "We can't . . ."

- start a new ministry; we can barely afford a pastor.
- give so much money away; we might need it later.
- send our staff into the community; they need to be doing more work for us.
- change the time of worship; those folks just need to wake up earlier.
- try it *that* way; we've always done it *this* way.

This statement can take on a variety of tones. As a pastor, I (Amber) have heard my fair share of them. As you read this section, listen to these tones and take time to ponder, "Which of these tones do I find present in me?" or "Which of these tones do I find present in my church community?"

Hesitancy

One way the killer phrase above is spoken is laden with fear and anxiety. This tone is *hesitancy*. It comes out quavering, perhaps just loud enough to hear. Those who express "We can't do that" with hesitancy have the strong urge to stay put rather than explore new territory because of the unsettling unknowns on the horizon. The dangers of now are perceived as preferable to the untold dangers ahead.

This is not just a tone found in traditional churches. In her book *Pastrix*, Pr. Nadia Bolz-Weber acknowledges that her church community of House for All Sinners and Saints experienced this tone when new people that did not match the mold of her current membership started attending. She writes, "My precious little indie boutique of a church was being treated like a 7-Eleven, and I was terrified that the edgy, marginalized people whom we had always attracted would now come and see a bunch of people who looked like their parents and think, 'This isn't for me,' and if that started to happen I would basically lose my shit."[3] As the

---

3. Nadia Bolz-Weber, *Pastrix: The Cranky Beautiful Faith of a Sinner & Saint* (Jericho Books, 2013), 182.

chapter unfolds, Nadia declares that her fear concerning the changing demographic of her church community prompted an initial reaction of finding a way to convince the "straight-laced, middle-aged men and soccer moms" to leave.[4] It was not until her church hosted a congregational meeting with the newcomers that they realized that having a church where people on the fringes and people in the mainstream could be in authentic relationships with each other was actually healing for everyone. Hesitancy almost hindered these healing relationships from forming.

Sometimes, like in this example, the reasoning behind hesitancy is founded in a sense of reality. There are truly big issues that many churches are facing right now, such as membership decline, financial scarcity, and decreasing societal influence. There are legitimate reasons for concern. Yet, the perceived threats are not always as grand as the correlate hesitation. Sometimes, the feeling of anxiety is simply an indicator that what lies ahead is unknown territory; it is a knee-jerk response to past interactions and experiments that did not yield desired results. In such moments, it can feel like so much can be lost by stepping forward, that "the indie boutique" might get replaced by a 7-Eleven. This feeling makes it difficult to summon the courage and curiosity to move forward. Though such feelings are legitimate, they do not in any way dictate that the outcome on the other side of being courageously curious will be detrimental. We can press beyond hesitancy and transform our anxious energy into curious energy.

Hostility

Another tone that can carry a message of "we can't do that" is anger. This tone is often evoked with a strong sense of loyalty toward what already is or has been. To part ways with the current patterns that have long been held is considered betrayal—a departure from that which is right and good. Sometimes this tone changes the killer statement slightly to say, "We *won't* do that" rather than "we can't."

When the lines of churches become rigid due to hostility, not only does the courageous curiosity become limited in those being hostile but the courageous curiosity of others in the community is also sti-

---

4. Bolz-Weber, *Pastrix*, 182.

fled. A council member lashing out in response to a curious question or idea can be experienced by the person who dared to be curious as a personal attack. It encourages withdrawal rather than engagement, and many have left churches because of the rejection of new ideas, experienced as a rejection of themselves. This is a particularly harmful atmosphere for young adults, as they sometimes arrive at church full of fresh ideas. Simply being their authentic selves is a manifestation of the embodiment of new ways of being. When others respond with hostility toward the newness they bring, young adults often experience it as a lack of care for them. When an adherence to tradition is mandated, young adults may feel that their authentic selves are neglected or not fully welcome.

When Malala Yousafzai, the youngest Nobel Peace Prize recipient in history, was running around as a young girl in her community in Swat Valley, she dreamed of and wondered about a world in which women and young girls could experience a life of peace, health, safety, and liberation. When she was a teenager, she used her voice to advocate for the rights of girls to receive public education like their male peers. This was courageously curious work that Malala was undertaking, but it was not welcomed by all who heard her. Malala became the target of the Taliban, religious extremists who did not think their tradition allowed the public education of women. These opponents responded with hostility to her courageous curiosity, striving to take Malala's life in order to destroy her and her dreams for women and young girls. Malala survived the encounter and continues to be an advocate for the education of women and girls to this day.[5]

Malala's example shows the extreme of how the hostility of "We *won't* do that" can be expressed, though thankfully, not always with success. The newness brought in by courageous curiosity may very well challenge current traditions, patterns, and ways of being in the church and in society. At the same time, newness may very well be exactly what is needed to live more faithfully in community as the image bearers of God. We won't know if we treat it as a threat instead of an opportunity.

---

5. Learn more about Malala Yousafzai and her story at https://malala.org/.

Courageous Curiosity and the Postures That Get Us There

"How It Is"

Lastly, the somewhat monotonous tone of "how it is" is one of complacency that is not concerned with moving forward in any particular direction. The way things are may not necessarily be perfect, but they are not seen as a bother either. The present conditions represent a comfortable place to dwell, causing no real urgency for anyone to embrace change. Curiosity slumbers here and can be difficult to awaken. This tone can be found in churches that are "doing okay in the moment": their financials are solid, no need to push for more; people are content with the available ministry offerings; no challenges are being issued by the pastor or congregation. This can especially be the case for churches that arose in the time of aberration, as stated by Rendle. Communities that feel stable in continuing to "do things the way they have always been done" don't often feel an urge to disrupt their own status quo.

While this tone is neither hesitant nor hostile, it is sometimes harder to break free from than the aforementioned killers of courageous curiosity. When people become complacent, it's sometimes a sign of disconnectedness from the thoughts and emotions found in oneself or in a church community. Complacency sometimes signals a detachment from the ever-changing challenges that impact our daily lives, and from the ever-coaxing voice of the Spirit that drives us beyond our comfort zones to share God's love with the world through word and deed. The task of relinquishing this tone can feel like trying to convince someone who is asleep that they are dreaming. If that someone does not know they are asleep, how can they be made to wake up? If a Christian community is in a blissful dreamland, how can they be convinced to strive for the possibilities beyond the box? The reality is, comfortable though it may be, complacency robs us of the opportunity to discover new ways of being in life together as a beloved community. Embodying beloved community is the impetus for moving beyond complacency.

In the year 2020, churches across the United States experienced an awakening to the limits of "how it is" with the massive disruption of the COVID-19 pandemic. The necessities of masking, distancing, and limiting exposure and transmission to vulnerable populations made it clear that "how it is" is not always "what is needed." I (Amber) was completing my pastoral internship during this time at a Lutheran church in Geneva, Illinois. Early on, it became abundantly clear that we could not do things as they had always been done. Instead, we needed to reimagine traditions in ways that both kept people safe and helped them to stay grounded in their faith and their relationships. We needed to discern new ways to maintain community virtually or at a distance (which unexpectedly made us more adept at connecting with those who were homebound even before the pandemic began). We needed to reconsider everything and plan everything tentatively, knowing that plans might require a pivot at any moment. Our advertising for events always included an asterisk: "*all plans subject to change." The pandemic forced us, and churches everywhere, to wake up from "how it is" to consider "what can be."

Unfortunately, not every church is able to leave behind "how it is" to heed the call of the moment. If someone tries to awaken a church that would rather stay asleep, the church's attitude may begin to take on a tone of hesitancy or hostility. Sometimes churches would rather cling to the illusion of health and vibrancy than open up to the possibilities that could lead to genuinely inclusive vitality. Thom S. Rainer, in his book *Autopsy of a Deceased Church*, calls this tendency "looking at the past as hero." Rainer explains: "The most pervasive and common thread of our autopsies was that the deceased churches lived for a long time with the past as heroes. . . . They often clung to things of the past with desperation and fear. And when any internal or external force tried to change the past, they responded with anger and resolution: 'We will die before we change.' And they did."[6]

We find in "the past as hero" a little of each of the tones expressed above: hesitancy, hostility, and complacency. By being honest about what quells the gift of courageous curiosity in ourselves and our congregations, we can find ways to open up beyond the limitations of "We can't do that" and lean into healthier postures that cultivate courageous curiosity.

POSTURES FOR PRACTICING COURAGEOUS CURIOSITY

Just as there are tones that kill courageous curiosity, there are also *ways of being* that inspire courageous curiosity: authenticity, emotionality, hu-

---

6. Thom S. Rainer, *Autopsy of a Deceased Church: 12 Ways to Keep Yours Alive* (B&H, 2014), 18.

mility, resilience, and reflection. These practices serve as the antidote to the killers of courageous curiosity named above, and will be useful in off-roading behaviors that thwart courageous curiosity. A practitioner is a person actively engaged in an art, discipline, or profession. As you consider the following postures, we invite you to see yourself as the practitioner.[7]

Authenticity

Authenticity, for this discussion, is defined as being true to one's own self, just as one is and just as one believes (holds values) in the moment being considered. This definition leaves a lot of room for one to continue to be shaped and to evolve in a moment. The definition is intended to make room for everyone to be fully present and unapologetic about showing up as one's whole self, even when one's selfhood does not resonate in dominant cultural ways of being.

Young adults today do a powerful job of modeling authenticity by laying claim to their identities and expressing their needs and desires. So often, older adults accuse them of being self-absorbed as they do this. However, to be oneself is not an act of selfishness—it is an act of self-sharing. It dismantles the illusion of and the insistence on sameness that have been emphasized in society and churches since the time of aberration. One size does not fit all, and beauty can be found in seeking to know another as the other is, as well as being known for who oneself is.

Getting present and then remaining true to genuine selfhood, extracting wonderment from within and then *sharing* that wonderment with others, is an act of courage in and of itself! But here's the reality: the only posture that will beget authentically courageous curiosity is one rooted in authentically courageous curiosity. Just showing up authentically might release someone else who was otherwise hesitant (a killer of courageous curiosity) to show up as an authentically curious person as well. Unleashing one's own authenticity is an invitation for others to let go of their own hesitations and instead to get curious. Sharing one's most authentic self might sometimes mean voicing a perspective that others may not share but is important to one's own identity. It might sound something like this: "I know that there is a party-line response to this question, but if I am to

---

7. Pay attention to how to apply these postures in the chapters that are to come.

remain true to myself, it is also important to name the complexities that are still very present for me around this topic." Statements like this can invite others to engage in the embodiment of authenticity as well, and this mutual sharing can lead to greater shared understanding.

It's also important to note the need for reciprocity in our authentic engagement with each other. Authenticity requires a certain amount of vulnerability to risk showing up and sharing our whole selves. I (Reesheda) am simply not willing to expose my truly curious self to one who is not also exhibiting the vulnerability associated with being truly and courageously curious along with me. So often, leaders request, almost demand, this posture, while not themselves being consistently willing to show up in their own vulnerable and authentic curiosity.

Practicing Authenticity

Here are a few ways to cultivate vulnerability and authenticity with others both in and out of the church:

- Admit and share when there is something you don't know that you might be wrestling with rather than hiding your moments of insecurity.
- Model sincerely that no one has the answers all the time as opposed to fabricating responses that lack depth, relevance, and meaning.
- Ask legitimate questions, as opposed to questions that are implicitly intended to judge, shame, indict, or instruct/teach from a didactically hierarchical posture/location.
- Actively and directly communicate to avoid being passive-aggressive, cynical, or sarcastic.

All these ways of being are inherently genuine and allow practitioners to be experienced as sincere and authentic. These strategies breed connection and deepen relationships that foster mutuality, reciprocity, and respect in ways that will enhance future meaningful moments.

Emotionality

Emotionality, for me (Reesheda), is one's own relationship to and ability to both process and respond to observable behavior that is related to the full continuum and range of human feelings. One's ability to see and have a response to an individual's or a collective's emotions is directly related to how effective that community will be at asking relevant, courageous questions. Embodying courageous curiosity without assessing the emotions that are present in a space/interaction can be negligent and harmful. Practitioners simply cannot practice courageous curiosity in a vacuum, void of emotional presence and emotional impact.

Emotionality helps people to know how to connect more deeply, both with ourselves and with others. Think of people as *emotional collaborators*. Emotionality is one's ability to read the feelings of one's own self and others, and to leverage that information to determine *how* to get courageously curious in ways that are healthy and ultimately beneficial to participants.

An example of how to get present to emotionality with others is to create space for people to name their emotions as a part of being with the community. That space making might sound a bit like this: "Many of us may be anxious to move on to the next agenda item, but before we do, I'd like to make room for us to get curious about an interaction that I witnessed in our meeting yesterday." Making space for people to name where they are emotionally increases the trust and rapport necessary for them to hold/carry an environment that makes courageous curiosity possible. This kind of rapport building can often mitigate and diffuse hostility: a natural-born killer of courageous curiosity. The more we can work together to manage our collective emotions, the greater the chances of courageous curiosity prevailing in our church communities and beyond. It is important to note the difference between *perceiving* the emotions of a person or a group of people and doing the work to find out what they are *actually* feeling. This is not about simply asking the coolest or even most provocative questions. Rather, this process couples courageous curiosity with emotionality, inviting people to construct and pose questions that cause them to feel seen in ways that challenge and inspire them to consider new ways of thinking and being in the world.

Practicing Emotionality

In practice, courageous curiosity that infuses emotionality looks like naming emotions and sentiments that are present *before* posing the challenge or discord. When practicing emotionality in courageous curiosity, it is okay to:

- Say what emotions *you are sensing*, and then *ask if your perceptions are accurate* rather than making assumptions.
- Ask if the timing/moment is right rather than prioritizing your own convenience or impulsivity to engage emotionally.
- Manage your own emotions rather than gatekeeping someone else's emotions.

Showing up as the most sincere version of selfhood (authenticity) and discerning the feelings that are feeding/fueling the moment (emotionality) are two characteristics that foster and develop opportunities to be courageously curious. It is important to see how these characteristics also build upon and intersect with one another to form a foundation for being audaciously wonder-full!

Humility

I (Reesheda) define humility as a willingness and openness to receive information and experiences that may be contrary to the most ideal version of how one perceives one's own self or community. This posture helps a person to grow and develop as an individual or with a community. This characteristic is vital to participating in courageous curiosity because in order to consider ways of thinking and being that are different from what one might be accustomed to or value, a person must be willing to momentarily suspend their position, in order to fully take in other possible ways of thinking and being. Humility allows practitioners to quiet the voices of authority inside of self and community, to allow room for other thoughts, ideas, and ways of being to be validated and considered.

Practicing humility at the intersection of courageous curiosity invites practitioners to name the beliefs and values that feel jeopardized. At this intersection, practitioners might say things like, "I believe in everyone having a say, and I want to get curious about your beliefs about leaders always making the decisions, but I am nervous about the implications of what it might mean for my long-held values that have guided and shaped my own life and being." People often feel this way but rarely share with others such vulnerable truths. Doing so requires a posture of humility. Humility requires vulnerability and a willingness to courageously face what might be changed by the new interaction, information, and values. This practice invites assistance, support, and community in holding disparate voices simultaneously. It also holds the potential to establish community *with* people and schools of thought that are quite contrary to one's own.

Practicing Humility

When practicing humility with courageous curiosity, we encourage you to:

- Lean into openness, transparency, and vulnerability rather than arrogance, pride, or power.
- Seek connections and engagement, even in the face of conflict, and resist the urge to disconnect.
- Embrace a posture of discovery rather than doubling down in your own values and convictions.

When practitioners become too certain of their way as the only possible way and their values as the only ones of value, there is very little room to be curious about what else might be possible or valuable. Humility allows practitioners to consider that more than one way of thinking or being can hold value and significance. Unless people are willing to suspend self-held values, they will forgo the opportunity to fully consider what else could coexist with, complement, or coincide with what already resonates within.

Resilience

Resilience is a particular kind of fortitude that is born as a result of enduring something difficult or challenging and coming out of it on the other side. Make no mistake: there is no other way to acquire resilience except by going through and enduring challenging circumstances. Admittedly, this is a hard road to tread, as it is not people's natural proclivity to sign up for challenging circumstances. Nonetheless, the tough terrain is the necessary road that leads to resilience. But at the end of that road is a new strength for staying the course in future difficult circumstances.

I (Reesheda) sometimes think of resilience as the consolation prize for experiencing hardship. While no one desires to endure turmoil, at least the adversity is accompanied by a growing resiliency.

Consider fragility as the opposing force of resilience. Think about the outcome of an interaction where a hard and perhaps inappropriate question is asked of a person who is fragile and lacking in resilience. What might happen under those circumstances? There is a much greater possibility of communication and relationships breaking down. But if even one of the people in the interaction embodies resilience, there is a greater chance of the participants being able to work *through* the difficult conversation together. This is the power of resilience.

Practicing resilience looks a lot like patience and listening. The addendum is that this patience and listening are happening in the face of offense and strife. An example might sound something like this: "I do not agree with what you are saying, and I think that your question is invasive, but I will momentarily give you the opportunity to further clarify your comments." Notice that in this example of practicing resilience, one does not have to abandon one's own truth, feelings, and authenticity. All these elements of self are present, but *how* these elements of self are articulated allows the courageous conversation to continue.

Practicing Resilience

When practicing resilience in courageous curiosity, it is important to:

- Bestow emotional maturity and grace rather than practicing revenge.
- Use power in leadership to wield peace and ease rather that expecting those with less power to be responsible for resolution.
- Stay in the struggle long enough to learn and be made stronger by it, rather than rushing closure or feigning politeness to manufacture closure.

As I (Reesheda) mentioned before, the people who have endured the most hardship in their lives are typically the folks who have the most resilience. That said, it will be important *not* to inadvertently burden the most-burdened people in a given situation or community with harnessing resilience all the time. Rather, when engaging courageous curiosity, engaging circumstances that allow more fragile individuals to practice resilience is powerful to ensure that the burden of bearing resilience is shared equitably.

Reflection

Reflection is the ability and willingness to process ideas, interactions, and circumstances that have occurred. Reflection allows us to better understand, gain new insight, and apply beneficial content to present and future circumstances. Reflection allows us to be progressive and develop mannerisms toward growth and development of self and others.

In order to benefit from reflection, one must be willing to entertain both objective and subjective narratives, which are complementary but serve two very different functions. Concurrently, one must be willing to be honest about the tandem realities of the objective and the subjective and the impact that each has on perceptions of self, each other, and the world. Additionally and consequently, one must realize that reflections, due to subjectivity, may culminate very differently, even if people share the same set of circumstances, in the same location, at the exact same time.

Reflection when engaging in courageous curiosity might look like coming back to a person (including yourself) and saying, "Upon further consideration, I can certainly see how your experiences might lead you to deduce the values and priorities you have articulated, even if mine are not the same as yours." Additionally, reflective practice might cause people to augment value system(s) based on evolving culture or circumstances that might preclude certain elements of beliefs of yore. Reflection begs the need for courageous curiosity and discovery in and of itself.

Practicing Reflection

Reflection is invaluable to the practice of courageous curiosity. Good practices will include:

- Thinking about one another's questions rather than being consumed with your own certainties.

- Considering your own discoveries (revelation) rather than resisting opportunities for epiphany.
- Registering the deepening of your understanding rather than pushing away thoughts that feel contrary to the ways you are accustomed to thinking.
- Getting present to ever-evolving and even more curious questions rather than limiting your engagement due to fear.

Rather than thinking that these engagements end when the conversation is finished, invite layers of continuum into courageously curious conversations, allowing them to linger, with the hope of reengaging them, continuing our relationships over time with one another. Allowing time to be lax and fluid, engaging thoughts and ideas within and with each other invites reflection, leading to further consideration and new opportunities for "second thoughts" to arise. Reflection invites nonlinear, organic, and informal thinking and processing that might not be afforded in a more linear and confined mental model. Admittedly, this is courageous work, as it invites practitioners to relinquish old ways of thinking and being, a sometimes warranted response to reflective practices and processes.

APPLYING THE POSTURES

There are many times that I (Reesheda) have been challenged to take on a courageously curious posture in my own life. One significant moment was when I began to ask myself how shared community spaces, often called "third spaces," could create opportunities for sacred community and epiphany *because* the space was not a church. I asked myself the audacious question: "What would happen if leaders created more liminal and ambiguous space, and continued to be the hands and feet of Jesus within the space (embodiment) in such a way that would draw people to participate and engage, regardless of faith tradition? Would they still feel like they had experienced spiritual formation and transformation together?"

So I took on the postures of courageous curiosity and embarked upon a discovery! With the assistance and support of the Austin and Oak Park communities in Chicago and collaborations with local resources and local vendors, the journey to create L!VE Café & Creative Space ensued.

Courageous Curiosity and the Postures That Get Us There

Together, community members built a space that literally and metaphorically held people in the most joyful and sorrowful of times. Often, as people would leave a community-building event held at the coffee shop, they would say, "Wow! I feel like I just left church!" Every time I heard someone say that over the five-year existence of the coffee shop, I said to myself, "Well, there is your answer." *This* is what happens when third spaces are created to bring people together intersectionally, across faith, socioeconomic, gender, and sexual orientations. It was a scary and audacious question that I had sought out and invited community to entertain together. Our collective, courageous willingness to be filled with wonderment and explore the question together has led to lifelong friendships, the development of businesses and partnerships, and a collectively new orientation to what "faith space" looks like. I eventually sold the coffee shop to the company that served as the coffee roaster, and that company has carried the coffee shop on. Imagine that—courageous curiosity has the capacity to generate visions that outlast the curious ones who originally conceived them! What must this mean for the church?

ENCOURAGEMENT FOR WHAT'S NEXT

It is our hope that this journey of exploring courageous curiosity together allows you, as a bearer of the *imago Dei*, to see this current moment as brimming with possibility for you, for your relationships, and for the church. We hope you were able to get present to some of the limiting beliefs that may have been holding you back from embracing your own engagement with courageous curiosity. We invite you to move beyond intellectualizing wonderment into a fuller embodied practice of discovery by way of authentic and genuine curiosity, as you now have a greater sense of what practices can inform your embodiment of courageous curiosity. The practice of courageous curiosity will create flourishing personally and relationally, to be sure. Poet/activist Amanda Gorman would remind us that quiet isn't always peace, and the norms and notions of what just is, isn't always justice.[8] Courageous curiosity invites us into a

---

8. Amanda Gorman, *The Hill We Climb: An Inaugural Poem for the Country* (Viking, 2021).

more genuine sense of peace and a more equitable form of justice that inspires change, transformation, and healing power in the church.

As more of the body of Christ engages with the postures of authenticity, emotionality, humility, resilience, and reflection, we challenge you to experience a resurgence in the full participation of the church in ways that are diverse, intersectional, and inclusive. This is the more robust manifestation of the church that is depicted in Revelation 7:9, the church that pleases God, manifests beloved community, and is a reflection of heaven on earth. This is the church that thinks beyond the box to wonder, "What else could we be?" in response to the calling of God and the needs of our neighbors.

As you go forth from this chapter into the rest of this book, and eventually into the work of the church, be fulfilled, strengthened, and enlivened by a resurgence of courageous curiosity in your life, practice, and call. May the church, your relationships, and your self be better for it. Selah.

2

TOKENISM OF YOUNG ADULTS

*Moving from Anxious Relationships Toward
Cocreative Communities*

Baird Linke
Rev. Kristen Glass Perez

OUR INVITATION

We begin with gratitude. We give thanks to the Creator of all things for our life and for all of you who are gathered across space and time as you encounter this text. We give thanks also for the circle around you of peers, friends, family, teachers, and all those who have traveled your path with you. We (Baird and Kristen) have spent many months in conversation and reflection with one another about our identities, our hopes, our joys, our sorrows, and our experiences in the church and the world. It is our firm belief that together elders and youth cocreate wisdom structures. We will share some of these reflections with you, from our own voices and stages, past, present, and future. Our invitation to you is to be in conversation and reflection with us, and with elders and youth in your circles. Our narrative is structured somewhat paradoxically. We will share pieces of our journeys and identities that are deeply rooted in our love of the church and in our lived experience of beloved community. At the same time, many of these pieces are also in conflict and contribute to our understanding of young adults experiencing tokenism in the church. We speak for ourselves and not for entire communities or for each other. We speak with distinct voices while pointing toward a shared understanding and experience. Our stories are centered in our identities. I (Kristen) am a cisgender white identifying-female pastor in her forties who lives in an urban setting. I (Baird) am a straight cisgender white male-identifying pastor in his twenties who lives in Montana.

We invite your voice and your experiences into this journey.

BAIRD'S JOURNEY

Many of my peers have drifted away from church without any particular disdain or resentment but with disinterest. Others have made the conscious choice not to engage with institutional faith communities for principled reasons of disagreement with the church or solidarity with those they feel the church excludes. Others still have been actively pushed out by communities that do not support them as they are.

I was raised in and nurtured by the church, and it is still important to me. Over the years I have noticed a common theme show up in my many conversations with older folks in the church who have asked about my relationship with the church. Generally, I am not asked about my faith or what value I find in faith communities. More often people ask what makes me different from my peers. Specifically, they ask what makes me different from their young adult children who aren't involved in church.

I try to be sympathetic to these questions. On a practical level, our communities need young people to have a future. Theologically, we want our communities to reach people of every kind, and it becomes important to reflect on our mission if we aren't meeting young people in their faith. On a personal level, though, it's clearly painful to these parents that their children aren't practicing the faith they were raised in.

I don't know how to respond to these questions. They aren't really questions about me, and I don't speak for my peers. But my experience of young adults, religiously observant, atheist, and agnostic/searching, is that they are not disinterested in questions about God and meaning and morals and community. In fact, many young people are hungry to explore those questions together. And we shouldn't be surprised—young people are people, after all, and people have been asking these questions for as long as they've had questions to ask. I'm actually *not* that different from my peers.

Don't get me wrong. I was a weird kid. There's a strong case to be made that I grew up into a weird adult. I was socially awkward and terminally eager to please. I didn't have much confidence in any of my abilities other than to absorb and regurgitate enough trivia to persuade people that, while I was clearly missing a beat or two socially, I was at least smart. The tried-and-true method of winning friends by being a self-conscious know-it-all.

The church was the place that helped me to calm down. I was accepted there despite my clumsy over-efforts to be liked, and people paid enough attention to coax out the parts of myself that I thought no one would care about. I was encouraged to learn and to sing and to ask questions. It didn't take too long before people noticed the Bible nerd who couldn't shut up long enough to be afraid of public speaking and thought: "Well, now, that looks like a pastor." They poured resources into me and my faith formation. I am deeply grateful for that.

My childhood congregations provided a consistent community (and for that reason, they might be easier to take for granted), but I was also lucky to be formed by outdoor ministry and campus ministry as both a participant and a leader. These specialized forms of ministry stretched my imagination of what faith and community could be for me, especially as I moved into leadership roles and began creating faith-based communities alongside people my own age. These communities challenged me to open up to the experiences and worldviews of others and to become more deliberate in my own perspective and faith.

My deepest friendships have come from faith communities, along with the bulk of my skills and hobbies. I learned to play guitar so I could be like the camp counselors I admired. I grew into my own as an outdoorsman by leading backpacking trips at Bible camp. My sense of calling to fight climate change and build resilient and just communities is the direct result of my upbringing to love God by loving my neighbor. My faith pulled me through my first experiences with loss and anxiety, and my deep love for learning and exploration is rooted fully in experiencing freedom through God's grace. My faith is the driving force behind every wonderful thing I have gotten to experience, and the church has, at almost every turn, supported, empowered, and encouraged me in both tangible and spiritual ways. If there were words to express my gratitude, I wouldn't need to be going on and on like this.

KRISTEN'S JOURNEY

My faith and spiritual life have been deeply formed by my Christian denomination and its institutions and ministries. I often reflect on the promises that my parents made at my baptism to nurture within me the gift of faith and uphold their baptismal promises to raise me in the context of a faith community. That courageous action to get the help of others in a congregation fundamentally altered the course of my life and would take me away from "home" over and over but would also show me that the church is wide and wherever there is the church, there is family. I think about them doing this as parents who were young adults, and I think about my first pastors who were young adults.

At the same time, my identities are deeply held and shaped by colonialism. In a paradoxical reality, it is that same colonialism that also brings me to the church. My paternal grandfather was born on the Leech Lake Reservation in Minnesota and enrolled in the Leech Lake Band of the Minnesota Ojibwe. His mother was from the White Earth Reservation. As a child, my grandfather experienced many of the harms and realities of the colonial church and its presence in indigenous communities. This deeply influenced his own understanding of religious practice, and he became a self-avowed "no church, ever" person. Furthermore, it instilled in him a sense of shame about his own native identity and ritual practices. He left his home as soon as he could and never wanted to look back. In his young adult life, he fully rejected the world of the church that had presented only harm in his life.

After enlisting in the navy and serving in World War II, he met my grandmother. She, from a family of Swedish immigrant farmers, was the definition of a traditional "church person," and her Swedish ancestors built the first Lutheran church in their small Minnesota town. Through their unlikely courtship, they were inseparable and married soon after meeting one another. When their first child, my father, was born, my grandfather shared with my grandmother that she could do "whatever" she wanted with religion as long as he didn't need to be involved. So, my father, born of Ojibwe and Swedish ancestors, was baptized as a Christian and raised in a Swedish-affiliated Lutheran church.

The experiences of my grandparents, nearly a century ago, have deeply influenced my life and career. I didn't learn the full history of my family until I was a young adult. It is only because of the history of my family that I have been connected personally and professionally to the Lutheran expression of the Christian tradition my entire life. Though I express gratitude and joy for those connections, I also experience generational grief and trauma over the wonder of what could have been and what might have been if my ancestors had had the freedom to live as they were fully created.

TRANSFORMATION PROMISES DISRUPTION

From 2017 through 2018 I (Baird) lived and worked in Buenos Aires, Argentina, with La Iglesia Evangélica Luterana Unida, and I had one of my most profound experiences with the Divine. It was a hard year. I had never experienced loneliness like that before. It was also a good year. I had to learn how to let others take care of me without having any ability to pay them back. And for the first time in my very privileged life, I experienced an environment that was not built with me in mind. That's not to say I didn't come in with some ambitious plans to grow as a Spanish-speaker, prayer, and world citizen.

One afternoon I was praying in the chapel attached to the group home I was living in, and I was having a heck of a time with it. I fidgeted on the hard floor and my mind ricocheted from one totally mundane thought to another, all while I gritted my teeth and tried to hold on to any scraps of contemplation I could summon. The minutes ticked by, and with every errant thought my heartbeat got louder and faster in my ears. Was I such a screwup that I couldn't even sit still right? Distracted as I was by this inner twitchiness, I barely registered the feeling that something very funny was happening.

My head pounding, I finally growled in frustration and slapped my hands, stinging on the floor, and asked out loud, "What the hell is wrong with me? Why can't I be peaceful already?" And that's when it happened. It didn't last long, but I felt like someone transcendent was laughing at me. This was completely unacceptable. I was trying to do something spiritual, goddammit. I asked with all sorts of self-important indignation, "What is so funny?" In this moment, I heard, without hearing, a quiet and kind voice say, "You are!" as if it were indescribably delighted with me.

For a moment I felt my pride rankle. I wanted to protest my dignity before this Great Big Laughing Something that I was not funny. I was a very serious—important, even—twenty-something with a butt that had grown numb from sitting on hard tile, yelling to the God who has loved me and blessed me my whole entire life about how unholy I thought I was. But something else caught me, and I saw myself in my mind's eye, trying to force Jesus to love me if I could just be good and still enough, sitting on a dusty floor and perhaps in need of a shower. I finally got the joke.

I tell you without exaggeration, I laughed with God. I laughed from the belly until tears welled up in my eyes and I wheezed for air. I marveled that God loved me so much that God could tease me out of a bad mood. I can count on one hand the number of times someone has been able to tease me out of being cranky, and this encounter with God is one of them. It was God's laughter, warm and sunny and toothy, and it changed me. I subtly sensed that the world was broader and more run-through with possibility than I had allowed myself to hope.

That vision hasn't left me. But it wasn't all I sensed. Something closed off within me, too. After that, there was no way quite back to the cynicism that my heart previously hid behind. I am hopeful now, founded on my faith in the laughing Christ. I can open myself to the pain of the world and the love of God—I can hold both woundedness and healing in my heart at once. This faith in healing has only made me more vocal about the woundedness. I left this encounter with God changed, the kind of change that the church seems to hope for, and I wonder what to do with it.

The world is packed to the brim with places hungry for transformation, but the church often seems most concerned with its own survival. Transformation promises disruption. For an institution in crisis, that's a risk that needs to be managed. For me and for many young people, it can feel like we are asked to display our transformation safely behind glass where it can be admired—celebrated, even!—safe from the possibility of demanding a new way of being from the community.

TOKENISM IS AMPLIFIED BY A "HYPERARCHY"

As a young adult I (Kristen) began to realize that of all my peers from the church system I grew up in—including my own sibling and cousins—I was the only one that remained connected to the institutional church of my youth and our family. And I was somewhat of an anomaly as pastor and professional in the church system. That was curious to me. It wasn't that "everyone else" didn't care about many of the things I cared about, but it was as if there was an open understanding that meaning-making community was elsewhere for most of the people that I knew.

I began to describe what I understood to be a "hyperarchy" of connection—that went alongside the hierarchy of the church. Of the young adults I knew and began to work with professionally, a few were involved in everything—from national to local levels—but especially at the national level. A working and colloquial definition of "hyperarchy" means that those who were connected were hyper- or extraconnected. Similar to hierarchy, there were a few at the top and they were everywhere. The hyperarchy produced outstanding opportunities for a few people, but it was largely based on having "young adult representatives" with no other attention for who a person was, beyond their age. There was no recognition of how varying salient identities were present. Tokenization seems to begin with hyperarchy. From where I sit now, I see this thread from the time of my grandfather through the present time, and I find myself wondering why we are still at this place. Where is it that tokenism, colonialism, and racism intersect in an attempt to disrupt the Divine?

Embedded in the Christian tradition is an understanding of creation as active, dynamic, and something in which God interacts with others, including human beings. As Phil Hefner describes, human beings are created to be creators.[1] The biblical witness has many examples of human beings actively working with God and one another to bring about the next thing. Noah and God work together to bring about a new era in which creation is *almost* recentered. God and Moses are copartners in the liberation of the people. Ruth and Naomi think, work, and actively plan together to ensure their survival. Mary and Elizabeth insist on the greatness of the Lord through their bodies and lived experiences. John and Jesus work as contemporaries to show the path of righteousness. The disciples of Jesus are called to witness the reality of God, now. There are people who are relentless to be healed by Jesus, like those so desperate for their friend to be healed that they come crashing through the roof to

---

1. Philip Hefner, "The Human Story: Created to Be a Creator," Lutheran Alliance for Faith, Science and Technology, December 16, 2013, https://tinyurl.com/78mb63d9.

get to Jesus. As the Christian church is established, Priscilla and Aquila are copartners with Paul and others to spread the gospel.

From the beginning, the story of God's people and the story of the Christian church are a space of dynamic change, cocreation, and active partnership. In these examples, all the people matter. Those that are healed are not simply props or passive participants in the work of creation. Why, then, would we expect a current church to be forged without the active cocreation of young adults? With this as a backdrop, we turn toward unpacking tokenism of young adults. For each of us, that looks different based on our own life journeys. We hope to show some overlapping themes and offer practical tools and strategies for cocreation instead of tokenism.

EXHAUSTED

I (Baird) am grateful for what my faith and faith communities have done for me. My time in Argentina and the transformation I experienced there were made possible by the generosity of faithful people (mostly strangers) in the United States and Argentina. And I am exhausted. I am tired of being called upon to explain my generation. I am tired of being put on a pedestal as an exemplar "young adult Christian" while listening to people complain to me about my demographic. I am tired of being treated like a talisman to ward off people's anxiety about declining church numbers. And I think it is important to talk about pain in relationships before it congeals into resentment.

I don't want to resent the church—the best parts of me are direct products of the love I've received in the church and from people following God. And I've had it easier than many. I fit the bill. I am a blond-haired, blue-eyed, straight, white, Lutheran man with a German last name from a respectable family with professional, happily married parents. I've never worried that some part of my identity would become a barrier between myself and my community. I've never met the first person of my race or gender or sexuality to be allowed ordination in the church. And I am still tired of being asked, over and over, for a magic spell that will get the young people back to church.

I am tired of hearing that the things my peers and I are worried about are too divisive to bring up in church. I am tired of hearing that the best we can hope for from God is a slightly more smiley way of being, when the world I have known is on fire. I have had a pit burned in my stomach by climate change since I was seventeen years old. I entered seminary while living in South Minneapolis during the largest demonstrations against racism since the civil rights movement. The United States was at war for my entire childhood. My adolescence was set against the largest economic collapse since the Great Depression. At every turn, my generation has borne witness to the failure of institution after institution to care for the least of these.

When we hear Jesus's words or read the prophet's cry for justice to roll down like water, we dare to hope that God is still on the move in a world that badly needs a savior. And too often we hear that now isn't the right time to talk about it. Of course, we are told, Jesus cares about racism, homophobia, sexism, poverty, and violence; and of course, the Spirit groans with creation; and yes, God is on the side of the poor and the meek, but giving is down this month and we don't want to give anyone a reason to leave. So, until we're in a less tenuous position, let's leave aside Amos's urgency. Leave aside Paul's courage and Mary's song for the lowly, and let's put the kingdom of God just a little more out of hand.

It is interesting to me that the conversation is always about who we are afraid to lose rather than who we hope to welcome in.

This is where the concept of tokenism enters the picture. Usually "tokenism" refers to the ways an organization makes the minimum effort to appear inclusive and diverse without fundamentally changing anything. It is essentially a process of objectification. People are cultivated for the type they represent more than for the stories, hopes, and gifts they carry within them. In the process, complex human beings are flattened into mascots, deployed to deflect accusations of stagnation and homogenization. (Our communities don't have a problem with "those people"! We know several of them!) When the church is worried about staying relevant but anxious about change, tokenism is a convenient coping mechanism.

I had an interview with an aging congregation. Nearly 70 percent of their members were over seventy years old, and they didn't have any members under thirty-five. The interview committee reflected this. Only one member was not retired. But at the end of our conversation they surprised me by telling me they had a high-school student on the committee, but of course they had class during our weekday afternoon meeting. Throughout the scheduling process they had never mentioned this high schooler, much less brought up the scheduling conflict. This was tokenization. They had asked a young person to be a part of the process in order to check that demographic on their paperwork and proceeded to leave them out of their considerations for the rest of the process. They didn't respect this person's opinion enough to make considerations for their ability to participate. This wasn't out of cruelty or malice but out of thoughtlessness and the goal of simplifying the messy process of scheduling a large group of volunteers. That's the rub. Tokenization is always a matter of practicality and not of relationship. That's why I believe tokenization is unworthy of faith communities.

This is one relatively mild example among many. Age is one of the many possible demographic indicators that could be leveraged to tokenize people, though it is different from the way tokenization weighs on people with marginalized identities. Racism, sexism, and queerphobia are all also expressed through tokenization and are not bound by age. That said, age-based tokenization came up as one of the most commonly shared experiences of the fifty diverse young adult participants at the visioning event that formed this book. Young people from around the country and from many different backgrounds described their experiences of feeling wanted by faith communities to tick a demographic box but not to be a part of transforming the community.

ACCOMPANIMENT LEADS TO AUTHENTIC RELATIONSHIPS INSTEAD OF TOKENISM

At this time, I (Kristen) have worked for twenty years in faith-based and nonprofit organizations, including higher education as both a program developer and a chaplain. One of the great privileges of being a university chaplain is accompanying people through life as it happens. People choose to share their life moments with me, and I receive those with gratitude and humility. I say "life as it happens" because life isn't always as we wish it was happening, but as it is. I often say to people who are unsure of what is next—let's begin with what we have, then go from there. You don't have to figure everything out; you just have to figure out the next thing. And then, the next thing. Perhaps a more graceful answer comes from Krista Tippett, who said, "Imagination is our gift as a species to move purposefully toward what does not yet exist and walk willingly through the unknown to get there." She adds that "reimagining the future works with a 'long sense of time.'"[2] The "long sense of time" is going to transform the meaning of this moment. But right now—there's a door. Let's move through it.

These are some of the things I've learned by moving through doors to unknown destinations. Faith communities wanting to disrupt the hyperarchy and move away from tokenism into cocreated communities will need to adopt a similar posture. Below are some tangible principles that help us cocreate rather than tokenize.

Go Where You Are Invited

At twenty-six, I began a new job as the director of a new program in a national faith-based organization. We had a four-figure annual budget. You read that correctly. That leadership experience showed me the power of grassroots organizing and the power of the collective. My primary investment was in people. I spent eighteen months going where I was invited, doing more listening than talking, convening networks and other groups to imagine something new. The result was that local networks facilitated development of the program that met the needs of their own communities. From that grew the capacity of the national program. That experience also taught me that there is a difference between power and credibility. Just because you have "power" doesn't mean you have credibility. Power comes with one's status or role; credibility comes from the community. Power is given, credibility is earned. Relationship trumps doctrine, at every level. When you go where you are invited, you are building capacity for credibility.

For college chaplains, everything we do follows the invitation of young adults. We don't do anything without the collective design of young adults, full stop. They are not endorsing decisions that I make.

---

2. Krista Tippett, "Three Callings for Your Life and for Our Time," Middlebury College Commencement Address, May 26, 2019, https://tinyurl.com/5rfvp3xy.

Instead, we are cocreating community and comentoring between age groups and identities. We recognize that there isn't a single person or community who knows everything about everything. And "success" is defined by meeting the needs of our community, which we set out to do.

The Best Self Is the Whole Self

Recall Baird's earlier narrative about his profound experience laughing alongside God. Each one of us is a whole person of mind, body, and spirit. This section began with reflections about accompaniment. Acknowledgment and accompaniment work together to build resilience. Megan Devine describes a beautiful sense of accompaniment through her description of acknowledgment as "being seen and heard and witnessed inside the truth about one's own life."[3] In my work, that is exactly what I want to do. Accompanying and acknowledging the wholeness of the young people in our communities is another way we actively work against tokenism.

Most of life is what I call accidental selfie. Let me explain. The usual things that we see on social media or send to people are cultivated; they are what we think are the best of us. Accidental selfie is when you turn your phone on to take a picture of the food in front of you but instead it snaps an image of you at the most unflattering angle. And you might get fifty screen bursts of that. When that happens to me, I recoil from the image of my selfie on the screen. That's not what I want to see—I don't want to be reminded of how I really look at any given moment. What if we started to think of those moments also as the best of us, because they are real. They are the answer to the question: How are you doing right now? Our lives contain so many moments—joyful, surprising, funny, inspiring. But they also contain moments of deep pain, sorrow, anger, frustration, and fear. We might all find it refreshing to share these real pictures, our real selfies. The topics in this book are a chance to do that—to look at our real selves, our real communities—and be in real conver-

---

3. Megan Devine, *It's OK That You're Not OK: Meeting Grief and Loss in a Culture That Doesn't Understand* (Sounds True, 2017), 56.

sation with one another. This is the radical yet simple way to disrupt the hyperarchy and tokenism.

Pay Attention to the Diverse Religious Experiences of Young Adults

Over the last five years, my life has been increasingly shaped by work alongside non-Christian communities and chaplains. I have hired and supervised Jewish, Muslim, Hindu, and Buddhist young adult chaplains and worked very closely with young adults from those identities. Much of that work also intersects with those who identify as spiritual but not religious. These communities have often been self-organized. They always host and plan ritual events and community-wide events that are open to all.

Tokenization of young adults is often framed only from a white, Christian perspective and is experienced very differently in nonmajority young adult religious communities. Feeling tokenized isn't necessarily the primary worry of young adults from these religious communities within the United States. There are more pressing concerns like a lack of knowledge about their traditions by those outside their religious communities, as well as very present threats, including Islamophobia, antisemitism, and anti-Hindu sentiment. Colonialism is still very real. These young adults have told me of their pressing and primary need to share rituals and practices with the broader culture, so that their peers might understand the religious, cultural, and worldview lenses they see through. There is also a strong desire to communicate that there is great interreligious diversity within each tradition. Perhaps this is a reaction to a different kind of tokenism—the one that doesn't recognize the internal diversity of non-Christian religious traditions.

TOKENISM SOOTHES INSTITUTIONAL ANXIETY

Lakes of ink have been spilled on my (Baird's) generation's distrust for institutions. It seems likely that this stems from the fact that systemic thinking is the only way to process the overwhelming chorus of pain streamed to us in real time. Humans have never been able to see real-time responses from normal people to crises on the other side of the world before. Nor have we had the ability to send direct aid with a few taps of a button. All this creates a plausible sense of responsibility for humankind's suffering that hasn't been possible in all of human history. Our brains are not set up to cope with the true depth of agony and injustice experienced by billions of people all at once. In the meantime, we learn every day of the new ways that the economic and political systems of the world siphon money, resources, and power from those who already have very little. The myths that veil our economic, religious, and political institutions in prestige are being peeled away. And layer by layer we find flawed, earnest, greedy, sinner-and-saint human beings underneath. The tension between this feeling of individual proximity to suffering and the institutional failure to address it drives an understandable sense of despair. In the face of powerfully flawed systems, how do we live out lives of faith in God that aren't passive abdications of our duty to our neighbors? That seems like a question faith communities should be interested in seriously asking.

Yet the mainline, white Anglo-Saxon Protestant churches in the United States are well adapted to being institutions of the mainstream of American culture. They don't have a history of shaking up the status quo. They have been known to adapt to the new center, but only after marginalized groups, like Black Christians in the civil rights movement, drag the country closer to its promises. History has shown that they rarely step out of a comfortable place of theological critique or quietism into a place of prophetic conflict. Still, people are transformed through their encounters with God and the world in these same churches, which then roll their eyes at the naïveté of the young people they raised to be hopeful. All the while, we hear the litany of anxiety for the future of the church murmured on and on.

Institutions of all kinds are systems designed to perpetuate themselves. "The church" (the thing consisting of communities of people, collections of assets, and reams of documents; not the spiritual reality bound and upheld by the Spirit) is no exception. The truly amazing thing about systems is that they create emergent principles—that is, they develop in unanticipated ways.[4] These emergent properties develop ad-

---

4. Donella H. Meadows and Diana Wright, *Thinking in Systems: A Primer* (Chelsea Green, 2008).

aptations in response to different pressures like financial constraints, environmental shocks, and competition.

The trouble is, these emergent adaptations are mostly unconscious and in response to pressures that seem disconnected to questions of mission and purpose. The interview committee's desire to smooth the scheduling process led to their disregard for their high schooler's needs, almost certainly against their organizing values. Anthropologist David Graeber describes the temptation of institutions to operate out of the narrow, practical demands of a specific pressure building over time to separate the actions of the institution from its values: "[Bureaucracy] appeals to us . . . it seems at its most liberating—precisely when it disappears: when it becomes so rational and reliable that we are able to just take it for granted that we can go to sleep on a bed of numbers and wake up with all those numbers snugly in place."[5] Because we are reliably unreliable narrators of our actions, organizational psychologists design studies to identify the "experiential" rather than the "expressed" values of a system in order to understand it. For example, a pharmaceutical business might express the value of healing the sick, while the experience of their business practices shows that they hoard the patents for life-saving medication or neglect supply chains to poor communities to maximize shareholder returns.

Faith communities are not exempt from this tendency. We can see this in dramatic ways, like the Southern Baptist Convention burying long histories of sexual abuse in the name of winning people to Christ,[6] and from mundane practices of tokenizing young people to assuage fears of decline. Unfortunately, we young people are pretty poor messiahs.

The church is setting itself up for an endless cycle of anxiety when we attach our understanding of the church's health to demographic data, especially a demographic marker as fleeting as young adulthood. For all we sing about the church being more than a building, the institution functions as an institution. The great temptation of the institutional church

---

5. David Graeber, *The Utopia of Rules: On Technology, Stupidity, and the Secret Joys of Bureaucracy* (Melville House, 2016), 74.

6. Chantal Da Silva and Kurt Chirbas, "Southern Baptist Leaders Release Once-Secret List of Accused Abusers," *NBC News*, May 27, 2022, https://tinyurl.com/3s9wetzm.

is to seek the tangible, numerical predictability that institutions always crave. But this is the logic of shareholders, not disciples.

Young people are not the church's savior, and we often respond the way people tend to when they have too much pressure put on them in a relationship. We leave. And those of us who stay often feel the burden of being made into a symbol rather than a person, a charm against the decline of the church and a place for the institution to deposit frustration, hurt, and resentment. No wonder so many of us are drawn toward the hyperarchy, which at least gives a sense of status or a career trajectory in exchange for objectification.

I am not cavalier about the church and the true and astounding good that only large organizations can do. I am a pastor, and I take my call as a steward seriously. I don't want to see the systems that the church has built and repaired and renovated and adapted to care for our neighbors fall apart. I owe a debt of gratitude for the church and how much it has invested in me personally and professionally, and I intend to pay it forward. The investment that the church makes in young people is transformative—we are transformed by God, and we want to point toward the God that transforms us. There is mutual frustration felt, though, when the church wants us to point back to the institution.

My gratitude and allegiance to the church are why I feel so strongly that we have to take on this self-reflection, no matter how painful it might be. The good news is that we are better equipped than many, with reflection, confession, repentance, and forgiveness at the core of our life together. These practices offend our ego. They remind us that we are not saved by our cleverness, by our earnestness, or by the righteousness of our cause. They remind us that we need each other, need transformation, need God. The challenge to the ego of all transformative institutions is the reality that in order to transform others, you have to be willing to be transformed by them.

Ultimately, the work of Jesus is liberation from sin and death in all its expressions, both spiritual and tangible. We are united with his life and death and resurrection in our baptisms and with his work in our love and acts of mercy for our neighbors and all of creation. This book contains examples of where God is leading young people into the world right now. The words on these pages are an invitation and a longing to have this conversation together.

THE SEVEN GRANDFATHER TEACHINGS RETURN US TO THE COLLECTIVE

Anishinaabe is a collective term that refers to a group of culturally related Indigenous peoples in Canada and the United States who share closely related Algonquian languages but have specific historical ties to the peoples of the Council of the Three Fires, which includes the Ojibwe, the Odawa, and the Potawatomi. A powerful image stands out as I (Kristen) think of elders and youth cocreating together. It comes from my experiences of the indigenous practice of making camp together.[7]

In making camp together so many things could occur . . .

- we had to commit to making the camp safe for everyone,
- we would learn from each other,
- we would make new relationships that could last a lifetime,
- we would do our part in serving and caring for each other,
- we would be mindful of the impact we had on one another with our words and our actions, and very importantly,
- we would practice reciprocity—showing our gratitude for what was shared and what was given.

We would then take all those experiences, new ideas, and new relationships back to our home communities and share—seeing the impact grow exponentially.

Camps are also seasonal. Each season of camp is really important— and its tasks, stories, and rituals can often only be done in that season. Each season has elements of magnificent things, terrible things, and mundane things. Without each element, we would not have the others, and they exist alongside each other. It is also true that there are seasons

7. Kristen Glass-Perez and Pamala Silas, "Land Acknowledgement and Invocation," Northwestern University Commencement, June 13, 2022.

Tokenism of Young Adults

in which we are ready to receive things differently than we are in other seasons. The same might be said about our journey through different generational stages of life. There is a time for elders, and there is a time for youth. Neither is to be disrespected, but rather, they are to be honored as their own seasons.

In the early 1900s ethnographer Frances Densmore interviewed Nodinens (Little Wind), an Ojibwe woman raised at Mille Lacs and White Earth. This is an excerpt from her account of winter:

> When I was young everything was very systematic. We worked day and night and made the best use of the material we had . . . when the ice froze on the lake we started for the game field. I carried half the bulrush mats and my mother carried the other half.
>
> My father was a good hunter. It was the custom to give a feast with the first deer or other game that was hunted. And all the other families were invited to the feast. . . . When we got to the sugar bush we took the birch-bark dishes out of the storage and the women began tapping the trees. Our sugar camp was always near Mille Lac[s], and the men cut holes in the ice, put something over their heads, and fished through the ice. . . . Toward the last of winter my father would say, "one month after another month has gone by, Spring is near and we must get back to our other work."
>
> In the great living and ongoing reality of the people of the creation, we meet in different seasons of camp. In this place—, we are gathered to begin to have a summit about these tasks that each one will do—and that really matters—and that we don't all do but all need to get done. We are interwoven. We are the co-creators. Being in camp is grounded in reciprocity, generosity, partnership, and slowed down to meet this moment with one another.[8]

When we make camp, we honor the season that we are in and then change with the seasons. In Anishinaabe history, the seven values or Grandfather Teachings that were gifted to the Anishinaabe are love, re-

---

8. Quoted in Frances Densmore, *Chippewa Customs* (Minnesota Historical Society Press, 1979), 68.

spect, truth, honesty, bravery, humility, and wisdom.[9] As I live an embodied life of multiple identities, these values ground me. They show the way even as I am called to be open to the ways that they challenge and teach us about what it means to be in community. As we imagine together about being church and continually make and break camp with one another—may we acknowledge new relationships, and all that we have received from each other. May we return safely home. May we be generous with our stories and share the skills and knowledge that we have gained while in camp together. May we be good stewards of the land—on whatever lands you call home. This is how we begin, in camp together, in a circle, to disrupt the patterns of hyperarchy, tokenism, and colonialism.

HOLDING HOPE IN TANDEM WITH REALITY

The events of the last years have upended life and our normal ways of functioning in communities. The COVID-19 pandemic created a profound loss of human life, economic hardship, and social isolation. Embedded within the pandemic are the omnipresent pandemics of racism, white supremacy, and loss of human life due to police violence and social and economic inequities. In particular, a mental health and loneliness epidemic, especially pronounced with young adults.[10] These factors, along with deep political divide, and renewed urgency for racial justice in the world, have left us forever changed. At the same time, these experiences contain moments of hope held in tandem with our challenging reality. The incredible work of scientists creating new vaccines and treatments for an emerging disease. The massive efforts of frontline healthcare workers caring for the sick and dying. Activists giving productive voice to profound frustration over justice delayed and denied. The stories of all of us, in ways big and small, reinventing our lives and our work in the face of deep challenges while also creating new ways of being community. This is the space of the church. An opportunity to be in camp

---

9. See the Seven Generations Education Institute, https://tinyurl.com/4np359nh.
10. Varun Soni, "There's a Loneliness Crisis on College Campuses," *Los Angeles Times*, July 14, 2019, https://tinyurl.com/3rhtf8n5.

with one another—in real communities with youth and elders together. It is a chance to go where we are invited, embodying the postures of curiosity, ready to practice reciprocity. It is a chance to be humbled by the vastness of the divine and be called to witness the new season unfolding. What is important to young adults is what is important to all of us.

There are plenty of reasons to read a book like this. Some may believe that one of those reasons is to figure out how to get young adults back to church. We don't want to dismiss that reason. There are gifts in community and in the church that we all want to share. Yet we have seen how if we aren't careful, getting young adults back to church can ultimately lead to objectifying—and alienating—the very people we want to be in community with. Instead, we want to invite you to engage with us and the other authors of this book. You are invited to listen with courageous curiosity, to seek to understand God's call for all of us and to be open to discovering what our path forward might look like, together.

3

DESTRUCTION AND RE-CREATION

Wayfinding in a Climate Apocalypse

JD Mechelke
Rev. Talitha Amadea Aho

OUR INVITATION

Our world is changing beyond recognition. The fact of change may not be surprising—our world is ever changing, and people of faith learn to cope with change. But this one is bigger. We are facing the end of climate stability. It is not coming; it is here. The world is ending—now—and we must learn how to continue after the end of the world as we know it. The church, along with all that is bound to the earth, must adapt faster than we could have believed necessary. Where is God, when God's creation is dying? In the rolling catastrophe of the climate crisis, people of faith must face the ongoing ending of worlds and invent a new spirituality of God-finding in the ruins. We must let go of the hubris hope that falsely proclaims a future victory over the climate crisis, a future of endless progress. We must dwell instead in hopelessness and learn to cope without hope. This sounds terrible, but it is a necessary and life-giving journey. In our personal spiritual lives we—JD and Talitha[1]—have made that movement from shock and horror to acceptance and creativity, and learned how God can be found in this new landscape.

What are the stories that help you make sense of the future? We all have them. All of us, religious or not, follow myths that help us understand where we've been and where we're going. The myth of progress is one on my mind. How have stories of progress helped organize your life? Onward technological innovation: after all, you know who invented the first lightbulb and the airplane. Expansion and discovery: onward,

---

1. JD is a PhD student researching and writing about political theology, vocation, and climate change. Talitha is a Presbyterian pastor turned pediatric hospital chaplain in Oakland, California. Both of us are white, queer, outdoorsy millennials.

whether on to Mars or into Chinese markets, even if forever haunted by the sins of Christopher Columbus. The American Dream: with enough hard work you will be better off than your parents—bigger bank account, bigger house, offspring of success and influence. The New City and the New Earth: that no matter the trouble we get ourselves into, God's providence will lead us from the stormy seas of the present onto a safe heavenly shore. But these days, as temperatures and oceans rise, time is out of joint. Things are getting worse, not better. As the climate crisis begins to make this myth of progress unbelievable, in the ruins of our time, what stories can we believe in? Can we find God in these ruins?

A ROLLING CATASTROPHE

For many around me (JD), moving out of a house and into a home-on-wheels didn't fit into the myths of their lives, or mine. It was my first fall living on the road. I'd planned to spend it in South Dakota's Black Hills—the land of the visions of Black Elk, heyoka and warrior of the Oglala Lakota nation.[2] The Black Hills are sacred land of the Lakota, a nation forcibly removed even after protection of a stern US treaty. A treaty that lasted no longer than the discovery of gold. The American stories of expansion and discovery, capital and extraction, turned hills and homelands into mines. Just like gold, something else was being extracted from sea to shining sea, made manifest by a "divine" destiny: fossil fuels. But extraction piles up externalized costs. With gold, that cost fell on the land and the Lakota: war, massacre, and forced displacement. With fossil fuels, that cost is an exponential growth of greenhouse gases in our atmosphere, now wreaking havoc on our collective home. Both gold and gas tell us stories of progress and ruin.

When I climbed into those sacred hills that September, I was assaulted by a heat wave that pushed temperatures forty degrees higher than average. It was as if the "mighty flowering tree"—the symbol of Earth and all that is bound to it in Black Elk's vision—caught fire. Living without air-conditioning or the reprieve of cool nights made temperatures

---

2. You can find more about Black Elk's story and vision in John G. Neihardt, *Black Elk Speaks*, the complete ed. (Bison Books; University of Nebraska Press, 2014).

above 100 unsafe. I couldn't sleep through the sweat and body aches. So I lay there under the heavy, grimy heat, worried whether my solar system's batteries would become inefficient and possibly dangerous in the noonday heat.

While being a nomad makes me more vulnerable to the sights and smells of our changing climate—heat, fire, smoke, drought, floods, storms—I'm also more mobile, more adaptable. Within a few days' drive I found mild fall weather two thousand feet higher in the land of the Ute in the north of Colorado's Front Range. In those weeks, down in the lowlands of the western United States, almost one thousand all-time heat records were being scorched. Time is out of joint.

On the other side of the country, the weather was extreme in a different way. The heat-storing Gulf of Mexico—warming twice as fast as the rest of the ocean—was refueling Hurricane Ian's strength as it pummeled Florida with winds up to 155 miles per hour and once-in-a-thousand-years level of rainfall.[3] For days I couldn't get hold of my mother. A thousand years passed while I sat with her last text from the bathtub: "Shit just got real."

When I arrived a few days after the hurricane had passed, I thanked the neighbors who helped my mom in the wreckage left behind. The house was uninhabitable. Ceiling caved in. Water everywhere. Sewage in the air. The backyard's massive live oak, older than George Washington's axe, had crashed into the canal.

Cell service was spotty. "We have to make this quick," I explained to my partner, Andrew. "Service cuts calls off at 60 seconds. No electricity. No water. Dad and I have just retrofitted the front yard into a campground. Thankfully we're used to living off the grid."

There have always been storms and fires, droughts and blizzards, but something is different now. Though unequal across our species, human activity has made possible the collapse of modern civilization. As global greenhouse gas emissions have yet to peak, our actions can no longer prevent this rolling catastrophe, only its intensity. Within my lifetime,

---

3. "Hurricane Ian's Path of Destruction," NOAA, October 4, 2022, https://tinyurl.com/mrfpjjch; "The Gulf of Mexico Is Getting Warmer," NOAA, February 1, 2023, https://tinyurl.com/yeywphvc.

the realm of the possible includes a world of 1.2 billion climate refugees, a world that—outside of Canada, Siberia, northern Europe, and Patagonia—would often be uninhabitable from direct heat.[4]

But climate crisis is not in the distant future, it is a rolling catastrophe that has already arrived. Pacific islands are vanishing and shrinking in rising seas; Pakistan is reaching organ-failure temps; in one year, an expanse the size of Syria burned in Australia; Utah's Great Salt Lake nears death, foreshadowing dust storms of arsenic and heavy metals. In southern Africa, the immense and storied baobab trees I once hid inside, some more ancient than the Tree of Jesse, are dying sudden and tragic deaths.[5]

For the last 11,700 years, human civilization has thrived in the relatively climate-stable epoch geologists call the Holocene. But a new epoch of climate volatility has emerged—the Anthropocene.[6] The Anthropocene is the proposed name of a new geological epoch defined by us humans, *anthropos*. From physical sciences' vantage, the Anthropocene

---

4. "Over One Billion People at Threat of Being Displaced by 2050 Due to Environmental Change, Conflict and Civil Unrest," press release, Institute for Economics & Peace, September 9, 2020, https://tinyurl.com/56a89s7k; Gaia Vince, "How to Survive the Coming Century," *New Scientist*, February 25, 2009.

5. To be clear, on the vanishing of Pacific islands, the relevant study attributes sea-level rise to a combination of both anthropogenic climate change *and* Pacific Decadal Oscillation. Simon Albert et al., "Interactions Between Sea-Level Rise and Wave Exposure on Reef Island Dynamics in the Solomon Islands," *Environmental Research Letters* 11, no. 5 (May 6, 2016), DOI 10.1088/1748-9326/11/5/054011. For another prominent example of sea-level rise, see Sönke Dangendorf et al., "Acceleration of U.S. Southeast and Gulf Coast Sea-Level Rise Amplified by Internal Climate Variability," *Nature Communications* 14, no. 1935 (April 10, 2023), https://doi.org/10.1038/s41467-023-37649-9. For more on Pakistan and the baobab trees, see "Postcards from a World on Fire," editorial, *New York Times*, December 13, 2021. For Australia see Kate Walton, "Mass Evacuation as Catastrophic Bushfires Worsen in Australia," *Al Jazeera*, January 4, 2020, https://tinyurl.com/yvkswdb7. And for the Great Salt Lake, see Margaret Osborne, "Drying Great Salt Lake Could Expose Millions to Toxic Arsenic-Laced Dust," *Smithsonian Magazine*, January 13, 2023, https://tinyurl.com/3cakkkfc.

6. "Working Group on the 'Anthropocene,'" Subcommission on Quaternary Stratigraphy, accessed December 9, 2024, https://tinyurl.com/fh2tsu42. See also *Newsletter of the Anthropocene Working Group* 9, December 2019.

names not only human-caused climate change (fossil fuel emissions and the greenhouse gas effect) but also a myriad of other human-driven changes: the movement of species, biodiversity loss, mass extinction, ocean acidification, catastrophic changes in the global nitrogen and phosphorus cycles. I find these technical terms helpful—Holocene and Anthropocene—because it forces me to radically shift the way I think about the future and the stories we tell about it. We can no longer act like humans in Holocene—the stories that have shown us the way won't help anymore. Not in the Anthropocene.

We've been replacing lawns with native fauna, avoiding single-use plastic, installing solar panels, joining local protests against fossil fuel development. But it isn't enough. It will never be enough. Our individual acts of repentance were never enough to wash away the systemic sins of extractive capitalism. Emissions, seas, and temperatures are still rising. Things are still getting worse. For the rest of my life, things will get worse. As the story of living in a world of perpetual progress perishes, what stories can we tell? What hope can we find? What God can be kept?

I (Talitha) have come to understand that climate change is not always a heat dome and a hurricane. Sometimes it is more ordinary. Sometimes it looks apocalyptic—like the months of red skies in California's fire seasons—but other times it is only apocalyptic to the people experiencing it, when your insurance is canceled and your pipes burst. The climate crisis has come upon us, not as a thief in the night but as a louder and louder drone in the background. It is a rolling catastrophe, hitting with some randomness but dependably hitting the poor and most vulnerable first. The climate crisis has not come slowly, but because it carries no banner to announce who wrecked this shoreline, who burned this forest, there are still those who do not see it. Even those of good will, trying to do the right thing for the climate, are often too focused on some future time when it will be worse than it is now. Yes, things will continue to get worse. But climate refugees (human and nonhuman) already exist.

I am an elder millennial. I had a hard awakening when I realized, as a thirty-something youth pastor, that I was not speaking the same language as the teenagers entrusted to my care. I was not able to minister faithfully to them because I kept taking comfort in out-of-date ideas, like my unconscious hope in the myth of progress. The teenagers had no such illusions. They called bullshit when they saw it.

People of my age and older have had a harder time coming to terms with the shock of the climate crisis because we grew up with stability. When I was a teenager, my peers and I were able to look at the earth and skies and to think, "This is the glory of God's creation." But your average teenagers at church camp this year are more likely to think: "This is the precious world we've totally fucked up." Those of us who are elder millennials and Gen Xers and boomers and "builders" grew up with a different story. We may have been taught to fear the possibility of nuclear war, but that was a binary situation: it would happen or it would not. In our youth we saw the world as good and humans as a mixed bag. Perhaps that is why it is so hard for many of us older leaders to wake up to the apocalypse. The younger ones have had no such illusions. A warming, stormy, suffering, and record-breaking world, the world of the rolling climate catastrophe, is the only world they know. So the young ones call it for what it is. Listen to them.

The church must come to grips with this reality. The church must face the ongoing ending of worlds and find her way through. She can no longer rely on programs of "creation care" as enough to satisfy a few ecological activists in the congregation—a field trip here, a sermon there. It was never enough, and we are all activists now. The climate catastrophe swallows up such token efforts as it rolls mercilessly across the world, crushing spirits in its wake. The church must shake herself awake and realize that in this global wreckage God cannot be found in the old places and the old ways. The generation coming of age right now is unable to find God in the world, because the world is coming apart at the seams. We must learn how to find God in the ruins.

Many of us will learn how to find God without a church building, as the climate catastrophe will not give special sanctuary to our sanctuaries. Some of the buildings will burn, or flood, or become unusable through more banal means such as financial considerations. There may be some freedom in this destruction, as some of us are weighed down by the excess and wastefulness of our collective belongings. The emotional cost of keeping today's small congregations in large spaces built by generations who believed in endless progress is significant: we are haunted by the memories of what the church used to be. Nostalgia can be deadly. We do not need to wait for a flood in order to downsize, lighten our load, find our essentials and give away our excess. Living more lightly, as responsible stewards of the resources given to us, will be a liberating and refreshing exercise.

But we (the church) are not just weighed down by tangible things. We also carry the weight of profound edifices of theology that need to be dismantled and left behind. The omnipotent *deus ex machina*[7] firmly lodged in the public imagination, the God who comes down out of the clouds and saves us from our catastrophe, must be jettisoned as we make our way forward in a world where we must do the saving together. This God serves us no longer, and if we continue to try to hold on, we will end up trapped and stuck.

The church must use all the creativity and innovation we can find, because God is not neatly painted in the ruins. The divine is still there, we trust, but the sign-markers are gone. We must learn and teach how to spot the presence, power, and purpose of God in these ruins.

PROGRESS WILL END US

We live in a time when God seems to be "10 zillion light-years away." A time when things may not get better. A time of climate catastrophe—a time of ending worlds, when the present *schema* of our world is passing away.[8] As if God was ever going to fix this for us. As if there haven't always been worlds ending.

---

7. *Deus ex machina*: a theatrical element in which a divinity appears to solve plot problems. The actor playing the divinity would be brought on stage by machine—perhaps lowered by a crane, flown in from the side, or raised through a trapdoor. When the *deus ex machina* appeared in the show, you could generally count on plot conflicts being resolved and the drama coming to a close.

8. Paul's letter to the church in Corinth is haunting: "I mean, brothers and sisters, the appointed time [*kairos*] has grown short. . . . For the present form [*schema*] of this world is passing away" (1 Cor. 7:29, 31 NRSV). For more on Paul's sense of time, see Giorgio Agamben, *The Time That Remains: A Commentary on the Letter to the Romans*, trans. Patricia Dailey (Stanford University Press, 2005). And on how it reads for our

Over a century ago, Black Elk saw worlds end before his eyes as a warrior witness to the Massacre at Wounded Knee:

> And so it was all over.
>
> I did not know then how much was ended. When I look back now from this high hill of my old age, I can still see the butchered women and children lying heaped and scattered all along the crooked gulch as plain as when I saw them with eyes still young. And I can see that something else died there in the bloody mud, and was buried in the blizzard. A people's dream died there. It was a beautiful dream.
>
> And I, to whom so great a vision was given in my youth,—you see me now a pitiful old man who has done nothing, for the nation's hoop is broken and scattered. There is no center any longer, and the sacred tree is dead.[9]

From the perspective of Black, Indigenous, and other colonized peoples, stories around the Anthropocene and our current climate apocalypse are stories of postcatastrophe, postapocalypse. For Kathryn Yusoff, "The Anthropocene might seem to offer a dystopic future that laments the end of the world, but imperialism and ongoing (settler) colonialisms have been ending worlds for as long as they have been in existence." In the North American context, for Julian Brave Noisecat, "To be Indigenous to North America is to be part of a postapocalyptic community and experience." In *Love After the End: An Anthology of Two-Spirit and Indigiqueer Speculative Fiction*, Joshua Whitehead reminds readers that "we have already survived the apocalypse—this, right here, right now, is a dystopian present."[10] This is why we insist on the ending of *worlds*, not the end of the world, like the fundamentalists of our tradition. We face

---

current climate crisis, Catherine Keller, *Political Theology of the Earth: Our Planetary Emergency and the Struggle for a New Public* (Columbia University Press, 2018).

9. Neihardt, *Black Elk Speaks*, 169.

10. Kathryn Yusoff, *A Billion Black Anthropocenes or None* (University of Minnesota Press, 2018), xiii; Julian Brave Noisecat, "How Indigenous Peoples Are Fighting the Apocalypse," *Emergence Magazine*, November 23, 2021; Joshua Whitehead, ed., *Love After the End: An Anthology of Two-Spirit and Indigiqueer Speculative Fiction* (Arsenal Pulp, 2020), 10.

a rolling and ongoing catastrophe within an apocalyptic present. Time is out of joint.

At first encounter, I (JD) struggled to reconcile these world endings with the stories I had been living my life around—economic growth, the continual expansion of human rights, unending progress, the American Dream. But sometimes there is no reconciling with the truth. The stories about unending progress have tricked us into believing that the truth will make us whole. Jesus did not promise that the truth would make us feel warm and fuzzy, or that it would give us a story to tell ourselves as we march into the future. He just said that the truth would set us free. But free from what? Standing before the abyss of that truth—the truth of the apocalypse we are living in—I was freed from the stranglehold of those stories of progress that have been ending worlds and will end the world. The truth sets us free from our fundamentalisms, from our easy and all-encompassing answers. The truth sets us free from the comforts of those lies we tell ourselves to make sense of truth's chaos. No wonder I feel out of joint.

It is true—in the New Testament, apocalypse doesn't refer to The End. Rather, as Catherine Keller reminds us, *apokalypsis*, "the Greek word for 'revelation,' means literally the 'removal of the veil.' It means not closure but *dis-closure*—that is, opening. A chance to open our eyes?"[11] A chance, I hope, to open our eyes beyond that story of progress that's been feeding us a fundamentalism leading us to extinction.

Seeing our present as apocalyptic jolts us out of stories about progress—one of the foundational myths of what some call *Western modernity*. These terms—"West" and "modern"—drip with power and history: the eighteenth-century Enlightenment, new technologies that sustain and destroy life, a move from tyrannical monarchy to flawed democracy, knowledge from reason rather than religion, and the further construction in thought and power of the "East" and the "West," the Orient and the Occident, colonization.[12] White/Anglo/American myths of salvation are

---

11. I encourage you to read Keller's revelatory dream reading of John's Revelation for our times. Catherine Keller, *Facing Apocalypse: Climate, Democracy, and Other Last Chances* (Orbis Books, 2021).

12. For more on the Western imperialist construction of the "Orient," see

bound up with myths of modernity and progress. For Walter Mignolo, a theorist of decoloniality, "Salvation has several designs, all co-existing today, but that unfolded over 500 years, since 1500: salvation by conversion to Christianity, salvation by progress and civilization, salvation by development and modernization, salvation by global market democracy (e.g., neoliberalism)."[13] Myths of progress are tangled up with colonization and Christian theology.[14]

Stories of progress have always been inhuman and insufficient, yet all-encompassing. That's the viciousness of progress—it turns everything into a binary between success or failure, progress or regression, developed or undeveloped, human or nonhuman, civilized or savage, white or nonwhite, owner or capital. For the anthropologist Anna Tsing, "the trope of progress is sufficient to know the world, both in success and failure." In the fight against climate change, the myth of progress forces us to imagine success through the lens of growth—growth of GDP, population, house-footprint, and the Standard & Poor's 500. Other possibilities focused directly on human and nonhuman flourishing are senseless to the

---

Edward W. Said's classic in postcolonial studies, *Orientalism* (Pantheon Books, 1978). See the Peruvian sociologist Anibal Quijano, paraphrased by Walter Mignolo, "there is no modernity without coloniality, thus, modernity/coloniality are two sides of the same coin." Before Quijano, "everybody thought of modernity as a totality and colonialism as an unhappy situation that advancing modernity vision and ideals would end. Quijano's proposal was that coloniality is a necessary component of modernity and therefore it cannot be ended if global imperial designs in the name of modernity continue. Coloniality, in other words, is the darker side of Western modernity." Walter Mignolo, "Interview—Walter Mignolo/Part 2: Key Concepts," interviewed by Alvina Hoffmann, *E-International Relations*, January 21, 2017, 2.

13. Mignolo, "Interview—Walter Mignolo/Part 2," 2.

14. Neoliberalism: Unlike previous forms of capitalism, neoliberal capitalism is a political theology, that is, a worldview that encapsulates not just economics but questions of politics, time, the nature of God and reality, and of what it means to be human. Adam Kotsko helpfully summarizes this worldview: "Whereas classical liberalism insisted that capitalism had to be allowed free rein within its sphere, under neoliberalism capitalism no longer has a set sphere. We are always 'on the clock,' always accruing (or squandering) various forms of financial and social capital." For a brief introduction to neoliberalism and what it means to call it a "political theology," see Adam Kotsko, *Neoliberalism's Demons: On the Political Theology of Late Capital* (Stanford University Press, 2018), 1–9.

myth of progress. For Tsing, "The story of decline offers no leftovers, no excess, nothing that escapes progress. Progress still controls us even in tales of ruination."[15] Colonized worlds were destroyed and enslaved, left in ruins, because they were uncivilized, failing, holding humanity back from the promise of progress. The nonhuman world was transformed into capital, warped into cheap commodities. From gas to gold, it was ours for the taking, it held the power of our progressive destiny. Or so the stories go. Like other stories that oppressively pretend to explain it all, progress gave us a story about *everything*—no leftovers. For progress, either success or failure, owner or capital, human or nonhuman.

That last binary—human or nonhuman—points to another theological entanglement in this story. Remember, the totalizing story of progress leaves no leftovers—not even theology, not even the question of what it is to be human. Over half a century ago, the historian Lynn White Jr. traced the "roots of our ecological crisis." Disturbingly long ago, from the research of his peers, White knew in 1967 the grave danger posed by our emission of greenhouse gases.[16] For White, the trunk and branches of our ecological crisis are found in the mid-nineteenth century of the Atlantic world,[17] a fusion of the theoretical work of science with the empirical work of technology, where "Nature" was something we could finally dominate.[18]

---

15. Anna Lowenhaupt Tsing, *The Mushroom at the End of the World: On the Possibility of Life in Capitalist Ruins* (Princeton University Press, 2015), 21.

16. Lynn White Jr., "The Historical Roots of Our Ecological Crisis," *Science* 155, no. 3767 (March 10, 1967): 1204.

17. I use the term "Atlantic world" here as opposed to the "West" because the former better encapsulates the entangled (and indistinguishable) histories of the European continent with Africa, South America, and North America. Said otherwise, colonization, indigenous genocide, and transatlantic slavery is just as "Western" as the Renaissance or the Enlightenment. See Paul Gilroy, *The Black Atlantic: Modernity and Double Consciousness* (Verso, 1993).

18. For the sake of brevity I have skipped a part of White's timeline: the way technology—the scratch plow—changed the distribution of land and with it our relationship to the land. White, "Historical Roots," 1205. This fusion comes out most brilliantly in Francis Bacon—a godparent of the scientific method, the Royal Society, and consumer industrialization—who instilled in "Modern Man" that not only is Nature separate from us but it is finally made subservient to us through

Yet, the real *root* of our ecological crisis is Christian theology. The (Jewish and) Christian creation myths secured, for many, Man (with the problematic, patriarchal capital *M*) and his dominance of Nature—"be fruitful, and multiply, and replenish the earth, and subdue it: and have dominion over [it]" (Gen. 1:28 KJV). Even though this particular translation of Genesis is highly contested, this violent (Christian) mistranslation has nevertheless functioned as the dominant foundation of the relationship between Man and Nature in Christian thought. Our stories tell us that we humans are fundamentally different. To be human is to be made in the image of God—*imago Dei*—to be enchanted with a gaze toward the future.[19] For White, this bred anthropocentrism, a privileging of all things human over the nonhuman. White, though, failed to show how "humanness" was tied to white property-owning men. The image of God was racial, gendered, and economic. White supremacy, patriarchy, and industrial capitalism defined human and nonhuman, progress and regression. Prior to Christianity, the multiple animism throughout the ancient world saw nature as enchanted with agency. But when animism was replaced by Christianity, the spiritual inhibitions of exploiting nature were dissolved—now natural objects had no enchantment, only Man and his *imago Dei*.[20] This theology of progress leaves no leftovers, not even what it means to be human.

---

our scientific-technological progress. But for White, this chasm between Man and Nature is merely perfected by Bacon.

19. Here we're describing how *imago Dei* has, unfortunately, functioned through the majority of Christian history—privileging the human over the nonhuman, men over women, property owners over those without, white colonizers over all others, etc. However, many have tried to rehabilitate and reconstruct *imago Dei* toward positive ends. For a fruitful example of this, see the chapter in this volume on courageous curiosity.

20. White, "Historical Roots," 1205. On this point about nature's disenchantment and the anthropocentrism of the human person in Christian thought, Akeel Bilgrami sharpens White's historical analysis. According to Bilgrami, the real change didn't happen with the coming of ancient Christianity (as White argues) but with early modern Christianity. There was a point in the early modern period when Christians stopped seeing nature as infused with the divine but instead as mechanistic (think Newtonianism), which led to a relegation of the natural world to inert mere natural resources. See Akeel Bilgrami, *Secularism, Identity, and Enchantment* (Harvard University Press, 2014).

But even more nefarious was the way our theology reshaped time. When ancient traditions—which believed in cyclical time—were overcome by Christianity, the Atlantic world took on a notion of time that was linear and progressive. According to White, "Our daily habits of action . . . are dominated by an implicit faith in perpetual progress which was unknown either to Greco-Roman antiquity or to the Orient. It is rooted in, and is indefensible apart from, Judeo-Christian theology."[21] Our Christian stories of salvation and the eschaton turned progress into an "iron law" of history.[22] As Christians, we claim to know the end of the story. But this theology has failed to face our vulnerability in a precarious world.[23]

Our theologies of progress allow us to hold on to a hubris hope—an unshakable feeling that everything will be okay, that we have time to sort things out, and if not, that Jesus will take the wheel. Hubris hope allows, for example, Jim Justice, the Republican governor of West Virginia, to simultaneously acknowledge the climate crisis while continuing his support for fossil fuels: "God will give us time for the smart people of the world to solve the riddle. If there truly is climate change going on, He will give us time."[24] If we know, as Justice believes, how the story ends, why worry about it? Those on the left aren't immune to this theology of progress either. Progressives are sure that both history and God are on their side. As Martin Luther King Jr. put it, even if the moral arc of the universe is long, it eventually bends toward justice. Yet even with genuine concern for social and ecological ills, this hubris hope allows us to

---

21. White, "Historical Roots," 1205.

22. See Clive Hamilton, "Human Destiny in the Anthropocene," in *The Anthropocene and the Global Environmental Crisis: Rethinking Modernity in a New Epoch*, ed. Clive Hamilton, Christophe Bonneuil, and François Gemenne (Routledge, 2015), 36–37.

23. Eschatology is the Christian doctrine of the future or the end times that undergirds political theologies of time as linear and progressive. Alternative visions of eschatology are more concerned with questions of hope, like with the theologian Jürgen Moltmann.

24. "Gov. Justice: President Biden Must Tap into West Virginia's Rich Natural Resources to Make America Energy Independent Again," press release, Office of the Governor, Jim Justice, March 11, 2022, https://tinyurl.com/ctj9pacr.

be satisfied with the status quo, to feel content that our old institutions will eventually solve the problem. We find shelter in a hollow faith in the inevitability of the future.

Hope can be useful. But when the object of hope becomes inevitable, hope degrades into hubris. Then we do not hope for progress, we are certain of it. We forged progress into an iron law of history, a golden calf of certainty. Our hubris hope has allowed the climate crisis to be treated like any other issue. I am grateful that mainline denominations have long left aside notions of the rapture and its premillennial end times. However, in its place, the church has taken up this false story of progress—not just of our individual selves but of our economies, communities, and countries. Instead of the world getting worse and worse until Christ finally raptures the good, we have a myth just as childish: unending progress, infinite growth, a universal arc inevitably bending toward justice. While the progressive Christian God of progress calls us to face the suffering of the world and calls us to work for "justice and peace in all the earth," nevertheless, with or without us, God bends the arc. No matter our ecological destruction, this God "will come to raise the living and the dead," bringing us into a "life everlasting." No matter how liberating our theology, no matter how much our God-talk calls us into the struggles of our neighbors, we still hold on to the *deus ex machina*, the God of exception who arrives with salvation in our final hour.[25]

Many of us have internalized the story of hubris hope, an optimistic story about our climate crisis: the problem is gargantuan, but with the right amount of spiritual, political, and corporate will, our current strategies, systems, churches, coalitions, and constitutions can keep the world from warming above the apocalyptic tipping point of 1.5° C. Warming above that threshold would act like a snowball growing larger as it rolls down a mountain. One example: The Greenland ice sheet would

---

25. A theology of a God of exception is most famously fleshed out in the work of Carl Schmitt, a Nazi jurist, in his *Political Theology: Four Chapters on the Concept of Sovereignty*, translated and introduced by George Schwab (University of Chicago Press, 1985). While, unfortunately, many of Schmitt's critiques of liberal democracy have held water, some scholars have found useful ways to critique his theology. For one, see Catherine Keller's critique of the God of exceptionalism in *Political Theology of the Earth*.

melt, pushing the oceans twenty-three feet higher—ten feet above my mother's bathtub.[26] But in this dominant story—the one where we prevail in the quest to avoid that snowball—we not only stop apocalyptic warming, but we usher in a new era, with the help of renewable energy and the technologies it propels, an era of utopian cities, a harmony between nature and society, equitable abundance, new heaven and new earth. In a warming world, this story has become unattainable and cruel.

The theological, political, and economic status quo—feeding us forced choices, hinging our hopes on the God of progress—has become an obstacle to our flourishing. We need to let those clay jars of hubris hope crack in the heat. The fundamentalist certainty that everything will be okay—that we will keep the climate below 1.5° C, and if we do not, that there is always the God option, the *deus ex machina*, the new earth of our eschatological futures. This hubris hope assures us we can keep on living as normal, that the status quo is sufficient, that our outdated constitutions will shepherd us, that our old models of managing church assets and membership will be sufficient (with perhaps the addition of a well-intentioned eco-justice committee), that the neoliberal stories that help us organize our lives and imagine the good life will continue to help us thrive (if they ever did). Without this faith in the future, it will feel like we lost something. We have. This hubris hope is a stumbling block for our imaginations, an obstacle to our flourishing in the apocalypse.

GOD IN THE RUINS

So what does this mean? It doesn't mean that we should scrap hope or that we should get rid of God. But it does mean that there are no guar-

---

26. Ove Hoegh-Guldberg, Daniela Jacob, and Michael Taylor, "Impacts of 1.5°C Global Warming on Natural and Human Systems," in *Global Warming of 1.5°C. An IPCC Special Report on the Impacts of Global Warming of 1.5°C Above Pre-industrial Levels and Related Global Greenhouse Gas Emission Pathways, in the Context of Strengthening the Global Response to the Threat of Climate Change, Sustainable Development, and Efforts to Eradicate Poverty*, ed. V. Masson-Delmotte et al. (Cambridge University Press, 2018), 175–312; "If All of Earth's Ice Melts and Flows into the Ocean, What Would Happen to the Planet's Rotation?," NASA, accessed December 9, 2024, https://tinyurl.com/626fec5e.

antees, no plot device or God that will suddenly resolve our previously unsolvable problems. It means we need to bathe, with Gregory of Nyssa, in the "brilliant darkness" where Moses found God.[27] It means that we need to let the hopelessness in, to be theologians of the cross, to call a thing what it actually is.

We often assume it's unhelpful to be truthfully blunt about the dim realities of the climate catastrophe—of letting hopelessness in. Yet this assumption is unsupported. Jem Bendell provides evidence—from case studies to peer-reviewed studies in psychology—that the unvarnished truth, even with its catastrophic implications, leads to action that opens our imaginations past the status quo. The hopelessness that often arises from facing the possibilities of catastrophe is not necessarily negative, Bendell argues. "The range of ancient wisdom traditions see a significant place for hopelessness and despair. . . . Hope is not a good thing to maintain" when the object of one's hope (like returning to the Holocene) is impossible.[28] In part, Bendell draws on Plenty Coups—the visionary Crow chief of the late nineteenth and early twentieth century—and how, in the face of catastrophe, that is, the annihilation of his nation and culture, he embodied a radical hope, a hope "that is directed toward a future goodness that transcends the current ability to understand what it is."[29] For Bendell, hopelessness in the face of the potential collapse of "industrial consumer society," as he sees the future, opens space for new hopes to emerge.

During my (JD's) first months in undergrad, I sat with tears on a boulder while I told Grammie that I was under shifting sand—I had been kicked out of home and college because I was gay. Though nothing like Plenty Coups's experience, my world was ending. Yet, the destruction of my world allowed me to see past its fundamentalisms, beyond the hubris hope of my "conversion therapy" that told me I was a walking

---

27. Gregory of Nyssa, *The Life of Moses*, translation, introduction, and notes by Abraham J. Malherbe and Everett Ferguson (Paulist, 1978), 95.

28. Jem Bendell, "Deep Adaptation: A Map for Navigating Climate Tragedy," in *Deep Adaptation: Navigating the Realities of Climate Crisis*, ed. Jem Bendell and Rupert Read (Polity, 2021), 61.

29. Jonathan Lear, *Radical Hope: Ethics in the Face of Cultural Devastation* (Harvard University Press, 2006), 103.

pathology that God and self-control could heal. In between drags from a Pall Mall, Grammie told me truths: "God loves you just the way you are. I love you, baby, no matter what." But when the smoke cleared, she told me lies too: "Everything happens for a reason. God will make this good. Everything will be okay." Now Grammie is dead, killed by a thousand vaccine lies. Grammie is still burnt to ash, and I will always carry the wounds of homosexual "healing." There is nothing good here, no God to tie the strands of death into good reason. But there is a God living in my wounds, a God hidden in Grammie's ashes—the same God hidden in the ruins of our time.

Something broke inside me when I finally faced the unvarnished truth of our ecological ruin. It was in the very early days of the pandemic, newly in lockdown, when we were humbled not only by a microscopic virus but also by what life does without the unending grind of consumer capitalism. It was in those days of fear, freezer-truck morgues, and the freedom of wild Earth that I read the first lines of David Wallace-Wells's *The Uninhabitable Earth*: "It is worse, much worse, than you think."[30] I remember the future, the world I constructed in my mind, drowned as I realized, even if we met the goals of the Paris climate accord, even in the best case of all scenarios, the place I was sitting would be underwater by century's end. How can the arc of justice bend on an uninhabitable Earth? I lost something that day. I lost the comforts of my progressive fundamentalism, that cozy assurance of a utopia on the horizon of the future. I lost my naïve faith in humanity, that we could solve the problems before us. I lost the innocence of that comforting lie Grammie told me—"everything will be okay."

I lost, too, an adherence to the creeds of the status quo. I lost an imagination that was boxed in by progress and the stories it tells us about how to find joy and purpose. I lost the forced choices of our neoliberal mythologies. This loss allowed me to imagine a life beyond the traditional house, beyond financial servitude to a landlord: a life on the road, off the capitalist economic grid, a nomadic life on public lands. This loss

---

30. David Wallace-Wells, *The Uninhabitable Earth: Life After Warming* (Random House, 2019), 3.

will mean something different to you. What have you lost as you woke up to the apocalypse?

Let the loss in. Keep hope at bay. Bathe in the "brilliant darkness" of our apocalyptic ruins. Don't blow the smoke away; stand still in the cloud of unknowing. Let this hopelessness fill the space between your bones; let it settle in the pit of your stomach. Let it sear through the weights of progress that are holding down your imagination. If you let it, hopelessness will shift your fidelities away from the status quo toward novel ways of flourishing in the apocalypse, toward a God that can be found in the ruins of our time.

Hopelessness cures us of a hubris hope. The philosopher and theologian John Caputo shows us the way toward a hope after the death of our hubris, after we let go of that fairy tale of progress and guarantees and the inevitable bending arc. For Caputo, "Hope is the risky business of calling for the coming of what we cannot see coming, of saying yes to the future, where nothing is guaranteed."[31] This hopeless hope gives us no guarantees of economic growth, providential progress, or bending arcs. "We are the ones whom God is waiting for . . . to pick up where God leaves off," Caputo tells us.[32] "Nothing says that the worst will not happen. No invisible hand ensures a good outcome. No Providence guides it like a ship to safe harbor." There is no guarantee of a hospitable planet for our individual or collective futures. The younger generations feel this in our bones, yet the church continues to feed us a lukewarm hubris hope that we will continue to spit out of our mouths.

When there are no guarantees, no providential backup plans, no *deus ex machina*, our existence and our planet become more fragile than we'd been led to believe. In the face of this fragility, we must refuse the God of progress, the God of guarantees, the God of victory. We must embrace a God of the ruins.

In the time that remains, we need to be foolish enough to follow the cross in the darkness of knowing ignorance, to find the back of God in

---

31. John D. Caputo, *Hoping Against Hope: Confessions of a Postmodern Pilgrim* (Fortress, 2015), 199.

32. John D. Caputo, *The Folly of God: A Theology of the Unconditional* (Polebridge, 2015), 118–19.

the incomprehensibility of the cloud. The cross is foolishness, after all, isn't it? The God we find in the ruins of our times shows what happens when we take the cross seriously. What if it really is finished? The God of the ruins asks us to stop and smell the stench—to call a thing what it actually is. No Easter lilies to mask the stink.[33]

If things really are more fragile, we must change. Our decisions matter. Our actions matter. Near the cross, we will find that this world and this life are more vulnerable, more fragile, more precious. In the ashes of that God of guarantees, in the ashes of that hollow God of hubris hope, if we look, we find a God of the ruins. There will be moments of resurrection in this rolling catastrophe. But we cannot let it be a resurrection *of* the ruins, a resurrection of Rome. Rather, we need resurrection *in* the ruins. Like the three women at the end of Mark's Gospel, we don't know what this resurrection will look like. But we know what it will feel like: terror and amazement.[34]

PACKING A SPIRITUAL GO-BAG

How can we find God when the signposts are washed away? What are we looking for? How do we seek?

Five wooden boxes stand in the forest near Binghamton University, where I (Talitha) attended college many years ago. The boxes are slatted, open to the wind, wood left natural and unstained. On them are pinecones, sticks, rocks, and a jar of water, arranged artfully by the gathered church. A child contributed a dandelion in full gray glory. A candle burns in a lantern on top. These boxes are the church building of a wild congregation, the "Church in the Wild."[35] Each week they meet and assemble

---

33. For more on the movement of Radical Theology to which I've been alluding in the last few paragraphs, see Christopher D. Rodkey and Jordan E. Miller, eds., *The Palgrave Handbook of Radical Theology* (Palgrave Macmillan, 2018). For more on knowing ignorance and the incomprehensibility of the cloud, see Catherine Keller, *Cloud of the Impossible: Negative Theology and Planetary Entanglement* (Columbia University Press, 2015), esp. chapters 1 and 2.

34. Mark 16:8—"So they went out and fled from the tomb, for terror and amazement had seized them; and they said nothing to anyone, for they were afraid."

35. For more information on Church in the Wild, see www.churchinthewild.org.

the boxes as an altar space, carrying with them what seems important. Their pastor invites them to bring the objects forward as they gather. When they disperse, the objects are dispersed also. Only the boxes and the candle are the same from week to week. I am three thousand miles away. I follow them on Instagram, listen to their podcasts, and sometimes attend their service during the coldest of winter Sundays when they relocate to Zoom. I have not touched the boxes myself. But they feel so important to me.

During one of the times in my life when I had to move more often than I wanted, and I felt rootless and stressed, I started putting a few sacred objects into a box. Putting my creative energy into that box—painting it, choosing important poems and little objects of beauty—I felt braver than before. I knew that if I had to pull up roots again I would be prepared. Yes, I would still have to disassemble my bookcases and find new routines, but at least I would have one box that would not be affected by the change. Wherever the box was opened, it would be just as it was before. My home on the road, my journey box.

As a pastor I used this method with our children and youth. Children's ministry needed to be outdoors during COVID times before the children got vaccinated. But we never could find the perfect location. We tried several, and eventually ended up in a large room with big open doors. While we journeyed around looking for the right place, each week I recruited someone to help me carry a twelve-foot rug out of the Sunday school room and unroll it wherever we would be. I brought a box full of items from the room, reminding them tangibly that our classrooms and their routines were just relocated, and not undone. We still know how to find God in this new place.

The youth group had to meet online, and so we sent a box to every house. It had a candle and matches, clay to make a candleholder, and snacks for fun. When we met online, we finished our meetings by lighting all the candles and praying. We know how to find God in dispersal.

Do you have a "go-bag"? For what disasters are you prepared? Californians have always been encouraged to have their emergency supply bags ready in case of an earthquake, but some of us never took that seriously until wildfire seasons got a little more scary. Some of us in other places have packed to evacuate for hurricanes or taken a bag of essentials down into a tornado shelter. What is in yours? IDs, important paperwork, precious mementos, several days' worth of water, food, medicine, N95 masks if you are bracing for wildfire.

Do you have a spiritual go-bag? Does your church? What are your essentials? The rug was not easy to lug around the church building; the candles were a better choice.

Those who have planted churches, moved churches, or merged congregations know how to do this kind of work; you know the flexibility and commitment you need to unhook yourselves from attachment to a certain sanctuary and its decorations. This task is not easy; plenty of pastors have gotten burned out from routine church renovations and the conflict they create. But where the congregation is willing, relocations and renovations can be fruitful and focusing periods. Those that thrive are the ones who know how to carry the absolute essentials with them in a go-bag or a box: a tablecloth, a piece of art, a plate and cup, a baptismal bowl, or whatever signifies to the gathered people "this is church." But the Church in the Wild takes this to another level: having just the box, no sacred objects inside, and trusting that each week we will bring or be able to find the things that can remind us of the sacred. This is spiritual wayfinding. We will know how to find God in the ruins, because we have been working to find God every Sunday in the ordinary wreckage of life.

Together we are looking for the signs of God in a world changing faster than we have the ability to comprehend. And each week, letting go as we dismantle the altar back down to the empty boxes. Because it is not the dandelion that matters, majestic as it may be. It is not the water itself. It is the finding that matters, the practice of asking the children, "What things can teach us about God today?" These children will grow up knowing that they are capable of answering that question.

I spend a lot of time in the ruins of people's lives. I work as a pediatric hospital chaplain. Things are wrecked and wretched all over the place. I bear witness as parents say good-bye to a child and turn to face the unfathomable world without them. I sit in meetings, prayerfully listening, as parents receive the explanation that their child will live but will not recover full brain function. I hear about diseases that cannot be cured but can be treated, at a high cost of discomfort, time, and energy. And I tell stories and play games with children who wonder "why did God let this happen to me?" In these rough spaces I am always on the lookout for the God of the ruins. It is a privilege and an honor to be in those terribly vulnerable moments where God is found in a new way. Sometimes God is not in the cure or the strength or the miracle; God is in the still small voice that helps you simply endure another day after your world ends. God is in the place where you find your new beginning.

There is a favorite tree here in the hospital courtyard—a 162-year-old magnolia—the largest magnolia west of the Mississippi. We call her Maggie. She is a representative of God outright, pure and innocent and flowering. A teenager enjoying Maggie's glory smiles as he states that he wants to "become a tree" when he dies, and we make plans for his remains to be buried with a grafted cutting of this very tree.

The tree is headed toward destruction, like the live oak in the backyard of JD's parents. It is slated to be cut down within a few years when the hospital expands. Some of us wonder if we can make a stand to protect her like the eco-activists of old keeping vigil in her branches, but we know that a gazillion dollars is on the line and the architectural plans have already been made for the new building. But where will we find God when her faithful representative Maggie is not there? We have plans for grafting, but the baby scions will take 162 years to approach Maggie's size and majesty. The sorrow of every bereaved family echoes in our hearts as we do our anticipatory grieving, preparing ourselves for a life without.

What do you want to become when you die? Maybe you want to become a tree like our teenage patient, or a mustard seed, or an ocean wave. Beyond our hopes to live on—whether in books or children or other legacy—when we have let go even of that, to what might we hope to be transformed? I want to be composted and nourish the earth with a trillion flourishing microorganisms. A friend hoped for a sky burial, being left on top of the highest accessible mountain for the birds to take of the body, and was disappointed to find that such burials are not allowed here. It is legal, however, to take some cremains and make jewelry out of them, to send them up in fireworks, or to literally tattoo some of the cremains into someone else's skin. "Organ donation first!" another friend reminds me, to which I always will say a thousand times yes, because I have been at both bedsides: the bedside where a family says good-bye to their child and sees them wheeled right into the operating room, and the bedside where a family rejoices in new life granted by a liver, a heart, a pair of lungs. Most of us will not die in such a way that organ donation is possible, so we must content ourselves with some other transformation. What do you want to become?

What does the church want to become when it dies? "It is in dying that we are born," the prayer attributed to Saint Francis goes. What will we give ourselves to? We may smile when an old church building becomes a bar or a roller skating rink,[36] or when a church gifts the land back to the native people from whose stewardship it was long ago taken.[37] But even after the disposition of the building is settled, still we ask: Where will the love and faith of the congregation go when the congregation disperses? What will she become when she is no more? Some say the church should be like a mighty oak, living long and strong, but I would prefer us to be a dandelion. Dandelions will survive the apocalypse, I feel sure of it. Unlike the majestic and mighty trees, their strength is in their short-lived vitality. They will grow in any available crack of pavement. They will find a way. They will bring nourishment, beauty, and joy to the children of tomorrow.

Things will get worse for the rest of our lives. Our old ideas of the good life will die. Many of the things we hold tight to will be shattered. But, even when we let hopelessness in, we don't fall into despair. We will cultivate new attachments.[38] And continue some old ones. Singing together will always be cathartic and euphoric. Falling in love will always be enthralling. A good meal will always bring satisfaction. Sharing a campfire will always bring warmth—to body and spirit. We will craft new ways to live a good life, even in the ruins.

So how do we find our way in this rolling catastrophe? How do we wayfind in the apocalypse? Not by thinking we can go back to the Holocene. Not by closing our imagination to the coming destruction. Not by

---

36. For more information on Church of 8 Wheels, see http://www.churchof8wheels.com/.

37. Terra Brockman, "A Church Returns Land to American Indians," *Christian Century* 137, no. 6 (March 11, 2020).

38. For more on cultivating attachments, see Bruno Latuor, *Down to Earth: Politics in the New Climatic Regime*, trans. Catherine Porter (Polity, 2018), 83.

buying into the myth of progress. Not with hubris hope. But with grief and hopelessness and a good cry. And then, once you've had that good cry and given your body enough time to salvage a sliver of acceptance, pack your go-bag, spiritual or otherwise, and fill it with what matters most for the time that remains.[39]

---

39. This conclusion, "what matters most," is indebted to a book that came to our attention very late in writing this chapter. We highly encourage reading Timothy Beal, *When Time Is Short: Finding Our Way in the Anthropocene* (Beacon, 2022).

4

LAMENT EMBODIED IN COMMUNITY

Accompanying Grief Toward Genuine Healing

Shaya Aguilar
Rev. Dr. Soong-Chan Rah

OUR INVITATION

We begin with a common space of grief and lament for the coauthors. One is a student (Shaya) experiencing the direct pain of communal suffering, and the other is a parent (Soong-Chan) experiencing pain from a distance as his child suffers. Our stories of the same tragedy speak to our need for embodied communal lament in a world heavy with grief.

I (Shaya) vividly remember waking up the morning of November 8, 2018. I had gone to sleep early the night before and was ready to walk out the door to face my three midterms. I picked up my phone to check the time and saw that my roommate Emily had sent a text to one of my close friends asking him if he was safe. He hadn't responded yet, but in the meantime a series of texts from family and friends started flooding my phone. "Are you okay, honey?" "Did you go out last night?"

I walked into my friend's room to find that they hadn't slept all night. It was then that I learned that a shooting had taken place at the local line-dancing bar, Borderline—thirteen people were killed, including seven college students, and a Pepperdine freshman, Alaina. I didn't have words to put to the feelings that were coming up. I didn't know how to show up to class knowing that a student who lived in the suite I had been in just a year before had lost her life. My friends and I had attended the same college night at Borderline the year before. It was a night full of laughs and memories—memories that I couldn't recall that day because they were now tainted by the tragedy of the loss of several students.

Around 10 a.m. the community gathered in Elkins Auditorium. At this time we didn't know how many students were lost; we just knew Alaina was missing. The silence in the room was palpable. Pepperdine's president, Andy K. Benton, then shared the news that Alaina was one of the victims, and that she had not made it out of Borderline alive. I will never forget the sound of the weeping that followed. I will never forget the audible distress embodied by a community in mourning. Tears that I had been choking back all morning now rushed down my cheeks. In a sea of crying people, I felt a wave of grief come over me. I didn't know what to do, where to go, who to talk to for comfort . . . so I went to class. The rest of the day is a blur to me.

Thousand Oaks wasn't just the town close to where I went to college; it was my hometown. The place I had lived since middle school. I didn't know where to go that day, so I grabbed my friend and went home. We went to a prayer vigil at the local church that night. I didn't have any tears by the time I pulled into my parents' driveway. I had intended to go back to campus, but once my mom saw the exhaustion on my face, I knew there was no way she would let me leave.

I went straight to sleep and woke up to my parents coming into my room at 3 a.m. the next day. They told me to grab what I needed and be ready to leave as soon as possible—I quickly learned that a fire that started a few hours earlier was now an imminent threat. Our neighborhood was put under mandatory evacuation. In the whirlwind that followed, I managed to grab a box of letters and my Bible. I failed to remember any of the essentials, but in that moment of complete exhaustion and confusion, my Bible took precedence over a toothbrush. Even as we left, I thought I would be back to campus by the end of the day. Little did I know that November 8 was the last day I would be on campus for a long time. The small brush fire ended up forcing the Pepperdine community to shelter in place as the flames engulfed the campus. My roommates along with many other students who were not from the area were stranded on campus without a car, trusting that Pepperdine would keep them safe.

What started as a small brush fire ended up burning 96,949 acres and forcing the evacuation of over 295,000 residents. The fall semester was moved to Zoom, and students wouldn't return to campus until after the Thanksgiving break, nearly three weeks later. With two tragedies coming back to back, it was clear that there was a growing need to help college students cultivate resilience. The freshman class became known as the "trauma" class. Less than a year later, this same class was sent home due to COVID-19. Pepperdine was once again a desolate campus—a campus that used to be full of life was deserted overnight.

Like many community members at the time, I didn't have words that could carry the weight of the grief that our community was holding. Two tragedies took place within the span of twenty-four hours, taking the life of thirteen students, taking the homes of families and students, and threatening the well-being of the entire community. The Pepperdine community came together in the face of trauma—the loss, isolation, and disorientation left the community longing for the space to grieve.

+++

It was my (Soong-Chan's) only daughter's first year at Pepperdine. The challenge of the first child going off to college was mitigated by the reassuring image of my seventeen-year-old at a Christian school in one of the nicest, most affluent, and seemingly safest neighborhoods in Southern California. The clincher was our campus visit where every stop featured breathtaking views of the Pacific Ocean. I relished the image of my daughter singing hymns on Malibu Beach while the Southern California sun and the ocean breeze enveloped her and her friends. Despite being based in Chicago, I made frequent trips to LA in her freshman year, visiting for her birthday in late October and a week later when I was scheduled to speak at a conference in Claremont. That second visit in November reinstated all my fears and evoked a lament through the experience of a vicarious trauma.

I had arrived a day earlier for my conference so I could meet up with my daughter. We went to the Malibu Pier for a great sunset dinner initially affirming the choice of Pepperdine as the perfect school. She had a rough start not unlike many first-year students, but she was beginning to make friends, particularly in her dorm of a dozen female first-year students. Both of us were in good spirits with a positive expectation and anticipation for the rest of the fall semester. A long drive got me to my hotel in Claremont, where I quickly fell asleep after a late-night check-in. My sleep was interrupted by a series of early morning text messages from my daughter. There had been a mass shooting at a nearby club that was hosting a college-night event. Pepperdine students were in attendance, including one of her suitemates. I immediately called back. Her suitemate was safe and back in their dorm, but there was a Pepperdine freshman who had been killed. I said that I would come out to Malibu as soon as possible. She said that she was safe and feeling better, now that she knew her suitemate was okay.

I rushed through my morning session and headed back to Malibu as quickly as I could. I met up with my daughter and hugged her tightly. When she was in high school, she had confided in me that since she was ten years old she had never felt safe in a large public gathering. At high school basketball games, at concerts, even at church services, she would always look around, wondering if she were safe from a mass shooter. And now, it had happened to her classmates. I sat with her, prayed with her, and tried to reassure her. The campus was conducting services of lament, and she said that she wanted to attend. I was scheduled to fly out on a red-eye flight and told her I could stay a few extra days, but she said that she would be okay. I headed to LAX glad that the Pepperdine community was trying to organize a communal lament over this communal pain.

After going through security, I was waiting for my late-night flight out of LA. My daughter called and said that a wildfire was spreading rapidly and heading toward the Pepperdine campus. She was told to prepare a "getaway" bag. I said that I would come back to campus right away, but she assured me that the evacuation was just a precaution. She called back to say that there would not be an evacuation and they were told to stay in place. I got on the plane assuming that all was well and that disaster had been avoided. By the time I got back to Chicago, the news had turned. The winds had shifted and the fire was spreading wildly. The campus of Pepperdine was under a "shelter in place" order—no one could get in or out. I looked for flights back to LA, but even if I did return, I would not be able to get to the Pepperdine campus.

Numerous emails and calls to the Pepperdine administration assured me that the Pepperdine campus was the safest place. The fire department staged fire mitigation and rescue efforts from Pepperdine because it was the safest place in the region. But the fear and anxiety were very real. I felt the fear and anxiety on our FaceTime calls. I felt the fear and anxiety every time I sent an e-mail or left a voicemail with university staff or friends in the area. Multiple assurances that the students were safe at Pepperdine did not mitigate the anxiety. Ultimately, the Pepperdine staff did know what they were doing, and the fire burned everything but the campus, which remained pristine and relatively untouched.

I was able to get on a flight back to LA the next day and get my daughter back home safely. She had experienced back-to-back traumatic events, but she had been with friends and classmates. She had experienced a communal lament during both the mass shooting and the wildfire. Her lament was the embodied pain experienced in the midst of trauma. My lament was the lament of helplessness as the parent of a child in danger so far away.

+++

The trauma was real, and so the lament had to be real. The trauma was experienced in the body and in a specific geographic location, and therefore the lament had to be expressed in a specific time and place. The trauma was experienced by a community, so the lament had to be communal. Lament could not be avoided because the pain, grief, and trauma were very real and therefore could not so easily be swept under the rug. While we experienced this very specific trauma through different lenses, the reality of this pain and suffering could not be denied. Grief and trauma required a response from both generations who experienced this painful reality.

I (Shaya) am coming to the text as a young adult as a part of the audience we are seeking to reach in the text. I am not only a young adult myself, I've also studied and written on the topic of emerging adulthood spirituality from a theological and psychological perspective as a student in Fuller Seminary's clinical psychology doctoral program. For the first time in four years, I'm approaching ministry with young adults more as an observer than as an active participant. I'm holding the tension of grieving the loss of a faith community that formed me and embracing a new community that is reinforming my theology of grief and lament. Lament, therefore, came out of necessity. Lament helped me to grieve without losing my faith. In time it eventually gave me a much richer appreciation for the stories throughout Scripture that capture what it means to cry out to God without turning away from my faith. It has also given me an appreciation for the role of narrative-informed trauma therapy. I see it as a necessity to cultivate a robust theology of lament for and with the church as an emerging clinician.

I (Soong-Chan) come to this project as first a father of two children who are in the generation that we seek to reach with this text. My immediate connection as a parent of two Gen Zers provides me with a different perspective as an outsider to this community but with a vested interest in and genuine concern for this community. I also approach this subject as a former pastor and a current seminary professor who has influence over and concern for those who are seeking to minister to a younger generation. In my ministry, I have seen the profound power of grief and the significant hold it can have on a community that refuses to acknowledge grief and the pain that comes with that grief. Lament, therefore, has become an important theme in my writing and in my teaching.[1]

GENERATIONAL GRIEF

All generations experience trauma in some form, yet there can be a division that happens when some people tend to internalize pain while others turn outward to express pain. Generational response to trauma varies within a community. Degrees of hyperindividualism, toxic masculinity, and conflict avoidance all impact how a generation deals with trauma. Stereotypes abound regarding how different generations may respond. The builders (the generation that survived the Depression and multiple world wars) are assumed to be the strong, stoic, and resilient generation that are impervious to pain and struggle. They have experienced multiple traumatic situations but have survived through their determination and the gritting of their teeth. Often, they internalized pain and suffering and did not engage in lament in order to assert and affirm their self-perception of exceptionalism and triumphalism.

As the builders pass on from US society, the boomers (born after World War II as part of a baby boom) inherit that self-perception of ex-

---

1. See my previous work on this topic: Soong-Chan Rah, *Prophetic Lament: A Call for Justice in Troubled Times* (IVP Books, 2015).

ceptionalism. Even if the boomers had not built like the builders, they certainly were exceptional for continuing American greatness and, therefore, not needing lament as a spiritual practice. Lament operated as a barrier to the boomers' sense of entitlement emerging from their exceptionalism and triumphalism. Gen X continued this sense of entitlement while living further and further away from the actual victories over very real challenges of the previous generations. Each of these generations were acknowledged as outdoing their parents' generation with higher income, a more lavish lifestyle, and an increasing sense of entitlement and exceptionalism.

Gen Y (millennials) and Gen Z (zoomers) emerged in rapid succession from generations that embraced exceptionalism and triumphalism. However, unlike previous generations, Gen Y and Gen Z had no guarantees of a better life based upon higher income and improving standard of living. Gen Y and Gen Z have lived through two pandemics in their lifetime: (1) COVID-19, which sharply curtailed any sense of exceptionalism and triumphalism, and (2) the pandemic of depression and anxiety, which has wreaked havoc across the generations but has performed on an epidemic level for recent generations, resulting in a collective social-psychological trauma.

As someone who falls between Gen Y and Gen Z, I (Shaya) find myself at a crossroads. I am not the only one to experience this generational malaise. Even within the same generation, the difference between being twenty years old and being thirty years old could feel like a chasm. It's no wonder builders, boomers, Gen Xers, millennials (Gen Y), and zoomers (Gen Z) struggle to find common language. This could not be more true when it comes to how church members of all ages are addressing their grief and pain. As a mid-twenty-something, I am now exploring what lies beneath my sadness and grief. Perhaps the greatest strength of the emerging adult generation is our willingness to lean in and ask *why*. The challenge is finding the right place to ask *why* and the right people to ask *why* with. Asking *why* requires balancing the tension of being in a place of present human ambiguity while holding to the promise that God is with us now and for all eternity. There is also the additional confusion of who God is—the essence of God's character that we cannot fully comprehend, at least not yet. This type of psychological, theological, and ecclesial ambiguity is an ever-present reality in the lives of the younger generation.

Our generation has more immediate access to available resources for expressing grief than those that came before us. For example, if you search for #grief, #grief support, #grief recovery on Instagram, you will find well over 4 million posts. The online resources explaining grief are seemingly endless. However, the space for human communal connection is very much absent, leading to further isolation and disconnect. We know it's not good to isolate when we're grieving, but the new spaces accessible to us through technology and social media do not provide the depth of community needed for genuine human connection.

Furthermore, the spaces once deemed safe and sacred for communal connection may carry a negative connotation for today's young adults. For example, if the church is the source of pain and grief, it is unlikely young people will turn to it for healing. Ideally, young adults would turn to mental health professionals to process their grief. More likely, they are turning to other platforms such as social media, even if they are inadequate, because they may find a sense of belonging where they can "control" who gets access to hurt them. Young adults are creating a new kind of shared language to capture their grief. The irony is that much of the language is actually emulating the lament theology expressed all throughout Psalms—honest, human, vulnerable, and longing for intervention and change.

THEOLOGY OF LAMENT

In contrast to social and even ecclesial norms, the Scriptures offer an alternative view of dealing with pain and suffering. The psalms, which reveal the worship life of Israel in the Old Testament, demonstrate the necessity of balance in worship between a joyful celebration and an acknowledgment of pain and suffering. If you were to divide the psalms between the two larger genres of Hebrew worship, about 60 percent would be hymns of praise while 40 percent would be songs of lament. The balance of both hymns of praise and songs of lament is consistently demonstrated among God's people throughout Scripture.

In contrast, lament as an expression of worship in the American church is largely absent. *Prophetic Lament*, a commentary on the book of Lamentations, recognizes that lament is notably absent in nearly every Christian worship tradition. Liturgical churches often omit laments from their readings from the Psalter. Less than 20 percent of the hymns in traditional worship services that rely upon hymnals could be considered hymns of lament. Christian Copyright Licensing International (CCLI), which tracks the use of contemporary worship songs, reveals a dominance of songs that reflect the theme of praise and triumph: "How Great Is Our God," "Happy Day," "Indescribable," "Friend of God," "Glorious Day," "Marvelous Light," and "Victory in Jesus."[2]

Old Testament scholar Claus Westermann categorizes the psalms into the two categories of praise and lament and asserts that "as the two poles, they determine the nature of all speaking to God."[3] Psalms and hymns of praise express honor and glory to God for the good things God has done. Lament expresses the need for God to intervene in the midst of pain and trouble. Lament can be defined as the appropriate theological, ecclesial, liturgical, spiritual response to the reality of suffering, pain, crisis, and injustice in the world. The second half of the definition points toward the need to see the reality of pain and suffering in the world. Both conditions must exist for lament to occur: the truth telling about a broken world and an authentic response to that reality.

US culture (and the US church) gravitates toward the narrative of exceptionalism in American history and society. This assertion of American exceptionalism leads to the absence of truth telling, since negative examples would challenge this dysfunctional and unbiblical assumption. The absence of truth telling about history and social reality presents a position in contradiction to the biblical practice of lament. A segment of the US culture and government is so focused on generating a sense of American exceptionalism and triumphalism that truth telling has been eliminated.

Florida's so-called Stop WOKE act is an attempt to censor education and has been applauded by many in the conservative white Christian

---

2. Rah, *Prophetic Lament*, 21–22.
3. Claus Westermann, *Praise and Lament in the Psalms* (John Knox, 1981), 152.

community. The law asserts that persons should not be instructed to "feel guilt, anguish, or other forms of psychological distress" due to their race, color, sex, or national origin. Truth telling about the social reality of pain and injustice has been outlawed by the state of Florida. The lack of truth telling reflects a profound obsession by the dominant white, male culture to be seen as doing good, a form of excessive triumphalism, particularly given the historical reality that the world is not good and the United States is not perfect. Instead of applauding attempts to hinder the full education of the individual, Christians should be at the forefront of truth telling. To put it in theological terms—Florida's Stop WOKE act is the inappropriate intrusion of the state into the church's ability to engage in the biblical practice of lament. The state is interrupting the church's ability to express the full worship of God. The absence of lament in the larger US culture is reflected in the absence of lament in the US Christian community, which has a biblical mandate to lament.

The psalms emphasize the importance of lament, which allows people to tell their stories truthfully and honestly in order to process their experiences. The psalms capture what perhaps is the closest thing to the Israelites' telling the full truth of the trauma they were experiencing. It captures what psychologists recognize as one of the critical components in trauma recovery: sharing your story, putting language to your grief and owning your lived experience for what it is—broken. Trauma sufferers often have trouble making logical sense of their emotions and experiences since nothing feels coherent. The psalms of lament convey this state of illogical thinking. Using these poems to create personal laments can be a helpful tool because poetry, like music, is processed in the right brain, which allows someone to write while the left part of the brain (Broca's area) is still impaired. Psychologically and emotionally, we need to make meaning out of our grief in order to move toward healing.

We cannot ignore the need for lament in communities of faith. "A church that goes on singing 'happy songs' in the face of raw reality is doing something very different from what the Bible itself does."[4] If the church provides the space where faith is practiced and formed, then the

---

4. Glenn Pemberton, *Hurting with God: Learning the Language of Lament* (Abilene Christian University Press, 2012), 25. See also Rah, *Prophetic Lament*.

traditional Sunday morning church service is leaving Christians with a lot of language to learn on their own. We often walk into a Sunday morning church service expecting a plug-and-play experience where people of faith can easily fall into passive acquiescence rather than purposeful participation as the body of Christ. As a part of the body, it is up to us to bring our minds, bodies, and spirits with us into the building. However, that can be hard to do when nearly every church member has experienced trauma of some kind. It is up to the church as the body of Christ to pave a way for people of faith to show up as their embodied selves, knowing that authentic participation as the body of Christ necessitates that we bring our full selves to the table. In the same way that we must learn how to speak and to write, we, as people of faith, must learn how to speak and embody the language of lament individually and communally.

Communal lament requires a community of faith that finds hope in the practice of lament. Our communal laments can join with and reflect the communal laments of Scripture and the church throughout her history. Through our contemporary lament, we join with the biblical laments where the full expression of pain is welcomed and embraced in the context of community. Even the individual expressions of lament in the psalms are experienced and expressed in the community. Old Testament scholar Bernhard Anderson states that "the psalms show that the individual finds his or her identity and vocation in the community that God has created. Within that community of faith one has access to God in worship; and within that community one participates in a great historical pilgrimage."[5] Lament in community is the necessary biblical practice that pushes God's people toward truth telling and the authentic experience of pain and suffering that is required in the journey toward healing and hope.

Today, in our individualized, isolated, and socially conscious Western church, hardly any time is set aside for lament to be practiced in community. However, the need for communal lamentation is becoming increasingly evident in the church. According to an article published

---

5. Bernhard Anderson, *Out of the Depths: The Psalms Speak for Us Today* (Westminster, 1983), 19.

by the Barna Group entitled "Six Reasons Why Young Christians Leave Church," 36 percent of young adults do not feel they can ask their most important life questions in the church. Additionally, 18 percent said that the church "does not help with depression or other emotional problems."[6] As a faith community, we have lost the ability to enter into one another's pain, let alone invite God into that pain with us. This necessitates the task to reestablish the language of lament in the church.

From the COVID-19 pandemic to racial unrest and political upheaval, the church is struggling to stay afloat in a storm where the waves threaten to dismember the body. The church has failed to embrace the language of lament, leaving many young adults to put words to the grief and suffering they experience on their own. Without the language of lament in its liturgy, the church's messaging can inadvertently become a cacophony of toxic positivity. Yet lament is seen all throughout Scripture and is used prominently throughout the history of the church.

The psalms are perhaps the most notable framework for lament in Scripture. Jesus himself cries out to God on the cross in Matthew 27:4, echoing the words from Psalm 22 when he says, "*Eli, Eli, lama sabachthani,*" that is to say, "My God, my God, why hast thou forsaken me?" God's one and only Son engaged in the practice of lament. We look to Jesus as the author and perfecter of our faith. We look to Jesus in order to learn how to pray. We must also look to him to teach us the language of lament. The church throughout history has offered up a lament. Martin Luther's posting of the Ninety-Five Theses can be seen as a lament over a church by one who loved the church but saw much brokenness in the church. Throughout its history, the church persistently offered laments when persecuted. In the more marginalized communities, such as the Black church and the immigrant communities, laments constitute a normal part of church life. And in the global church, we see how a church steeped in injustice, poverty, and brokenness cries out to God through lament. Despite the American church's inability to lament, the church universal and the church global offers the redemptive power of lament.

---

6. "Six Reasons Young Christians Leave Church," Barna, September 27, 2011, https://tinyurl.com/26r36d3k.

AN EMBODIED PSYCHOLOGY OF LAMENT

At their core, our cognitive mental processes are sensorimotor, situated and action oriented.[7] In most situations in our daily and communal contexts, we do not have the time to think for the sake of thinking abstractly. We are thinking in order to make decisions about how to behave, interact with our environment, and interact with other people. The human brain does not reach full cortical thickness until well into the second decade of life. This means that I (Shaya), after nearly twenty-six years, have a fully developed brain (at least from a neurobiological perspective). The first twenty-five years of my life have been years of immense formation, when my brain was being molded and shaped by external influences and pressures—pressures that carry both positive and negative connotations for the ways in which I see the world around me.

One of the primary ways we are being formed during the first two decades of our lives is through relationships. An integral part of understanding our formation is understanding the role that attachment plays in shaping our brain's neural pathways. The study of attachment offers a rich theological and psychological basis for understanding our innate relationality. The early relationships we have as children set the precedent for our relationships moving forward, but we are also constantly evolving and capable of adaptation throughout our lives, meaning that our attachment styles are not fixed. Psychologist John Bowlby found that children who established a secure relationship with their caregivers were more likely to be receptive to change and variability during their development, while those with insecure, avoidant, or disorganized caregivers were more likely to respond in or recoil into rigid ways of coping.[8]

Our brains are not only shaped by our relationships, they are shaped by our earliest narratives. Mirror neurons in the brain enable us to imitate those around us. The communities into which we are integrated matter in our development. Mirroring matters because we are constantly

---

7. W. S. Brown and K. S. Reimer, "Embodied Cognition, Character Formation, and Virtue," *Zygon* 48: 833.
8. John Bowlby, *Attachment and Loss: Attachment*, vol. 1 (Basic Books, 1969).

adapting to the lives of those around us, which means that there is always space to learn what it means to live virtuously or without virtue. If the calling on the lives of Christians is to live as Jesus lived, then it seems that one of the virtues Jesus held dear was sitting with others in their grief and pain. Lamenting in community was central to Jesus's life. And it is an inevitable part of our lives today. Nearly every story we learn growing up—whether it be a part of our nation's history or the history of our family or a children's story, like the stories in *Aesop's Fables*—involves a component of learning and lament. Philosopher Alasdair MacIntyre wrote that when you "deprive children of stories, you leave them unscripted, anxious stutterers in their actions and their words."[9] In our neurobiology, there is a strong case for Christians to see lament as a virtue to be embodied as opposed to a theory to be understood. We are not merely thinking beings. We cannot think ourselves out of our grief and pain. We need community to compel us to see beyond our circumstances. We need others to see us, hold us, cry with us, and be for us. We need each other. We need to be held in the loving presence of another not just because we will feel better, but because in doing so, we are living into what it means to live like Christ in the world today.

If we come to understand our grief as being embodied, we need to challenge the narrative that grief is sequential. This depiction of the stages of grief as linear stems from a Western understanding of grief and loss. Marilyn McCabe found that Western cultural understandings of grief do not fully allow the individual to heal because they prevent the person grieving from maintaining emotional or physical closeness to the thing they are grieving.[10] Shinobu Kitayama and Dov Cohen along with Panagiotis Pentaris have found that in non-Western cultures, part of the grieving process allows the person grieving to maintain a close connec-

---

9. Alasdair MacIntyre, *After Virtue: A Study in Moral Theory* (Bloomsbury, 2011), 251.

10. Marilyn McCabe, *The Paradox of Loss: Toward a Relational Theory of Grief* (Greenwood, 2003). See also J. Cernero, B. D. Strawn, and A. D. Abernethy, "Embodied Grief and Primary Metaphor: Towards a New Paradigm for Integrative Bereavement Groups," *Journal of Psychology and Christianity* 36, no. 4 (Winter 2017): 326.

tion with the person or people who have passed on.[11] McCabe argues that moving away from the thing we are grieving may not actually be in the best interest of the one who is mourning. To lose closeness with the thing, group, or person we are grieving is to become disoriented to who they were in relation to the person they lost.[12] An emotional wound that results in relational rupture in a church context could lead someone to walk away from their faith or faith community entirely. Yet, this severing of relationship leaves the person grieving in a state of disorientation as they try to not only heal spiritually but also to heal psychologically from the loss of formative relationships. The purpose of exploring the psychology of grief is not only to leave us with a psychological foundation for lament but to suggest that lamenting in the communities that have hurt us, which for many young adults includes the church communities that formed them, is one of the ways that we can steward ecclesial spaces for profound healing to occur.

A prominent example of an embodied liturgical practice in the church is taking communion.[13] The physical breaking of the bread and the drinking of the wine is one way we actively participate in simultaneously lamenting the crucifixion of Christ and celebrating that he rose again for the redemption of humanity. Lamenting and celebrating are not isolated experiences; experiencing joy can come in the mourning.

This embodied psychological model of grief necessitates that we participate in liturgies of lament together. This does not negate the need to establish safety for young adults to reengage with the communities that have hurt them. Sometimes the hurt requires the grieving young adult to walk away from a particular communal context. This decision can be deeply painful and divisive, but as the church, we have to be ready to love and to embrace those who have been hurt by the church, which should have been better at loving young adults in the first place.

---

11. Cernero, Strawn, and Abernethy, "Embodied Grief," 328.
12. Cernero, Strawn, and Abernethy, "Embodied Grief," 329.
13. Cernero, Strawn, and Abernethy, "Embodied Grief," 330.

UNTANGLING TRAUMA TODAY

While many people have referenced 2020 as the worst of the pandemic, many licensed psychologists believe we are still being "actively traumatized" and won't see the full impact until much later.[14] "You're not able to assess the damage while the tornado is still raging."[15] Isolation of young adults was rampant prior to the pandemic, but now, young adults are fleeing the communal spaces and sacred places, not because they have found the answers, but because they crave relationships that can provide a means for them to confront the raw realities of being human.

Young adults are standing at the threshold of so-called sacred places seeking respite and comfort yet find themselves unable to step across the threshold because of the hurt that the church is actively complicit in. What many church communities have failed to embrace is that "trauma does not need to be brought *into* the discussion of theology because theology already has grounds to speak about trauma."[16] To follow Jesus was never about choosing cheap joy. It was about embracing a new way of being human. The Psalms speak to the desires of the human heart to find safety in God. Trauma counseling teaches that the number one priority for trauma survivors is establishing safety as the first step in treatment and to find respite for one's soul, one's body, and one's mind.[17]

Establishing a communal language of lament requires a recognition of the communal and individual traumas that every member of a congregation or community brings with them. In light of the recent literature on trauma recovery, an integrated, embodied approach could create space in church communities for learning the language of lament. This embodiment includes not only our physical selves but an acknowledgment and acceptance of our cultural, social, and ethnic differences.

---

14. Anita Phillips, "Barna: The State of the Church," Barna Group, May 7, 2021.
15. Phillips, "Barna."
16. Alex R. Wendel, "Trauma-Informed Theology or Theologically Informed Trauma? Traumatic Experiences and Theological Method," *Journal of Reformed Theology* 16, no. 1–2 (April 8, 2022): 3–26, 18.
17. Wendel, "Trauma-Informed Theology?," 18.

Today, most people who have experienced trauma of some kind often express a feeling of being stuck. The church is also stuck in patterns of avoidance and complicity when it comes to confronting systemic abuse. We all must find a way forward. But we must move forward as one body made up of a tapestry of beautifully diverse and necessary parts. "By bringing diverse voices that have been ignored or marginalized into a pulpit as an expression of the gospel, a hermeneutic of lament can open the way to practicing hospitality for interpreting and reading biblical texts in diverse ways."[18] It starts with amplifying the stories of those who have historically had their voices silenced or taken away.

And sometimes it starts with starting over. It starts with walking away from the places that have formed our faith because to stay is to leave behind a part of our humanness. To live in the *imago Dei* is to embrace the entirety of our humanity. Any church that wants to be a place of healing must radically embrace the other. That means recognizing the inherent worth and dignity in all human beings, not just those human beings who share the same experiences we do.

Young adults are not alone in crying out for institutions to show up authentically. They desperately want to see Christians taking a stand for those on the margins. They are searching for spaces that make them feel safe and desire to do the same for those that society has deemed the least of these.

If the church keeps failing to name our collective grief, where does that leave us? It leaves us chronically anxious, depressed, confused, and desperate. It leaves us living in a polarized climate, questioning whether the church cares more about its ideology or the people it's responsible for caring for. We are desperate for a meaningful narrative to name our grief.

While there may be differing definitions of "church hurt" used in a myriad of ecclesial contexts, we acknowledge the reality of the experience of "church hurt"—however defined by different faith communities.

---

18. Eliana Ah Rum Ku, "A Call for Practicing Hospitality Based on Lament in Preaching for a Wounded Community," *Journal of the Academy of Homiletics* 42, no. 2 (2022): 15–26, 23.

Our assertion is that the appropriate response of lament over "church hurt" has been absent and has resulted in the furthering of that pain. The variety of lived experiences requires a communal response. This response should acknowledge how "church hurt" has been internalized and embodied in ways that make it challenging to grieve and lament together in a faith community.

Often grief and lament are conflated with the loss of faith, but that may not be an accurate assessment. To lament is to be honest. It is to pray with our full selves: mind, body, and spirit. In the church's attempts to remain relevant, hopeful, and joy-filled, it has lost its theology of suffering. Healing and joy can come in the mourning. Grief isn't a futile surrender of our agency. Lament isn't a shallow plea. Grief and lament are a radical reminder that healing is not linear. Our grief is a terrifying acknowledgment that healing isn't cheap. Lament is the necessary full expression of our humanity to a God who feels distant. "Lament is an appeal to God's compassion to intervene and change a desperate situation."[19] Honesty before God can be the beginning of hope.

The church must be better. It must be better at its welcome and embrace. We need those tangible reminders of the Lord's provision when the world distorts God's face. We are image bearers—broken, abused, yet still begotten—we bear the image of the one whose goodness we long to taste. Jesus himself still cried out: Abba, Father, please take this cross away from me. He grieved, he suffered, and he died. To grieve is to be human. To lament is to join with Jesus in dying to self. We can't continue to outrun, numb out, and deny ourselves. Our grief will consume us if we try. We are desperate to be known. Church, please be better, we cannot live this life of faith alone.

EPILOGUE

After six years of being a part of the Pepperdine community as an undergrad student, graduate student, and staff member, I (Shaya) walked away, not forever, but for now. I left Pepperdine knowing that I had outgrown a community that formed me in ways for which I am deeply grateful. It is

19. Anderson, *Out of the Depths*, 76.

also a community that left me yearning for a deeper sense of belonging as a woman in ministry. Leaving a church or Christian institution is a story that many young adults are currently walking through. They leave when their full humanity or the fullness of those they care for is not welcomed or accepted. No institution is perfect, but young adults are holding the hope that these institutions will be better at bearing the image of God because while many are leaving, not all have the privilege to walk away.

My (Soong-Chan's) story differs from Shaya's in that I don't have the freedom to walk away. My identity, life, career, livelihood are steeped in the very system that has oppressed me at times. Maybe that's the jaded reality for parents or those from a previous generation. We lack the opportunity, capacity, maybe the courage to walk away from the very systems that have oppressed or continue to oppress us. The space to lament feels absent even for those of us who have been steeped in the system.

When the places we deem safe perpetuate systemic abuse, societal, political, and racial injustice, it's hard to imagine moving forward into a new community of any kind. Can we come back home to our core identity in Christ, embracing the parts of the self that had to be denied to stay safe? That's what trauma does: It challenges us to reimagine and reestablish what normal looks like. The language of healing is elusive, but it is the biblical call of lament, the language of healing that is "not yet." Meanwhile, we continue to move ahead seeking new spaces where the fullness of our humanity is expressed.

Lament requires previously silenced voices to be heard. We must invite the silenced voices of each generation to—in the words of the psalmist—"pour forth their speech." The voices of Gen Z are not extraneous but essential. Can the church offer this space for the marginalized to collectively make meaning out of their grief? The call is to lament together, to carry the cries of our neighbor, to hold the hope with and for those who have been hurt. The church is both the oppressor and the healer; it's time we start embodying this collectively, acknowledging each other's hurt.

For both of us, the crisis of the double traumas at Pepperdine University a few years ago reminded us that there are no easy answers when an unexpected or even expected tragedy occurs. The power of lament was the ability to grieve together in community. Even being able to write together about a shared trauma from different spaces allows for ongoing healing. While other traumas have come and gone since the devastating week at Pepperdine, we recognize that grief and healing are ongoing painful realities that all generations experience. Perhaps shared trauma is what brings a community together, and shared lament is how a community heals together.

5

HEALTH AND WHOLENESS

Trauma, Anxiety, and Our Call to Mental Health

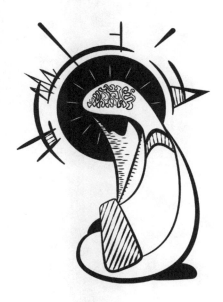

Sarah Brock Iverson
Jia Johnson

OUR INVITATION

We're glad you're here! Because our unique experiences with mental health are deeply shaped by the bodies, situations, and ZIP codes we are born into, we think it's important for you to understand a little about the people who wrote this chapter. I (Sarah) am a white, cisgender, Lutheran millennial woman who was raised in rural Minnesota, now working as a physician assistant at a women's health clinic near Minneapolis, where I engage in mental health care daily. I am passionate about the church, challenging the church, and supporting the force for good that the church can be. I (Jia) am a mix-raced, cisgender woman who identifies as Black. I am unchurched, spiritually eclectic, and live with invisible disabilities. I am a mission-driven social entrepreneur, mind-body somatic coach, and founder of Freedom Dream Collective, a mission-driven organization committed to supporting the holistic well-being of social changemakers.

Our lives, like yours, reveal that humans are complex creatures. We are storied people. We are formed and shaped by both nature and nurture. Decisions not made by us, whether they be within families or institutions or systems and structures, shape our existence. They determine how we navigate and respond to our inner world and the world around us. They determine what resources we have or do not have to support our well-being and the well-being of those around us. At the same time, we each have agency. Through self-determination, advocacy, and collective power, we can shift culture, practices, and ways of being that serve the common good of all, including our individual selves.

The young adults who inspired this book project are well aware of these lived realities and the importance of mental health. As a collective voice, we desire the church to create communities of belonging. A community that responds to the urgent need to create a culture that prioritizes mental health education and awareness, fosters the destigmatization of mental health and illness, and promotes openness and authenticity. It is our hope that the church would be better equipped to engage in conversations, resourcing, and resiliency around mental health. We (Sarah and Jia) hope to offer inspiration and insights that support you in shifting your church culture to one that prioritizes the mental wellness of your community.

UNPACKING MENTAL HEALTH AND TRAUMA

A few years ago, I (Jia) spoke to a group of undergraduate students in a public ministry degree program in Minnesota. I was there to speak about my work as an abolitionist, relational educator, and spiritual activist. One of the many professional hats I wore in the past was the director of the Solidarity Building Initiative for Liberative Carceral Education, most commonly known as SBI. SBI is an initiative of McCormick Theological Seminary to offer higher education to incarcerated students at the Cook County Department of Corrections.

After my presentation, one of the students asked me when the first time I visited a jail was. No one had ever asked me that question before. I instantly remembered my first time. In 2013/2014 my family and I drove thirty minutes to the county jail in my hometown to visit my younger brother. He spent about a year and a half in the county jail on false charges.

What I have come to learn from personal and professional experience is that most incarcerated people were victims of injustice long before they found themselves incarcerated. This is also true in my family story. At a very young age, my brother and I were exposed to the physical, psychological, and emotional trauma of racism. His experience as a young brown boy was far more egregious than mine. And he was exposed to street drugs by an adult who was an educator and entrusted with nurturing his development. My brother's lived experience over the years led to compounded acute trauma and secondary trauma for me and my family, eventually leading him to become part of the 1.2 million Americans who are criminalized and incarcerated for substance dependency and mental illness, making me part of the one in four Americans who have had a sibling incarcerated and my family part of the 6.5 million adults who have an immediate family member currently incarcerated in jail or prison.[1]

In addition to the secondary trauma I experienced within my family dynamic, by the time I was in my early thirties, I had experienced the trauma of intimate partner violence and sexual assault. According to the Centers for Disease Control and Prevention, "Over half of women and almost one in three men have experienced sexual violence involving physical contact during their lifetimes. More than four in five female rape survivors reported that they were first raped before age 25, and almost half were first raped as a minor (i.e., before age eighteen)."[2] The details of my story are unique to me and my family, but the experiences of trauma and its impact on mental health are ubiquitous. We are counted among the many.

The Impacts of Trauma on Mental Health

The Substance Abuse and Mental Health Administration of the US Department of Health and Human Services states, "Mental health includes our emotional, psychological and social well-being. It affects how we think, feel and act, and helps determine how we handle stress, relate to others and make choices."[3] At every stage of human development, mental health is essential. Factors such as biology; genes and brain chemistry; life experiences, including trauma and abuse; and family history of mental health challenges shape and inform one's mental health.

While mental health is not the same as mental illness, they are connected. Mental illness falls under the umbrella of mental health.

---

1. Madeo Admin, "Half of Americans Have Family Members Who Have Been Incarcerated," Equal Justice Initiative, December 11, 2018, https://tinyurl.com/4hyz72np.

2. "About Sexual Violence," US Centers for Disease Control, January 23, 2024, https://tinyurl.com/8kdjyj98.

3. "What Is Mental Health?," Substance Abuse and Mental Health Services Administration, April 24, 2023, https://tinyurl.com/zrhv3zx4.

Someone can have a mental illness and have all the tools to support the flourishing of their mental health. At the same time, one can have poor mental health without mental illness. Research indicates that 50 percent of people living in the United States will be diagnosed with a mental health condition or mental illness, and one in eight people are living with a mental health disorder. The most common are depression and anxiety disorder.[4] Other conditions include bipolar disorder, substance use disorders, schizophrenia, obsessive-compulsive disorder, eating disorder, and posttraumatic stress disorder (PTSD). Support and resources for maintaining one's mental health are vital regardless of where one falls on the spectrum of mental wellness.

Resmaa Menakem, in *My Grandmother's Hands: Racialized Trauma and the Pathway to Mending Our Hearts and Bodies*, says this about trauma:

> When something happens to the body that is too much, too fast, or too soon, it overwhelms the body and can create trauma. Contrary to what many people believe, trauma is not *primarily* an emotional response. Trauma always happens in the body. It is a spontaneous protective mechanism used by the body to stop or thwart further (or future) potential damage. Trauma is not a flaw or a weakness. It is a highly effective tool of safety and survival. Trauma is also not an event. Trauma is the body's protective response to an event—or a series of events—that it perceives as potentially dangerous. This perception may be accurate, inaccurate, or entirely imaginary.[5]

Trauma is how the human body protects itself from anything that disrupts its sense of "belonging, dignity, and safety."[6] It is also true that

---

4. "Mental Health and Mental Disorders," Healthy People 2030, US Department of Health and Human Services, accessed January 18, 2025, https://health.gov/healthypeople/objectives-and-data/browse-objectives/mental-health-and-mental-disorders.

5. Resmaa Menakem, *My Grandmother's Hands: Racialized Trauma and the Pathway to Mending Our Hearts and Bodies* (Central Recovery, 2017), 7 (emphasis added). A fourth trauma response has since been identified—fawn—which is the body's stress response to try and please someone to avoid conflict.

6. Staci K. Haines, *The Politics of Trauma: Somatics, Healing, and Social Justice* (North Atlantic Books, 2019), 133, Kindle edition.

some people groups experience higher rates of trauma for longer periods of time and over generations due to their race, gender, religious beliefs, economic status, sexual orientation, and the like, compounding the effects of trauma and overall mental health. One way this happens is through embedded trauma.

Resmaa states, "An embedded trauma response can manifest as fight, flee or freeze—or as some combination of constriction, pain, fear, dread, anxiety, unpleasant (and/or sometimes pleasant) thoughts, reactive behaviors, or other sensations and experiences. This trauma then gets stuck in our body until it is addressed. We can have a trauma response to anything we perceive as a threat, not only to physical safety, but to what we do, say, think, care about, believe in, or yearn for."[7] This definition of embedded trauma or unresolved trauma offers nuance and, in many ways, normalizes the experience of trauma and provides insights into understanding this very human experience. Seventy percent of adults in the United States have experienced some type of traumatic event at least once in their lives.[8] What we know to be true is, we cannot speak about mental health without also recognizing the impacts of trauma in people's lives. They are intertwined.

Telling Our Stories

It was not until I was in my early thirties that I began to face the reality of my own story. Addressing my poor mental health became a necessity. It was the first time someone (my spiritual advisor) referred to my lived experience as shaped by trauma. I was shocked and offended. At that time, terms like "trauma," "mental health," and "mental illness" were "taboo." Like most people, I had internalized the language of trauma as something fundamentally wrong with me as opposed to something that had happened to me. Trauma was for other people but not for me.

I grew up in a safe middle-class neighborhood in the stereotypical nuclear family. While I am of mixed identity, Black, Spaniard, and Syrian,

---

7. Menakem, *My Grandmother's Hands*, 7.
8. National Council for Behavioral Health. This statistic represents 223.4 million people.

I grew up in a color-blind household. In learning about my own history and origin story, I have come to understand that assimilation into color-blind ideology was a means of survival for my parents and, in some ways, a means to preserve their mental health. But in reality, it was a false sense of comfort and protection that did not equip me with the tools to navigate the realities of interpersonal and systemic oppression I encountered growing up, making me vulnerable to internalized oppression.

Like the majority of the American population who has not sought treatment for clinical-level mental health issues and the 25 percent of those who do not seek help for fear of stigma and invasion of privacy, I (and my brother) did not have the mental health tools to help me process and metabolize the traumas I had experienced.[9] In the absence of healthy coping mechanisms, my mental health suffered, impacting my quality of life. I turned to unhealthy coping mechanisms that merely compounded the physical, psychological, emotional, and interpersonal effects of the unresolved trauma. In my brother's case, he was eventually criminalized and incarcerated for his mental health condition.

My lived experience, my relationship with my sibling, and my work with individuals who have experienced incarceration have exposed me to the reality that in the United States, rather than providing people who have mental health challenges with a warm bed and compassionate care, we criminalize, stigmatize, and incarcerate. Oftentimes the very institutions that claim to provide therapeutic, rehabilitative, and supportive environments are the ones that create the most harm. This is also true of the church. As I coauthor this chapter with Sarah, I cannot help but recall the many times I sat in pews riddled with anxiety, PTSD, and depression, listening to sermons urging people to get involved and serve the church. Every time I heard that message, I felt a deep sense of guilt

---

9. "Here we provide insight into help seeking behavior reported by ~45,000+ respondents in 2021 through the Mental Health Million project. We find that over half of all people globally with clinical level mental health risks do not seek any help for their challenges. The major reasons are not knowing what kind of help to seek and thinking that seeking help won't make a difference. In the United States, only 25% of those not seeking help cite stigma or not wanting others to know as a reason." "Mental Health Has Bigger Challenges Than Stigma," Sapien Labs, 2021, https://tinyurl.com/2388hfjj.

for not having the bandwidth to serve. I was merely trying to survive. At the same time, I felt alone and ashamed. I was alone because I did not have a community of support that could help me understand what I was experiencing. I was ashamed because the history of my lived experience was antithetical to purity culture.[10] I recall confiding in a pastor only to receive a blank stare followed by a Scripture and a mini-sermon on how perfect love casts out all fear. What I learned from that pastor was that my experience was a result of not loving God enough. I was broken and in need of fixing.

I am guilty of calling myself or someone else broken, implying that I or they must be fixed. The more I am intentional about being attentive to nurturing my mental health, the more I wholeheartedly believe no one is broken. We are all wounded people in search of healing. I am convinced sin is less about moral failure and more about unresolved trauma that results in harm to self, harm to others, harm to the community, and harm to Earth and other-than-human kin. We carry in our bodies experiences of deep pain and hurt. Some of us have been given the tools, space, and resources to heal our wounds, while others have been deprived of the resources to heal.

I share my story because I firmly believe that part of how we begin to dissolve the stigmas that keep us silent is by speaking our truth. It is by speaking our truth that we find solidarity. It gives people the courage to come out from hiding and find support and resources in a community that sees and hears them because they, too, share the experience. What would it look like for the church to create a culture where people can come out of hiding and be truly seen and offered the space and resources to flourish their mental wellness?

UNPACKING MENTAL HEALTH AND ANXIETY

It was Christmas Eve. I (Sarah) was a new physician assistant and the only one working in the small-town clinic that day. My gut tried to reassure me that the patient's chest pain was indeed a panic attack. Medical school had done a good job of training me on how to keep bodies alive and

---

10. For more, see chapter 8, "Sex Is a Gift," in this volume.

find which organ was malfunctioning. So, I ordered an X-ray of the lungs and an electrocardiogram of the heart. But all the textbooks and hours of studying in the library hadn't fully prepared me for the very real and physical ways every body held a story. How muscle fibers, brain neurons, and hormone-signaling pathways could carry the effects of anxiety and trauma for years—resulting in very real physical symptoms. It took me even longer to see how anxiety was taking a toll on my own body.

Epidemic of Anxiety

I don't listen to the news anymore on my drive to work because I have lost confidence in (some of) our leaders and (some of) our news sources. Mostly, I have lost confidence in my ability to not let the constant onslaught of crisis-laden, injustice-steeped news spike my own anxiety. And if I were to turn on the news, there would be stories about people losing confidence in our government, police force, school systems, justice system, and climate—to name a few.

Theologian Jürgen Moltmann once claimed that all of the world's wealthiest countries are plagued by anxiety. He contends that it is "not anxiety about any particular thing" but rather "general malaise, a loss of confidence—an undefined attitude to life which continually expects the worst."[11] As I read his words, I highlighted and circled the phrase "loss of confidence." That phrase that Moltmann used to describe 1970s Germany aptly describes the epidemic of anxiety that clings to us today.

When we lose our confidence in the world around us, our brains start doing unhelpful things with that uncertainty. Our prefrontal cortex, the "most evolved" part of our brain and the center of critical thinking, thrives on making predictions and plans about the future. If the prefrontal cortex perceives a lack of information or inaccurate information, then it starts spiraling through all the possible outcomes—including bad or unlikely ones. Like any muscle memory, the more this pattern of spiral-

---

11. Jürgen Moltmann, *Experiences of God*, trans. Margaret Kohl (Fortress, 1980), 37.

ing occurs, the stronger those "spiraling" neurons become and anxiety takes up residence.[12]

An estimated one-third of US adults will experience an anxiety disorder in their lifetime.[13] The prevalence of anxiety and depression, which can often co-occur with anxiety, is increasing. Rates of anxiety and depression in US young adults increased by 63 percent from 2005 to 2017.[14] Please reread that last sentence. Young adults are struggling. Then the COVID-19 pandemic hit, and the problem became worse. Anxiety and depression increased 25 percent across all age groups during the first year of the pandemic.[15] We are all struggling.

Statistics describe the incidence of anxiety *disorders*. That includes people diagnosed with generalized anxiety disorder, panic disorder, obsessive-compulsive disorder, phobias, social anxiety disorder, PTSD, agoraphobias, and separation anxiety disorder. What the numbers don't account for is that everyday anxiety and stress affect all of us, leading to systemic and collective anxiety. This is the anxiety that is polarizing our country. The anxiety that makes us build walls, cling tightly to our guns, hoard our money, and fear those that are different from us. It robs us of our curiosity and creativity. It breeds a self-centeredness that is unhealthy for ourselves and the world we interact with.

Anxious Bodies

As a health-care provider, I see firsthand the physical manifestations of this culture of anxiety. I've witnessed a patient, days into a panic attack,

---

12. Judson Brewer, *Unwinding Anxiety: New Science Shows How to Break the Cycles of Worry and Fear to Heal Your Mind* (Avery, 2021).

13. "Any Anxiety Disorder," National Institute of Mental Health, accessed December 12, 2024, https://tinyurl.com/2s3zsyxj.

14. Emma Kauana Osorio and Emily Hyde, "The Rise of Anxiety and Depression Among Young Adults in the United States," *Ballard Brief*, Winter 2021, https://tinyurl.com/mr3meau3.

15. "COVID-19 Pandemic Triggers 25% Increase in Prevalence of Anxiety and Depression Worldwide," news release, World Health Organization, March 2, 2022, https://tinyurl.com/238npjwb.

curled up in a ball on my exam table, with numb hands and feet from days of hyperventilation. I've seen women suffer chronic headaches and abdominal pain that completely resolve once they leave an abusive relationship. In the height of COVID-19 stay-at-home orders, I had a patient who saw specialist after specialist trying to figure out a cause for her chronic shortness of breath. Then she tried an antianxiety medication, and she was finally able to breathe deeply again.

Some anxiety is more discreet. I have had episodes of chest tightness throughout my life. Usually the episodes were in response to an upcoming stressor (like finals in college); the tight feeling would last a few days and then disappear for several weeks to months. A couple of years ago the episodes became more frequent and eventually the tightness became constant. The feeling didn't make sense to me. I had a happy relationship with my partner, close relationships with family and friends, and was doing well at work—so I couldn't make sense of the anxious cloud that sat on my chest. As a provider I work hard to break through mental health stigma every day with patients: I was the one that helped others work through their anxieties, and I didn't want to admit that I needed help too.

I spent a few months pretending I didn't have anxiety, ignoring the tightness in my chest. As a healthy, young adult, I knew the heaviness in my chest was unlikely my heart or lungs, but, in my denial, I tried taking antacids (because maybe it was heartburn!). I had my primary-care provider check my thyroid function (hoping it was hyperthyroidism). I thought maybe it was muscle pain (so I stretched and took ibuprofen). Nothing helped. I decided it was just the stress of being a health-care provider in a pandemic.

Ignoring the anxiety made it worse. I have a very calm demeanor, so fortunately (or probably unfortunately) no one around me noticed I was struggling. Finally, I made appointments with a therapist and a psychiatrist. My therapist helped me see how the chest tightness was the result of unhelpful thought patterns that my brain had sunk into. She helped me get curious about my anxiety instead of getting mad at it or ignoring it. Learning to notice and be curious about how my brain worked slowly helped me make little changes in my life and rewire my brain into more helpful, life-giving thought patterns. My psychiatrist started me on medication so that I could do a better job tackling the hard work of cognitive behavioral therapy (CBT).

Through therapy and getting curious, I was able to see how much my anxiety was affecting my life. As my anxiety began to dissipate, I noticed that I enjoyed my job more, had more patience for my family, was less exhausted after work, and communicated more easily with my partner. I observed that when I was anxious I was more judgmental and less outgoing, thoughtful, and patient. I will probably always have moments when anxiety gets the best of me. Mental health and wellness is a journey, not a destination. I'm learning how to incorporate better habits of self-care in my life. Recognizing how and when my mental health is struggling allows me to find my way back to the joyful, loving person God created me to be.

The Body of Christ

When anxiety hits, we turn inward. I have seen this in myself, my patients, our country, and the church. We imagine the worst scenarios, expect the worst of others, and see scarcity without abundance.[16] If left unchecked, these expectations breed fear and hopelessness. In our bodies, anxiety increases the activity of our sympathetic "fight or flight" nervous system, which increases heart rate, constricts blood vessels, and strains the heart. Digestion slows, the immune system becomes weaker, cortisol increases, and inflammation rises. All the essential functions of a healthy body, including sleeping, eating, and fighting off disease, become more difficult. The only thing the body is better at in this state is seeing danger, fighting, and running away.

My day job is tending to physical bodies, but I also worry about the church body. Not only is the church body made up of individuals struggling with their own mental health and carrying the weight of our country's collective anxieties, but there's deep-seated anxiety about the future of the church. There is decline in church participation and seminary enrollment. Traditions that have long been a part of the church

---

16. Refer to chapter 11, "Reclaiming 'Enough.'"

are dying with a generation. The church of the future is unclear. This is causing anxiety.

The world is rapidly changing—so it's appropriate for the ears of the church to perk up, notice the changes, and get a *little* anxious—enough to motivate self-reflection and curiosity. Unfortunately, anxiety has instead taken hold of the church in unhelpful ways. An anxious church gets defensive when, let's say, a young adult questions the validity of an age-old tradition or points out ways the church might be contributing to systemic injustice. An anxious church turns inward, imprisoned by its expectations, seeing more threats than opportunities.

The apostle Paul describes the church as a body with distinct, unique body parts working together to be something greater than the sum of its parts, highlighting the interconnectedness of humanity. He writes, "But God has so composed the body, giving greater honor to the part that lacked it, that there may be no division in the body, but that the members may have the same care for one another. If one member suffers, all suffer together; if one member is honored, all rejoice together. Now you are the body of Christ and individually members of it" (1 Cor. 12:24–27 ESV). Paul wrote these lines for a very specific audience in a very specific time, but I imagine that he might include similar lines in a letter to our churches in our polarized and anxious country.

Think of the immune system of the church body as the church's resiliency. Chronic stress suppresses resiliency, making it more difficult to recognize and address something toxic. The blood vessels of the church could be the conduit between scarcity and abundance. Chronic stress causes vasoconstriction, causing the church, like the human body, to hold more tightly to its resources instead of letting them flow out easily and freely. Think of the church's ability to problem-solve as its digestive system—the ability to break down overwhelming concerns into smaller, more manageable concepts.

Inflammation is the chronic stress felt by the people of the church. A healthy body can address and take care of inflammation before it gets systemic. A healthy church knows how to recognize individuals in crisis, instinctively turns toward the hurt, and does the hard work of healing and reconciliation before it becomes systemic. A church overcome by anxiety, with a suppressed immune system, doesn't recognize little pockets of inflammation (i.e., greed, ego, distrust, fear). Additionally, it doesn't have the energy to properly address and heal, and thus the inflammation spreads to every system of the body (i.e., homophobia, systemic racism, white nationalism). As communities of faith, we are called to pay attention to these symptoms of anxiety and work to heal them.

OUR CALL TO MENTAL HEALTH

In *My Body, My Earth: The Practice of Somatic Archaeology*, Ruby Gibson writes,

> The essence of healing is really quite simple. What it all boils down to is that you must learn to love your story. You know what I mean—the personal issues, the family dynamics, and the burdens of humanness. You may not like your story or think you deserve what you've inherited, but you've got to learn to love it in a way that transforms it. Otherwise, you will keep passing the unhealed or fragmented stories forward, generation to generation, until someone grabs a hold of them and decides that they have the capacity to remember the truth, heal the wounds, and create a different story.[17]

Our call to mental health is to be healed and made well. Wellness is holistic healing—spiritual, physical, emotional, social, and economic. There is so much to heal.

Andre Henry, a singer, songwriter, best-selling author, faith leader, and activist, speaks openly about his struggles with mental health, suicidal ideation, and the systemic causes igniting our mental health crises. In recent posts on his Instagram profile, he pushes back on the narrative that mental wellness is solely an individual "problem" and sheds light on the societal and cultural ills that create unsustainable conditions impacting mental wellness. He shares: "If everyone 'needs' therapy, the problem gotta be the environment. . . . If six hundred people get sick from eating at Chipotle this week, we gonna' ask, 'Well. What's goin' on at Chipotle?'

---

17. Ruby Gibson, *My Body, My Earth: The Practice of Somatic Archaeology* (iUniverse, 2008), 5.

If millions of people are struggling with their mental health and dying early from chronic disease, we gotta ask 'Well. What's going on with society?'"[18] He goes on to say, "The best suicide prevention is building a society worth living in. A living wage is suicide prevention. Access to free and high-quality healthcare is suicide prevention. Student loan forgiveness is suicide prevention. Access to free, quality education is suicide prevention. Access to clean water and healthy food is suicide prevention. The end of mass shootings is suicide prevention. Gender-affirming care is suicide prevention. The end of police brutality and endless war is suicide prevention. The end of supremacy culture is suicide prevention. We can't make life hell and then pathologize people who don't want to live. That's torture."[19] Henry tells the story of millions of people, including me and possibly you. It is heavy.

As I (Jia) sit with Henry's words, I notice the tension in my chest and a knot in my throat, and my body contracts as my breath gets shallow. The anxiety is almost paralyzing. It is as expected. We are human and living in untenable conditions. We all live under the same cultural and societal conditions that deplete and rob us of emotional, psychological, and social well-being. Our mental wellness is under assault. For those living on the wrong side of the race, class, and gender line, the consequences are far greater.[20] Some of us are struggling against this culture of hustle and grind fueled by capitalism and supremacy with roots in slavery and colonization. While others are gatekeepers and complicit in fueling burnout culture. And others participate out of survival and a need to make ends meet.

Henry invites us to wrestle with the conditions that have created this individual and collective mental health crisis.[21] According to Tricia Hersey, "Capitalism has cornered us in such a way that we only can comprehend two options: 1: Work at machine level, from a disconnected and exhausted place or 2: Make space for rest and space to connect with our

---

18. Andre Henry, "Why Therapy Isn't Enough, I Need a Revolution," *Medium*, June 14, 2023, https://tinyurl.com/yf5zyns6.
19. Henry, "Why Therapy Isn't Enough."
20. Read more in chapter 7, "Liberating the Sanctuary."
21. Tricia Hersey, *Rest Is Resistance: A Manifesto* (Little, Brown, 2022), 23.

highest selves while fearing how we will eat and live. This rigid binary, combined with the violent reality of poverty, keeps us in a place of sleep deprivation and constant hustle to survive."[22] The remedy to a culture of exploited mental wellness is a cultural revolution of "radical community care."[23] I imagine radical community care unapologetically centering holistic mental wellness for ourselves and others.

When I think of the revolutionary radical community care I have experienced in my life, I am reminded of the tribe of men who broke through obstacles to carry along, lift, and lower down a disabled man who lay on his mat. They set this man before Jesus so that he could be healed. Jesus looked upon the men and saw their collective faith and said, "Friend, your sins are forgiven" (Luke 5:20; cf. Luke 5:17-26; Matt. 9:1-8; Mark 2:1-12). Jesus asked the man to get up, pick up his mat (his stuff), and walk. The man stood up, gathered his belongings, and walked home to his community of belonging, praising God.

The word "sin" is loaded with baggage. It has been used to justify violence, shame, and exclusion. In my theology, sin is what happens when there is unresolved trauma and woundedness. As the old saying goes: hurt people hurt people. I want to be clear that "sin" in this story is not this man's disability. Sin is the cultural and social response to what is deemed other, not "normal," or contrary to the status quo.[24] The New Testament is filled with stories of people who are marginalized for poor mental health, mental illness, physical disabilities, social location of incarceration, poverty, and the like. They were excluded from communal care, religious practices, and economic resources permissible by the social, cultural, religious, and political powers of that time. Sin separates and divides us from the bonds of love and care that are innate to our humanity. It was Jesus in the midst of the community of faith that healed and restored the man for his individual and communal flourishing.

This call to a cultural revolution of radical community care that Tricia Hersey advocates for is the very same message Jesus proclaimed and embodied when he said, "Love your neighbor as yourself" (Mark 12:31 ESV).

22. Hersey, *Rest Is Resistance*, 56-57.
23. Read more in chapter 11.
24. Read more in chapter 7.

Health and Wholeness

The message is not abandoning oneself in pursuit of loving others, nor is it to abandon others in pursuit of loving self. It is to love yourself well and then love others with that same love. To truly love, bell hooks suggests, "we must learn to mix various ingredients—care, affections, recognition, respect, commitment, trust, as well as honest and open communication."[25] hooks's love ethic is one of being well, and from this place of wellness we embody love in action.

While we don't know much about the men who carried the man with disabilities, we can ascertain that these men were well enough to carry their neighbor to Jesus for healing. They moved courageously. They were stopped by nothing. They were unbothered by what others would think or say. They worked harmoniously together—radically—to ensure, beyond themselves, that someone had the opportunity to be made well. They chose to participate in radical community care, embodying hooks's love ethic. Radical community care starts when we reclaim our agency and use our influences of power to shift culture, practices, and ways of being that center radical community care by prioritizing mental wellness.

While writing this section, I was onboarding a new team member, Juah Washington, at the seminary where I worked. I intentionally chose to hire her during our slow season so that she could ease into her new role. We moved slowly through her training, allowing her time to digest and integrate each phase before moving on to the next one. We set boundaries around time, discussed how to work with each other, and set limits to how much work is sustainable.

I shared with her what to expect from our work culture: If I need to scale back on programming, I will because I refuse to burn out myself or my team. If we need to shift deadlines, we do. I set realistic expectations about what can and cannot get done and invite others to do the same with me. I make time for meditation and breathwork when necessary. Rather than moving from a place of urgency, I make decisions based on priority and flexibility and invite others to do the same. Because I am aware of my positional power, I am open and transparent in helping my team understand me as their direct supervisor. If I know my energy feels rushed and overwhelmed, I let them know so they do not assume they

---

25. bell hooks, *Salvation: Black People and Love* (William Morrow, 2001), 5.

have done something wrong. As part of professional development, we meet to discuss Hersey's text *Rest Is Resistance: A Manifesto*.

During one of our debrief sessions, Juah noted how vastly different this work environment was compared to the places where she worked in the past. The shift to centering mental wellness away from the pressures and demands of productivity presented a learning curve for her. I invited her to share her experience. She writes:

> The element of onboarding that required the greatest mindset shift was the invitation to make rest [my mental wellness] a responsibility. A priority that was just as important, or even more important, than the mastering of new learning curves, new systems, and new tasks. It was a violent confrontation to the previous conditioning that was accepted subconsciously: that toxic cultures are what you must settle in while there is a demand to produce. Resting [centering mental wellness] has allowed me to breathe, see, repent, be kind, discover peace, acknowledge the confines that are restricted, and embrace gratitude with a tight grip—almost vowing never to surrender my mind, body, and spirit to pressure over peace.[26]

Juah Washington's experience underscores the transformative power of centering mental wellness as a form of resistance against toxic productivity cultures. In embracing radical community care, we honor the inherent worth and dignity of every individual, recognizing that our liberation is bound together. Let us forge a path toward a future where compassion, empathy, and mutual support are the cornerstones of our churches and communities, and where mental wellness is not just an aspiration but a fundamental human right.

Our call to mental health resonates in the voices of bell hooks, Andre Henry, Tricia Hersey, and the imperative of radical community care. Just as the men who carried their neighbor to Jesus demonstrated, radical community care requires courage, collaboration, and a commitment to wellness for all. As we confront the mental health crisis and pervasive culture of burnout and exploitation, we must prioritize holistic well-

---

26. Juah Washington, personal correspondence with author.

being and systemic change. By embracing hooks's love ethic and Henry's advocacy for societal transformation, we recognize that mental wellness is inseparable from collective liberation. Through intentional practices and culture shift, we challenge oppressive structures and reclaim agency over our lives.

MENTAL WELLNESS IN COMMUNITY

My (Sarah's) younger sister is just starting out her career in theology and church leadership. Over dinner recently she pointed out to me that organized religion is one of the major public forms of group nervous system regulation. Communal singing, chanting, and reading combined with intentional silence and synced movements (like kneeling, sitting, standing, bowing) all help stimulate the vagus nerve and soothe the primitive, fear-prone, reptilian region of the brain.[27] The church, in practices it has held for thousands of years, has embedded in it mental wellness practices that have been soothing heightened nervous systems long before modern neuroscience could describe it as such.

For the modern church to comprise centers for healing and wholeness, it must tap into the sacred holy practices that have helped the church survive this long, address the ways the church has caused harm or stifled healing, and partner with local mental health resources so as to not overspiritualize individual mental health needs. How might churches contribute to mental wellness as communities of radical care?

Fostering Mindfulness Practices

I don't know what word Jesus would have used to describe those moments when he stepped away—be it to the garden, the desert, or just the other room—to just be. Did he call it prayer, meditation, mindfulness, contemplation? Regardless of the label, Jesus clearly understood the importance of pausing to reattune himself to his body and the present—and by extension, to the Holy Spirit.

---

27. Anna Belz-Brock (Episcopal Children and Youth Minister), in discussion with the author, April 2023.

Mindfulness has been described as "paying attention in a particular way: on purpose, in the present moment, and nonjudgmentally."[28] Mindfulness, by grounding us in the present, can free us from the trauma of the past and the anxieties of the future. We can practice mindfulness anytime, such as while washing the dishes or driving to work. However, one of the best ways to help our brain strengthen its mindfulness "muscle" is meditation. Thanks to modern neuroscience, we now know that a regular practice of meditation, even after just a few weeks, causes physical structural changes to the brain. A landmark study in 2011 showed that just eight weeks of meditation and mindfulness training resulted in "increased neural circuitry" or, to put it another way, "increased grey matter density of the insula."[29] A larger anterior insula means a stronger connection between the cortex (center for more advanced reasoning) and limbic system (the more primitive emotional center that plays a key role in triggering the "fight or flight" response). Strengthening this connection helps prevent an overreaction (like getting angry or anxious) from a particular stressor.

How might a few minutes of meditation be woven into worship, Sunday school, or a church council meeting? What if meditation became a habit and the "calming" neural networks of our brains became stronger than the fearful, reactive networks? What might shift if we were more grounded and present when we gathered?

Destigmatizing Medication Management

Medication changes lives and saves lives—whether it is for high blood pressure, depression, anxiety, cancer, or heart disease. Unfortunately, while psychiatric medications can be instrumental to some bodies' healthy flourishing, a cloud of shame surrounds those medications.

---

28. Jon Kabat-Zinn, *Wherever You Go, There You Are: Mindfulness Meditation in Everyday Life* (Hyperion, 2005), 4.

29. Britta K. Hözel et al., "Mindfulness Practice Leads to Increases in Regional Brain Gray Matter Density," *Psychiatry Research: Neuroimaging* 191, no. 1 (January 2011): 36–43, https://doi.org/10.1016/j.pscychresns.2010.08.006, quoted in Caroline Oakes, *Practice the Pause: Jesus' Contemplative Practice, New Brain Science, and What It Means to Be Fully Human* (Broadleaf Books, 2023).

I have had more than one young adult patient who, struggling with their mental health, wants to try taking a medication but can't because their parents won't approve of it or "don't believe in" medication for mental illness. So they say they are just going to get by until they are off their parents' health insurance or move out of their parents' house. What parent wouldn't support their child starting cardiac medication if their heart was struggling? So why do we hesitate when it's the brain?

Our culture has perpetuated the story that seeking medical treatment for mental illness, especially treatment with medication, is a sign of weakness. We are led to believe that if we just prayed more, exercised more, focused on others more, or worked harder, then the symptoms of anxiety or depression would go away. And while prayer, exercise, strong social networks, and meaningful work can all help us thrive, they cannot replace medical treatment when someone is ill. To overspiritualize mental illness and psychiatric treatment is to deepen the chasm between individuals and healthy flourishing.

According to the Centers for Disease Control (CDC), "one in five adults (52.9 million) in the United States were living with a mental health disorder in 2020. However, less than one-half of adults living with a mental health disorder received mental health services in the past year."[30] We, as faith communities, need to push for the healthy flourishing of all people. One way we can do this is to help break the stigma surrounding mental health treatment by sharing stories. Normalize seeing a mental health provider when mental health is struggling or just for a mental health checkup. Normalize taking psychiatric medications when they're needed or beneficial. Normalize the fact that there is no such thing as normal. For some people their normal is needing to take antianxiety medication just as needed, while others manage their mental illness without medication, and some need daily medication for several years.

Jennifer Marshall, a young mother living with bipolar disorder, started sharing stories about her life via an anonymous blog. She soon

---

30. Zachary J. Peters et al., "Emergency Department Visits Related to Mental Health Disorders Among Adults, by Race and Hispanic Ethnicity: United States, 2018–2020," National Health Statistics Reports, no. 181, March 1, 2023, https://tinyurl.com/tjyarz3p.

realized how great the need was for more storytelling platforms for people living with mental illness. She went on to be one of the cofounders of This Is My Brave, a storytelling theater show where individuals share their real stories about living with mental illness.[31] What might happen if your faith community hosted a virtual showing of a This Is My Brave production and held space for discussion afterward? Whose life might change? What relationships might deepen?

Cognitive Behavioral Therapy

One of the evidence-based tools psychotherapists use to help individuals deal with recurring unhelpful emotions like anxiety or depression or process trauma is cognitive behavioral therapy (CBT). The foundation of CBT is the idea that our emotions, behaviors, and thoughts all connect to each other, and making changes in one area can result in changes in the others. It is a way to help address inconsistencies in what we think, feel, and do and the values one aspires to live by. For example, if you're feeling anxious or irritable, trying to simply talk yourself into feeling a different emotion isn't helpful. It can be more helpful to look at the thoughts or behaviors that are feeding that emotion. Cognitive techniques invite us to get curious about the thoughts and beliefs we hold that lead to that anxiety and then gently rewrite those beliefs into something more helpful. Maybe that belief is "I am never going to get my work done" and something more helpful would be "I am not defined by the work I accomplish. I am enough." Then behavioral techniques invite us to reinforce those helpful thought patterns through our behavior. For example, if the thought we are reinforcing is "I am enough," then learning to draw clear boundaries between work-related demands and time for rest and family is an important behavior to learn and practice.

While we as communities need to continue doing the hard work of creating spaces that promote mental wellness, we also need to know how to help individuals connect with mental health professionals when

---

31. "Our Story," This Is My Brave, accessed December 12, 2024, https://tinyurl.com/u9d45ud8.

needed. How might the Holy Spirit be inviting the church to receive help and mental health support from evidence-based counseling practices?

For many, finding a good therapist is an answer to prayers. Whether the goal of therapy is to treat clinical anxiety or simply to nurture our souls in an anxiety-laden world, an hour of therapy can be a sacred thing. Theologian Charles Marsh describes his experience with anxiety and psychotherapy in his memoir *Evangelical Anxiety*. He writes, "Like prayer, the analytic dialogue (of therapy) slows down to ponder, to meander, to piece together, to redeem; both inspire the mind toward hope under the influence of an empathetic listener."[32] Historically, the church has asserted that pastors and other church leaders were the "empathetic listeners" sufficient to treat mental illness; pretending that talk therapy is just talking about your problems. By doing this, the church has been a stigmatizing barrier to life-giving clinical treatment and wellness tools. Just like someone who sprained their ankle can't pretend that doing their usual morning workout is the same as going to physical therapy, we can't pretend that talking to someone that cares is the same as seeing a trained clinical therapist. We, the church, can support the holy work of psychotherapy by getting to know our local referral networks and working to eliminate barriers to care (cost, transportation, child care, stigma).[33]

CONCLUSION

This book and chapter were inspired by young adults who are looking for a church and willing to get curious.[34] Curiosity changes lives. As I (Sarah) shared earlier, getting curious about my own anxiety allowed

---

32. Charles Marsh, *Evangelical Anxiety: A Memoir* (HarperOne, 2022).

33. Mental Health Connect is a collaboration of faith communities in Minneapolis doing this very thing. The collaborative provides mental health educational programming in faith communities and employs Mental Health Navigators who help individuals navigate mental health services and resources. "Mental Health Connect Today," Mental Health Connect, accessed December 12, 2024, https://tinyurl.com/5etvyu3a.

34. For further discussion on postures of curiosity, refer to chapter 1 in this volume, "What Else Could It Be? Courageous Curiosity and the Postures That Get Us There."

me to better understand it and address it with resilience. For Jia, getting curious about her story and the trauma that shaped it invited her to reconsider her relationship to and participation in cultures that perpetrate harm and cocreate a new way of being that embodies bell hooks's love ethic. Now imagine the church sitting down with a therapist ready to get curious about its own mental health. Think back a few paragraphs to the principles of cognitive behavioral therapy—the technique psychotherapists use to help individuals see the connections between what they think, feel, and do.

What if we applied those same techniques to the church body? Cognitive behavioral techniques are an invitation to get curious about what drives us and then use the new insight to make changes. Cognitive behavioral therapy necessitates the need to adapt to what is needed now—not what was needed in the past. It also comes with an aspect of "fake it until you make it." When trying to rewrite how we interface with the world, new habits we are forming might not feel natural at first and we might not be all that convinced that these new actions will pay off. But as clinical psychologist Seth Gillihan writes in his book *Mindful Cognitive Behavioral Therapy*, "Action changes us." He writes, "If we approach something we fear, maybe it's not actually dangerous. If we treat ourselves kindly, we must be someone worth taking care of. If we invest in a cause, we must care about it. Action changes us. Behavior is therapy."[35]

Gillihan goes on to remind us that those small steps we take and changes we make to become more of who we are supposed to be may feel small and inconsequential but are imperative for a body to thrive. He writes, "A single breath is a trivial act, but not breathing is an emergency. We accomplish the big things in our lives by doing the little things one small step at a time." So a small first step may be just asking the question: How are we doing? *How are we really doing?* If we're grieving, do we have time and space to grieve? If we're exhausted, are we giving ourselves permission to rest? If we're anxious, what are the stories we are telling ourselves that are causing that anxiety? We must ask without

---

35. Seth Gillihan, *Mindful Cognitive Behavioral Therapy: A Simple Path to Healing, Hope, and Peace* (HarperOne, 2022), 51.

judgment and answer with humility. If the church is going to address the anxiety about its future and heal the trauma of its past, it's time for those of us in the church body to get more curious. It's time to create communities that prioritize mental health education and awareness, foster the destigmatization of mental health and illness, and promote openness and authenticity.

6

WHY ARE YOU SO ANGRY?

Power, Fear, and Anger Among Historically Powerful and Historically Powerless Communities

Rev. Drew Stever
Rev. Dr. Eric H. F. Law

OUR INVITATION

"Do you want power?" the facilitator of the community-organizing training asked.

I was shocked to see that not one person raised their hand to say, "Yes. I do want power." The facilitators asked the group why this was.

One person chimed in: "I don't like what power does to people. It manipulates. It hurts. It divides people." More students echoed those comments. The majority of the class agreed: Power was bad. Power was evil. Power was sinful.

The facilitator asked the group, "Is 'bad' the *only* thing power is?" A couple of beats went by without anyone saying anything. The same person who chimed in initially said, "Well, no, I guess not. If power can be used to manipulate people for evil, I suppose it can be used to inspire people for good as well."

What was learned that day was that there is power that divides and power that unites. And, depending on your cultural and social location, your relationship to either expression of power may be a relationship of fear or dominance, or a relationship of empowerment and unity. Throughout history we can see expressions of power enacted by the "historically powerful"[1] that spark fear in those who are historically power-

---

1. We use the terms "historically powerful," "historically oppressed," or "historically powerless" in this chapter to acknowledge the fact that certain racial, ethnic, economic, or gender groups had in the past possessed power of influence and manipulation while other groups did not. We are not saying that a person or group is powerful or powerless in the present context; we are simply referring to how their identity may connect with the powerful or powerless groups as documented through history.

less. Specifically, cisgender, straight, white men have historically and successfully used power to control and cause fear. As a result, those who are LGBTQIA2S+, people of color, people with disabilities, and anyone who doesn't identify as cisgender, straight, white male feel fear—for our safety, our livelihoods, and our community. One way to respond to this fear is to respond to the powerful with violence, which in turn causes the powerful to respond with even more violence, continuing the cycle of destruction. Another way to respond to fear experienced by the powerless is to respond constructively, using power in ways to unite both the powerful and the powerless and bring healing. Despite these constructive ways, many from the historically powerful groups still react with fear. The fear felt by the historically powerless is a fear for our safety, while the fear felt by the historically powerful is a fear of discomfort. The historically powerful have set the standard for what is considered normal, appropriate, and safe, and when that is jeopardized, they fall into unhealthy and often violent expressions of fear and anger. This chapter will highlight a different standard for power that we can seek to embody through the person and example of Jesus.

We (Drew and Eric) share from our lived experiences of being a part of historically oppressed communities. We have witnessed the institutional church fail to live into the example of Jesus when it comes to power and community, as well as fail to acknowledge its own relationship with the fears of those who are historically powerful and abuse power.[2] Our reflections come from the young adult experience by leaders who are both elders and young adults in their faith professions. One of our intended audiences includes young adults from historically oppressed communities. We hope that this demographic finds affirmation of their experiences within the institutional church and that they find hope in moving forward in who they are and how they are called to lead in ministry. The other intended audience includes the historically powerful, in particular those in higher church leadership who are proclaiming a message of wel-

---

2. When we speak of the "institutional church," we speak of the systems, policies, and rhetoric put in place by humans. When we speak of the "church," we speak of the *ecclesia*, the body of people that make up the community of faith that follows Jesus's teachings.

come and inclusion within the church. We hope that this demographic is able to recognize the anger-inducing oppressive systems they are a part of. We hope the leaders within the institutional church can understand how they, too, can be and are part of a solution for a community of faith more aligned with God's word.

This chapter explores different expressions of power, fear, and anger through story—our own and those of others, and through the stories of Scripture. By comparing healthy and harmful patterns of these human emotions, we hope readers will notice where they may have contributed to harm in the past and identify holy and healthy responses to fear, anger, and power that they can begin to put into practice.

REV. DREW STEVER (PRONOUNS: THEY/HE)

My relationship with power, anger, and fear has evolved over the years. I was identified as "female" at birth and was raised in the white, female context. My parents and sister are white. The neighborhoods I grew up in were mostly white. Our family attended a predominantly white Lutheran congregation in the ELCA,[3] and my sister and I attended predominantly white schools. My experiences were formed with those settings as the backdrop. I learned that power could be used to instill fear, and anger must never be shown, especially by women.[4]

As I grew older, I saw how fear was viewed by the historically powerless. Fear of those in power kept us in line, kept us submissive, and kept

---

3. The Evangelical Lutheran Church in America is one of the largest Christian denominations in the world. The term "evangelical," however you interpret it, references the original meaning of the word: to proclaim. Our tradition practices the proclamation of God's all-inclusive love and care for all creation—including the LGBTQIA+ community. The ELCA voted in 2009 to allow openly LGBTQIA+ clergy in same-sex monogamous relationships to serve. Prior to 2009, clergy could be open, but they could not be in a publicly disclosed relationship. As a result, many clergy chose to remain closeted and keep personal relationships secret.

4. Eric H. F. Law, *Fear Not: Living Grace and Truth in a Frightened World* (Chalice, 2019), 48–64. Law described four ways that people respond to fear: fear-conqueror, fear-bearer, fear-miner, and fear-exploiter. All four of these "roles" are demonstrated in Drew's story.

us silent—all of this undermining our well-being. When the trauma of keeping one's anger to oneself is unable to be processed and is instead stored within one's body, it can directly affect one's health.[5] We are cognitively and psychologically learning that behaving "correctly" in the face of oppression is to remain silent, and as such, to suffer silently, and our biological makeup is learning the same as well.[6]

I came out as transgender in 2016. I began transitioning in a time when a known sexual abuser, a white man, was elected to the highest political office in the United States.[7] My excitement was mixed with dread. The rhetoric that supported the historically powerful and bashed the historically powerless grew louder and spread further around the country. My fear of the historically powerful grew as this new administration quickly became a threat to all historically oppressed communities. And with my fear, my anger grew too.

Unfortunately, I did not have a healthy avenue to direct these feelings. My fear and anger manifested into abusing substances. The level of hypervigilance, obsessive doom-scrolling, and arguing with strangers online took a toll on my health. In hindsight, I know now that anger was a form of fear and grief. I was afraid that at any moment I could be targeted by some angry, ignorant person and get attacked or killed. I was angry because, as I transitioned into the appearance of a white male, I knew what harm white men have caused throughout history, and all I wanted to do was live. I was angry because I believed the church could have done more and can still do more than posting prayerful captions on social media. I was afraid because the church does a really good job naming injustices, but it does not do a good job taking action against injustice as it is happening.

I was committed to getting to know my anger to better understand how I could use my privilege as a white man to respond quicker, to unite, to heal, and to empower. Power, as I have transitioned, has become a

---

5. "How Trauma Affects Our Health," Center to Advance Trauma Informed Health Care, accessed December 13, 2024, https://tinyurl.com/yncv4664.

6. You are invited to read more about this in chapter 5 in this volume.

7. White men in America represent the foundation of what it means to be powerful.

tool that many in historically marginalized groups use to bring people together. I am still wary of power and the people who hold it, but I do not completely reject it. With all the violence we witness and experience in the world, I am still angry, too. The church has had the opportunity to take action in response to abuses of power, but it has dragged its feet. It has been silent. It has been absent. Part of this I know to be because of fear. I want to believe the church wants to do the right thing but doesn't know how. We have been telling the church how to respond, what to say, and how to move, but the church has either silenced the historically oppressed because what we have to say is uncomfortable, or perhaps it is too enmeshed with historically powerful systems of operating that it cannot remove itself to try anything new. This is why we are angry.

REV. DR. ERIC H. F. LAW (PRONOUNS: HE/HIM)

When I was going through the discernment process for ordained ministry at the age of twenty-three, my Episcopal diocese sent me to a three-day psychological evaluation. It was a requirement, and the report would be part of my file. The first evening, I had to complete a set of assessment tests like the Myers-Briggs instrument. I was surprised to find that one of the tests was a vocabulary test, which set off an emotional alarm in me.

I had immigrated from Hong Kong to the United States only seven years before, and I didn't speak much English when I arrived at the age of fourteen. I struggled to get through English classes in high school to get my written and spoken English good enough to graduate and get accepted to Cornell University. I graduated with honors, and I thought I had proven myself and had "arrived." I still spoke with an accent different from how English was spoken in the United States. I did the best I could with the vocabulary test, knowing that there were quite a few big words I didn't know.

The next day my tester pulled out the result of my vocabulary test and said, "Your vocabulary is not very good." My defenses went up. He continued, "I am concerned that you will not be able to do the work in seminary at a master-degree level."

"Do you speak Chinese?" I asked.

He said, "No."

"A thought in Chinese is no worse than a thought in English!" I continued in anger, "I graduated from Cornell with honors. I am sure I can do the work in seminary."

That was the end of the conversation about my verbal ability. A few months later, I was sitting in front of the Commission on Ministry, which would further evaluate me and determine whether I should continue my discernment process. One of the committee members read from a piece of paper: "This is from your psych evaluation report. It says you are easily upset." I felt anger welling up in me; I wanted to say, "Why was I given a vocabulary test? Isn't my academic record good enough? I was being targeted because I don't look or speak like other people whom they were testing." But I didn't. However, I did explain what happened calmly and added, "Aren't all these tests about assessing my ability to learn and to express myself independently of what language I speak?" And that was the end of the conversation on my English ability. If only they knew, I would go on to publish ten books in English, three of them still assigned for seminary courses.

On my path to ordination in the Episcopal Church, there would be more hurdles to jump over, stirring my anger at the institutional abuse of power. During my field education, a white priest reported to my bishop that I was no good at working with the Chinese elders at the Boston Chinese Ministry, an organization I helped found while in seminary. He actually sat me down and told me he had done that all for my own good. Later, a cisgender priest reported to my bishop that I was gay and should not be ordained. You bet I was angry. Yet I knew I could not safely express this anger outwardly to the people in power, like my bishop.

I was lucky to have allies in the Commission on Ministry and the other Asian church leaders. They allowed me to be angry and helped me find ways to cut through the abusive noise to name what was important. And time and again, what was important was that I was a person with gifts that the church needed, not the other way around. These allies used their power to advocate for me. Not only did they affirm my gifts for ministry, they further sealed the deal by threatening to resign from the Commission on Ministry and broadcast to the world what would have happened if the bishop removed me from the list of candidates for ordination.

Power, Fear, and Anger Among Historically Powerless Communities

They played the political game to get me through the system. I was grateful, but I also wondered how we can move toward a better and more faithful way: to change the system of abuse by addressing the church's fear of the unknown, as well as the unhealthy ways of dealing with anger by historically oppressed leaders.

AN EXERCISE IN POWER

It is important to pause and reflect on power and our own experiences of it. Power is defined, in secular terms, as the ability to influence others and manipulate the environment. But what does this mean in your life? When teaching, Eric often asks groups to reflect on a time when they felt powerful and a time when they felt powerless. Take a moment to describe and reflect on a situation from your own life.

- Who was there?
- What role did you play?
- How did you know you were powerful/powerless?
- What did you do with the power that you had? Or, What did you do with the state of powerlessness?

As participants work through these questions individually and share and listen to others' stories in small groups, they discover the many dimensions of power and how it impacts their lives in real terms. Some find it easy to name the powerful events in their lives; some find it difficult to admit they have power. Some find it difficult to name a time when they were powerful because they feel powerless most of the time. Others find it hard to name a powerless time because they perceive themselves as powerful most of the time.

Power defined as the ability to manipulate the environment and influence others is not bad in itself. Jesus, in the cleansing of the temple, used his physical power to change the environment by driving people out that were causing harm, profoundly influencing the crowds. He angered the money changers and dove-sellers and likely caused fear in them. He made room for the lame and the blind in the temple and brought them closer to God's healing power. He influenced the children's perception of God. So words like "manipulate" and "influence" are not inherently bad. It's *how* we use our power to influence that matters. If preachers use the power of their role to propagate fear, hate, and division, preachers are abusing their power. But if they decide to preach in ways that bring people closer to one another and God, they are using their power constructively and faithfully.

Similarly, anger is neither good nor bad. It's one of many human reactions to our environment. It's important to mention that anger also is a common response to grief, especially grief that has been ignored, grief that has not been lamented.[8] When anger is fueled with fear and abuse of power (political, physical, and sometimes military) and when there is no community effort to channel that anger constructively, the results are bad. Property can be destroyed, and people get hurt physically and mentally.

The abuse of power that the historically powerless are angry about shows up in a variety of ways. Here are some examples of this seen through the lens of the young adult experience:

- *Legalism*: There are explicit, implicit, social, and systemic rules that are created by historically powerful groups and are applied unevenly, favoring one group and depleting the already historically powerless groups. When a young adult breaks the social or systemic rules that haven't been explicitly explained and is punished, while a church elder is forgiven, this is an abuse of power.
- *Political Favoritism*: Those who get along with the already powerful are favored. When a young adult questions the actions of those in power and is told to be quiet, or they're "too young" to understand, this is an abuse of power.
- *Secrecy*: In order to benefit and protect those with power, those in power guard information, resources, and harmful behaviors as secrets. This is done often in the name of "confidentiality," allowing them to protect power. This is an abuse of power.

---

8. Recall the insights shared in chapter 4 on the importance of grief and lament, and our culture's (and church's) pattern of avoiding this holy path to repair and healing.

- *Control Through Money*: The system tokenizes historically powerless groups by keeping them in low-pay, undersupported jobs. This is often done by forcing historically powerless groups to fight over limited financial resources, creating division and a scarcity mind-set. When a young adult is told they have amazing gifts, there's plenty of opportunity for growth and that the church has been looking for someone like them to be a leader, but then they are paid below a living wage with no supervisional or institutional support, this is abuse of power.
- *Status Quo/Denial*: When someone from a historically powerful group does not use their power to expose and stop the injustice and abuse of which they are aware, the abuse is deemed acceptable and becomes normal and creates a status quo. This is abuse of power.

This is not an exhaustive list, and the examples are interconnected. Our purpose here is to invite readers to recognize these and other ways power is abused. When a historically powerless person is asked, "Why are you so angry?" this list might explain why. We are angry because these abuses of power are not new to young adults in the church today but reach back for generations. Faith leaders, young and old, are tired of addressing those in power and receiving no productive response. What we are witnessing is a surge of burnout from leaders voicing concerns about abuse, without receiving an adequate response. As a result, many talented, diverse young leaders are leaving ministry and leaving faith communities.

We recognize that one chapter cannot and will not change an entire system. However, in order to even begin changing the cycle of abuse within the system, those in power must begin by doing their own work and intimately acquainting themselves with their anger, grief, and use of power. Additionally, the historically powerless must begin to learn ways of expressing anger in holy ways to stay well and strong in order to cut through the abuse and transform our communities and environments.

People from historically powerless groups know that expressing anger is not only healthy but necessary for change. We must explore where this anger comes from, always asking ourselves, "What am I angry at?" As historically powerless people, we ask ourselves this on a daily basis so that we can stop the cycle of abuse by moving away from sin and causing harm to our neighbors and instead direct our angry energy toward changing the injustice that we are angry about. Jesus shows a pattern of anger and power that rejects the system that tries to enforce the comfort of the powerful. Instead Jesus's work begins in healing the powerless. In following his story, we can witness how anger functions in exposing abuse of power, overcoming our fear, and continuing to build a community of healing and empowerment. The patterns we see in Jesus's handling of power gives us alternative ways to respond to the injustices experienced in our contexts. The Gospel of Matthew 20–21 will offer a guide for our reflection, along with contemporary narratives.

Jesus Heals

> As they were leaving Jericho, a large crowd followed him. There were two blind men sitting by the roadside. When they heard that Jesus was passing by, they shouted, "Lord, have mercy on us, Son of David!" The crowd sternly ordered them to be quiet; but they shouted even more loudly, "Have mercy on us, Lord, Son of David!" Jesus stood still and called them, saying, "What do you want me to do for you?" They said to him, "Lord, let our eyes be opened." Moved with compassion, Jesus touched their eyes. Immediately they regained their sight and followed him. (Matt. 20:29–34)

Those in need of healing are told to be quiet because they are disrupting the status quo. These were the very ones Jesus was sent to heal, and in doing so, he was inviting others to do the same. The crowd misunderstood. They had become infatuated with the idea of the new Messiah being this big, powerful, mighty, and militaristic leader, much like Aaron or Moses, but they could not comprehend that Jesus's ministry of healing and reconciliation was not at all what they had envisioned.

The sin Jesus addresses in this narrative is the sin of assimilation.[9] The blind men did not behave in a way that the crowd deemed "normal," so they were rebuked. Jesus cut through the rebukes and denounced as-

---

9. The act of making oneself smaller in order to fit within the norms created by the historically powerful.

Power, Fear, and Anger Among Historically Powerless Communities

similation and addressed the blind men directly, asking, "What do you want me to do for you?" Without question, Jesus "immediately" restored the men of their sight, and the healed followed the healer. By witnessing Jesus heal others, the crowd required healing of its own so that they could understand and live into what Jesus was asking of them.

In the 1980s, Eric was a newly ordained Asian American priest working as the full-time campus pastor at the University of Southern California. After hearing complaints from other Asian leaders about him turning down part-time Chinese ministry job offers, he launched a youth and young adult Asian American ministry. The first gathering was a success, with forty-five participants from the greater Los Angeles area, and grew in four years to a national annual event.

As the ministry grew, there were rumors that Eric was starting his own Asian church and would be stealing "sheep" from the local Asian churches. Several priests and parents would not send their youth because they heard the youth were talking about sex and drugs in these gatherings. Like the fearful crowd in Matthew, other leaders misunderstood the work God was up to through Eric because it didn't look familiar, and they feared that it threatened their status quo. In response, several adults were invited to observe.

Despite the "boycott," the next gathering was attended by over fifty young people. They stated that the purpose of the gathering was to develop young adult leadership so that they can return to support their respective congregations. The program included Bible studies, worship, and segments on being Asian Americans and Christian. More importantly, participants were able to ask questions on any topics without judgment and receive supportive reflection from one another and the adult leaders. The observers were amazed at how the young people respectfully responded to each other's questions with grace and truth from their experiences.

At one point in the conference, an unlikely young adult stood up to declare that his experience in the previous three years at the youth and young adult gathering had inspired him to seek ordination in the church. He cried, all the young people cried, and the adults cried. Eyes were opened.

Why Are You So Angry?

Jesus Gets Angry

> Then Jesus entered the temple and drove out all who were selling and buying in the temple, and he overturned the tables of the money changers and the seats of those who sold doves. He said to them, "It is written,
>> 'My house shall be called a house of prayer';
>> but you are making it a den of robbers." (Matt. 21:12–13)

After healing the blind men, Jesus arrived in Jerusalem to a triumphant welcome. The mood abruptly shifts, however, when he enters the temple. Jesus was angry because the religious establishment allowed the money changers and the dove-sellers to exploit the poor. They used the rules associated with the ritual of making offerings at the temple to achieve personal financial gain at the expense of the poor. The rules stated that the temple only accepted a certain kind of currency and that "Anyone who cannot afford a lamb is to bring two doves or two young pigeons to the LORD as a penalty for their sin—one for a sin offering and the other for a burnt offering" (Lev. 5:7 NIV).

In the process of making a profit, they blocked the powerless from having access to what people at the time considered "holy." Jesus, upset by this injustice, expressed his anger by destroying the tools that were being used to leave others out.

> In 2018, a young person entered a worship service in Chicago in drag. The pastor invited the young person to stand up and stand in the aisle in front of everyone to see. The pastor said to this person, "Can you leave my church and go put on man clothes? . . . If you're a man, dress like a man. If you're a woman, dress like a woman. . . . My salvation is more important, and God is holding me accountable." While some people applauded the pastor's comments, a person videorecording the exchange left the service fuming with anger. Christian James Lhuillier shared that church is supposed "to be a place of change, a place of deliverance." Lhuillier raged against the pastor's decision to publicly embarrass this person in front of the congregation, commenting on how exclusionary experiences like these are what cause people to suffer severe mental illness and commit suicide.

The historically powerful (the pastor) gets angry that someone (the historically powerless) violated rules that were set by the powerful. Meanwhile, the historically powerless get angry because while the church claims to be an inclusive community, its actions demonstrate otherwise. Its actions not only exclude but harm and dehumanize.

Jesus Heals (Again)

The blind and the lame came to him in the temple, and he cured them. (Matt. 21:14)

Jesus got angry, so he made a mess. What Jesus did not do was bring violence upon others. Instead, he destroyed the structures that fuel greed, individualism, and abuse of power. In response, the money changers were left to clean up the mess, and those who had come to this "holy place" to be healed finally gained access back into their communities. The historically powerless witnessed someone standing up to the historically powerful. They wanted to know more.

Jesus's response is antithetical to what we are often taught about anger: you get angry and you go after the people you're angry at and strike back. Here, we witness Jesus doing something very different with anger: he got angry, destroyed the tools of oppression, and turned to the ones who had been hurt and excluded and healed them.

> Rev. Hazel Salazar-Davidson experienced a traumatic event while at work in the winter of 2021. She was diagnosed with PTSD. It was determined that she would have to take some time away from work to heal. In the time of her absence, her employer stopped payments and stopped contributing to her health and retirement benefits without notifying her. A widow with three children, Pastor Hazel found herself in a position where she would radically have to depend on the support of her community. After assembling a team of support to help accompany her through this season, her team sent an email to Pastor Hazel's community, asking them to consider giving a financial gift to help support her and her family. Overwhelmingly, her community and many strangers showed up and helped her reach her goal. When the

systems within the institutional church broke down, and when they did not and could not support one of its own leaders in healing after suffering harm from the church, the community of the people directly around Pastor Hazel and beyond the boundaries of the institution were the ones to respond and support. Their anger at the injustices she experienced was directed at caring for her well-being.

Jesus Advocates for the Children

> But when the chief priests and the scribes saw the amazing things that he did, and heard the children crying out in the temple, "Hosanna to the Son of David," they became angry and said to him, "Do you hear what these are saying?" Jesus said to them, "Yes; have you never read,
> > 'Out of the mouths of infants and nursing babies
> > you have prepared praise for yourself'?" (Matt. 21:15-16)

Back at the temple, after the healing of more people, the religious leaders were angered by all the healings and annoyed by the children shouting, "Hosanna to the Son of David," leading to another round of discourse with Jesus. Perhaps Jesus didn't fit the profile of what they assumed a messiah should be. Jesus rebuked the powerful while defending the children: *"From the lips of children and infants, you, Lord, have called forth your praise."*

Children have a way of noticing what is important, ignoring the grown-ups' rules and biases. Jesus was affirming through the children, who shouted "Hosanna" after observing the healing of the blind and the lame despite it being against the rules.

> In May 1968, university students protested reforms within the university system and brought the entire country of France to a complete halt. In June of 1976, during the apartheid in South Africa, thousands of students organized to protest against the unequal education they were facing as a result of unjust laws. Despite the violent backlash, the students continued to organize, drawing international attention and paving the way for the end of the apartheid era. March for Our

Lives, a student-led organization founded in 2018, leads protests against gun violence, advocates for gun safety laws, and gets young voters mobilized. In Tennessee in 2020, six teenagers organized the region's largest protest against racism and police brutality after the death of George Floyd.

Young people have been shouting "Hosanna to the Son of David" for generations. They have been demonstrating the holy anger Jesus displays in Scripture. They have made sure that their classmates and their peers are not alone, and they remain inspired and committed to dismantling the systems and tools that bring about oppression and abuse. The children—the historically powerless—have been shining a light on where things are broken.

Jesus Rests

He left them, and went out of the city to Bethany, and spent the night there. (Matt. 21:17)

I (Eric) have been a pastor for decades, and for much of that time I overlooked the significance of this short verse. Bethany is a two-mile walk from Jerusalem. Jesus had already been walking eighteen miles, arriving in Jerusalem from Jericho, spending a long time in Jerusalem, talking to all sorts of people, and yet he still made the trip to Bethany for the night before returning to Jerusalem the next morning.

Why Bethany? Bethany is where Jesus goes to raise his good friend Lazarus from the dead. It is the home of Simon the Leper. It is where Jesus ascended back into heaven. It is where Mary anointed Jesus's feet with perfume. Through the lens of historically powerless experiences, this act of anointing by Jesus's friend Mary has multiple connotations, but one of utmost importance to the historically powerless: family. Bethany was a place of sanctuary for Jesus. It was where his chosen family was. It was where he could go if he needed to get away from the chaos and injustices of the big city, or when he was tired and needed to pause throughout his ministry. It wasn't anything special to the average person, but it was significant to Jesus and his life. Bethany was home for Jesus.

It was imperative for Jesus to rest.[10] He didn't do it to isolate himself from the world or to give up. Instead, he did it to recharge, to recenter, and to remember what it was he was called to do, who called him, and why he was called to do it. Bethany gave him the space for these things.

> During a clergy gathering, Eric was walking with colleagues toward the main hall where they would gather for the first plenary. By this time, Eric was a senior priest with over twenty-five years of experience and most people knew him. The person walking next to him was a tall white priest whom he did not recognize. Eric thought he must have just joined the diocese, and to be friendly, he introduced himself and tried to strike up a conversation. It became very clear very fast that this person did not want to talk to him. Anger welled up in Eric unexpectedly and he thought, "I shouldn't have let my guard down. I should remember what I look like." Before he got any further into this recurring destructive mind-set, Eric heard voices calling him. He looked up and saw two friends—a Chinese woman priest and an African American priest—waving at him, gesturing that he should join them. Eric immediately left his unfriendly colleague and cut through the crowd. As he arrived, they knew what Eric was feeling and he did not need to explain. The African American priest said with a knowing smile, "So you were just 'raced.'" Eric, for that moment, was home to Bethany.

Jesus Gets Back to Work

In the morning, when he returned to the city, he was hungry. And seeing a fig tree by the side of the road, he went to it and found nothing at all on it but leaves. Then he said to it, "May no fruit ever come from you again!" And the fig tree withered at once. (Matt. 21:18–19)

After spending time with his chosen family, Jesus returned to Jerusalem. On his way, he became hungry and came across a fig tree. In

---

10. Matt. 14:23; Mark 6:46–47; John 6:15; Luke 6:12.

Scripture, fig trees are representative of Israel.[11] Jesus began his return to Jerusalem, refreshed from rest, while also renewed with holy anger about the injustices caused by the leaders of Israel. Injustices that harmed the very people he had just spent time with in Bethany and the people rejected at the temple. Seeing the fig tree and thinking a fig might make a good snack, he walked up to it but saw nothing on it except leaves. He cursed the fig tree, all while cursing his people Israel, for the ways they were fruitless in their labors and commitment to God's covenant. The barren fig tree served as a reminder for Jesus of the work yet to do. His holy anger continued.

> Drew is a pastor for a church that is trying to figure out who they are and how they want to be in the world after coming back together from the pandemic. The work is hard. Drew and his partner converted their garage into an art studio as a place to retreat to during the week. On his Sabbath days, he goes to the garage to create, to rest, and to pray.
>
> There is intention when entering the space—you need to take time to set up your station, get the tools you need, clean the clutter, and set your intention for the work. This often includes setting the phone down somewhere far away from the workstation, or shutting it off. The time of rest requires focus on rest so that returning can be more abundant and full.
>
> Just as there is intention in arriving in the space, there is also intention in leaving it. You can't hide away in the garage forever; at some point, you do have to return to the work outside of the garage. When Jesus went to Bethany, he didn't forget about the injustice he witnessed in Jerusalem. He didn't forget about the religious leaders misusing religious law. He went to Bethany to recenter his spirit. He remembered his purpose: to speak truth to the ones that had forgotten their purpose and remind them of the One who sent them.

---

11. The Israel being referenced is contextual to the Israel of Jesus's time and place. Israel was a larger group of people that Jesus himself was also a part of. Not unlike young leaders in the church now, Jesus offered critique of the communities he was from.

WHAT JESUS'S ANGER IS AND WHAT JESUS'S ANGER IS NOT

In order to move toward an acceptance and hopefully a practice of holy anger, the church must recognize what holy anger is and what it is not. When examining Jesus's expression of anger, we can see that his anger is: a call to the historically powerful to recognize and witness injustice, a reminder of what God's people have been called to do and be, a reminder that it is God who has called us, not the world, and a reminder that God's power is greater. For the historically powerless, Jesus's anger is an empowering message of truth and a testimony of liberation for those who have been imprisoned. Jesus's anger is not abusive, shaming, ridiculing, or excluding. It is not retaliatory, nor does it cause harm to other people. It may not always be easy to digest, or comprehend, especially by the historically powerful. But it is not belittling, sexist, ableist, or racist. Jesus's power does not cling to policy or rules, or societal norms created by the historically powerful. At the heart of Jesus's anger is the dismantling of oppression and the uplifting of the oppressed.

When comparing the anger expressed by Jesus with the anger expressed by the historically powerless today, we find many similarities. The anger most often expressed by the historically powerless is an anger in response to injustice. We have witnessed and experienced direct harm, restrictive policies and laws, and have had to remain hypervigilant in spaces that do not welcome us in our fullness. The anger we express toward the church is an expression of our exhaustion, frustration, confusion, and grief. While we voice our needs and calls for change within the institution, often little changes, and when it does, it arrives at a glacial pace. That being said, our anger does not move toward violence. We have our Bethanys to retreat to, to rest, to recover, and to return. We return to this work because we have each other to remind us what we were called to do, who called us to do it, and why we are called. Our power is communal and sacred.

The same cannot always be said about the institution. When the historically powerless express anger, the historically powerful have a tendency to respond with fear. This can look like scripted, emotionless apologies, thoughts and prayers on social media, or actions that instill fear and force silence. The historically powerless represent many different cultures, all that bring unique gifts to the church. Rather than being curious about and celebrating these diverse gifts, the institutional church responds by enforcing strict policies so that we maintain the status quo, living into the sin of assimilation. When harm has been done by church elders toward leaders from historically powerless communities, the anger we express is often ignored. We watch our colleagues fade into our memories and no action for reparation takes place.

The anger expressed by the historically powerful is misaligned with the anger expressed by Jesus. Where Jesus responds with anger to injustice and oppression enacted by the institution, the institution responds with anger *to* those experiencing the injustices and oppression.

This is why we are angry.

So what now? How can the church realign itself with the teachings and actions of Jesus? Where is this pattern already being supported within the church? Is it possible to steer a multicenturies-old institution toward a more just purpose? What does the church need to shed itself of in order for this to become possible? Or, is the institution so big that all hope is lost? Here are some direct actions the church can take in order to move toward greater alignment with Christ's teachings.

1. Name wrongs and imperfections.

Reflect on how it feels in your body when you know you've done something wrong and need to make it right. Reflect on what encourages you and what prevents you from mending relationships. Do you consider naming wrongs as weakness, or do you find it to be powerful?

> They said to him, "Lord, let our eyes be opened." Moved with compassion, Jesus touched their eyes. Immediately they regained their sight and followed him. (Matt. 20:33–34)

2. Ask for help. Sometimes, we need to ask for help from the least likely of people.

Consider how often those in power ask for help and reflect on how the Roman centurion compares to those examples. Reflect on the boundaries one might need to cross in order to seek adequate help and care.

> When he entered Capernaum, a centurion came to him, appealing to him and saying, "Lord, my servant is lying at home paralyzed, in terrible distress." And he said to him, "I will come and cure him." The centurion answered, "Lord, I am not worthy to have you come under my roof, but only speak the word, and my servant will be healed." (Matt. 8:5-8)

3. Engage in listening sessions. Action plans are even more powerful.

Reflect on how you respond mentally and in action (or inaction) when someone asks you for help. Wonder about what might prevent you from responding with action. Imagine what it might look like if you responded without hesitation to someone's cry for help.

> The official said to him, "Sir, come down before my little boy dies." Jesus said to him, "Go; your son will live." The man believed the word that Jesus spoke to him and started on his way. As he was going down, his slaves met him and told him that his child was alive. (John 4:49-51)

4. Encourage the church to acquaint itself with holy death.

In the Gospel of Mark, Jesus predicts and announces his death three times. Despite this, the disciples still didn't understand Jesus and were afraid to ask him about it. Reflect on how often in the church calendar our communities talk about or preach about death. How often do we gloss over Jesus's death and resurrection as just part of the story, when in fact it has real implications for what it looks like to follow God? Imagine what the rhythm of churches might look like if we reflect on the rhythms of nature—the cycle of life and death and new life.

> They went on from there and passed through Galilee. He did not want anyone to know it; for he was teaching his disciples, saying to them, "The Son of Man is to be betrayed into human hands, and they will kill him, and three days after being killed, he will rise again." But they did not understand what he was saying and were afraid to ask him. (Mark 9:30-32)

5. Insist that the church talk about its relationship with fear, anger, and power.

The historically powerless have done this work. The historically powerful, the church, must do the same. Reflect on your reaction when you witness someone else's anger. Take inventory of what fear feels like physically and mentally in your body. Think back to how you have responded with holy anger and harmful anger in the past. Ask yourself: Where have I felt powerful? Where have I felt powerless?

> But immediately Jesus spoke to them and said, "Take heart, it is I; do not be afraid." (Matt. 14:27)

FINAL THOUGHTS

"Why are you so angry?" This is a question many historically powerless persons have been asked by those in the church. This chapter has aimed to illustrate examples of anger and uplifted Jesus's "holy anger" as a standard we all should follow as we seek to address oppression and injustices.

- Jesus heals so we can see the truth.
- Jesus gets angry at the tools of oppression used by the powerful religious establishments.
- Jesus heals the powerless and excluded (again) while breaking the rules put in place by the powerful.
- Jesus rebukes the powerful and affirms the children, inviting the people to recover a fresh way of noticing things that are important.
- Jesus goes "home" to Bethany to recover and reconnect.
- Jesus goes back out to challenge the powerful and get angry again.

Depending on your relationship to power, Jesus's holy anger pattern may affirm your experiences. Rest assured that we will continue to be angry, but we will go home to Bethany to recharge and we will go back out empowered by holy anger to heal God's people.

Why Are You So Angry?

For the historically powerful in the institution of the church, we hope you will receive this holy anger as a gift and seek opportunities to listen to and receive the anger of the historically powerless in the church. The real question is after the system acknowledges our anger, will the system have a gracious space for the angry ones to move through the holy anger pattern? The church must create a time and place for the powerful to recognize their discomfort and fear of losing what they have. The institution must ask for help and allow themselves to be ministered to. There needs to be a place where we all can go after the anger and healing work is done to rest. The church must learn to value and give authentic praise for the contributions young people bring to the community. We must learn the true value of creativity, difference, and holy questioning. If these are not done, we run the risk of triggering more abuse of power and more destructive anger. These are the choices that individuals and institutions have to make if we are to follow Jesus. The decisions we choose will determine whether both the historically powerless and historically powerful have the time and space for holy anger. By honoring that space, we turn our focus to healing and reconnection to the Divine, restoring our relationship with one another and with God.

7

LIBERATING THE SANCTUARY

Beyond Marginalization, Intersectionality, and Inclusion to Reach Liberation

Abby Grifno
Dr. Jimmy Hoke

OUR INVITATION

We are calling upon the church, congregants, leaders, and believers to reimagine the church in a way that centers liberation and not only sees but fully embraces the many differences among its members. As part of this liberation, we also have to call churches to accountability for the marginalization we have been at the root of. In order to imagine a liberated church, we have to abandon the harmful structures that exclude marginalized people and that prevent liberation.

In the chapter—especially when we discuss inclusion—you may notice that we do not always agree. Sometimes what Jimmy says may feel like it is in tension with (or even contradicts) something Abby says. This is okay: we want you to see how we, as two authors who agree about the importance of liberation, can differ in the steps we take to get there—just as we differ in our experiences of marginalization in the church and the world. I (Abby—she/her) was born and raised in Austin, Texas, and now work as a high school English teacher. As the daughter of an immigrant and half Hispanic and half White, I often feel as Gloria Anzaldua best said, "in the borderlands" of identity, rarely accepted as either of my ethnicities. I (Jimmy—they/he) am a white scholar of queer and feminist biblical studies and a queer campus and congregational leader living in Minneapolis. My experiences (good and bad) as a lifelong leader in the Presbyterian Church (U.S.A.) and college professor have molded my radical queer and feminist agenda. We believe that our differences make us, our chapter, and our commitment to genuine liberation stronger. We hope this can be a model for readers to learn to name and embrace difference.

We want to start this chapter with a vision, and we invite you to join us. Discussing the marginalization of our communities can feel bleak, or even hopeless. But we want to remind readers that there is indeed hope. The challenge is large, and the fruits of our labors are unlikely to be felt immediately. Liberation is worth imagining. Liberation is possible.

IMAGINING LIBERATION

I (Abby) grew up with summer camp an important part of my life. The camp songs still play in my head. Every week of camp would end with the softest, slowest song we knew, "Sanctuary." The lyrics are repetitive, allowing anyone from 4 years old to 100 to catch on quickly. We'd all hold a piece of yarn, singing the song, and cutting it into simple bracelets that served as a reminder of our connectedness. The song's beginning line, repeated throughout, is, "Lord, prepare me, to be a sanctuary." This line is telling—it's not about the building or the place but the people.

And what exactly is a sanctuary? We're familiar with it being a holy place, where we gather. But in the song, it's more than that—we know a sanctuary is more than that too. It's a place of refuge, a place of acceptance. It's not necessarily a church, and it may not even be a physical location. But it's still a place you can go no matter the need, no matter your condition. As a teenager leading camp, I found this idea easier to grasp; you don't hit or name-call, you apologize for mistakes, and any conflict is addressed by prioritizing relationships. Everyone was welcome, everyone was given the same supplies for the same activities, and at my church, thankfully, no one was turned away for a lack of funds. And yet, as adults, much of this has been lost. We have naturally been hardened by our world and the desperate realities we live in. It is easier for many to be callous or closed off.

We've forgotten how to be a sanctuary. In a liberated church, we remember.

A liberated church would be full—and not in the sense that every pew has someone in it. I mean that the church is full of all kinds of kinds. Full of people exploring themselves; full of people with lives inside, and outside, of the church; and full of acceptance. To me, a liberating church doesn't mean everyone sees everything in the same way. There will be people who brush their teeth before coffee and those who do it after, moms who choose to keep their career and mothers who find their calling at home, and those who choose not to be mothers at all. There will still be times of serious disagreements—over how the church budgets, or how to respond to injustice in the community.

But in this future church, no one would have to Google if LGBTQIA2S+ people are accepted before they step into the building, no one would have to worry if their kids could afford the youth group trips, or if they would have to awkwardly decline to provide coffee once a month. Instead, everyone could just belong and be, connect and learn. Together we would experience grace and hope in a world that can sometimes feel hopeless.

I (Jimmy) imagine a transformed church that is not waiting for marginalized populations to come inside because the church has decentered tradition in order to center and start with the people who are currently marginalized the most. Liberation *feels* like a radically decentered church. But I cannot quite put words to what that could look like.

In her short story "The Ones Who Stay and Fight," N. K. Jemisin imagines Um-Helat, a sort-of-utopian planet where, the story's narrator seems to argue, liberation has occurred. Differences are celebrated, and people are not marginalized because everyone is considered "different." The narrator celebrates, but they assume the reader is skeptical: *Don't you believe?* they ask before describing more. Almost sighing, they finally describe a man who has been contaminated by the ideas of our own world: he believes that some people are inherently better than others, that a hierarchy of differences should marginalize many and privilege a few. One of the "social workers" tasked with the duty of protecting Um-Helat kills him. The story ends with his child, sad and angry after having seen this, and asks the reader, again, to believe and fight to teach and save this child from the anger rooted in having absorbed her father's toxic ideas.[1]

Jemisin's short story disturbs brilliantly.[2] But it is also easily misunderstood: many readers walk away satisfied: *a liberative utopia like Um-Helat is impossible.* They cannot look past the man's death: this would not happen in

---

1. The full story is freely accessible online in print and audio. N. K. Jemisin, "The Ones Who Stay and Fight," *Lightspeed* 116 (January 2020), https://tinyurl.com/3x pc5v4f. Originally published in Jemisin, *How Long 'til Black Future Month?* (Orbit Books, 2018).

2. Jemisin's story is an homage and critique of Ursula K. LeGuin's "The Ones Who Walk Away from Omelas."

a utopia. But I happen to believe that utopia and liberation are possible. Like Jemisin, I believe you have to fight for it. Fighting for liberation means murdering marginalization and refusing to stop at the fiction of inclusion.

As I've tried to imagine what liberation would look like in the church, I keep coming back to an ecclesial version of Um-Helat. A liberated church is not a utopia that we achieve once. A liberated church constantly reimagines itself as it fights impulses toward marginalization, oppression, and injustice. A liberated church recognizes that it cannot include people who refuse to change; it cannot "be nice" in the face of "good people" who are "set in their ways" when those ways are racist, transphobic, antiqueer, sexist, ableist, classist, or otherwise discriminatory. A liberated church recognizes and condemns the violence of marginalization and refuses to give it sanctuary.

UNDERSTANDING MARGINALIZATION

Experiencing marginalization makes it hard to imagine liberation. There are also those who use Christianity as a way to further agendas that are far from aligned with the Bible or God, but this chapter won't spend much time on how some have intentionally used religion to marginalize others. Instead, this chapter is focused on the roles we each play in the continued marginalization within the church. We may not be actively marginalizing or hurting groups of people—although some are—but we may be sitting on the sidelines of monumental moments, bystanders through our inaction in fighting for others.

Our Experiences of Marginalization

The Lutheran denomination I (Abby) grew up in is overwhelmingly white in many parts of the country. Hailing from a Hispanic family, I stood out as different from other church members. I was too young to remember our family's experience at our first church; my mother bore the brunt of the racism our family encountered there, forcing us to leave. Fortunately, I never experienced that kind of unwelcome in my church home.

For me, marginalization happens in the little moments; in being pointedly asked where I'm from, or if I can translate Spanish even though

Beyond Marginalization, Intersectionality, and Inclusion to Reach Liberation

I never learned it. It exists in the tokenization I feel at improving the diversity numbers at the places I work while simultaneously not being considered "Hispanic enough" by coworkers. For many of us, these tiny microaggressions are mirrored in the church. The church often becomes another opportunity to experience isolation, well-intended but harmful questions, and tokenization. To feel any sense of peace, many of us have to work to ignore these small assaults. Bringing them up can feel unnecessary or overcritical (it's not) and can stir the pot when we already feel a situation is precarious. Growing up, I learned ignorance was easier.

The monumental moment I experienced came from a time when I distinctly *didn't* feel marginalized. This meaningful experience highlighted for me how much we are missing out on, when marginalization is happening in our churches. Every three years the ELCA hosts a National Youth Gathering (NYG) where thousands of Lutheran teens—and their adult chaperones—congregate for a week. It includes massive worship services, huge volunteer efforts, and a variety of events that are both exhilarating and exhausting.

Except it wasn't NYG that was *the place* for me. For me, the place of belonging was at the event that preceded it; the Multicultural Youth Leadership Event (MYLE) took place in the same city as the gathering. MYLE was meant to acknowledge the disparity in ethnicity and races represented in the church and lift up those voices. MYLE was, for me, the main event. While I often worry that "multicultural events" will feel awkward or performative, my experience at MYLE was the opposite. I was surrounded by both people who looked like me and people who had completely different backgrounds. Our differences were what helped us find belonging. Throughout the week, there were deep conversations about the church, race, marginalization, and colonialism. These deep conversations were tempered by gatherings and worship from around the world that were just as thought-provoking. I've never had an experience like MYLE anywhere else.

MYLE gave me a taste of what it's like to have spaces created for you, for all. Places where our differences are gifts to be celebrated, not something to ignore or accommodate. I wonder, what would happen if churches didn't just try to limit marginalization but actually went all in on creating the exact opposite—places of radical belonging?

+++

The church has never been a space where I (Jimmy) have been able to be my queer self. In high school and college—a time when I sensed a call toward ministry—I was acutely aware that I could not be ordained in the PC(USA) if I was a "practicing homosexual." I did not come out to anyone (other than myself) until I was twenty-one, and it is not coincidental that this was a few months after I realized my vocation was in academia and not ordained ministry. Today, queer young adults in most mainline denominations are no longer prohibited from ordination, and their denominations allow their pastors to marry them to a partner of any gender identity. Yet the marginalization of queer people still happens in churches.

When I think about my ongoing experience of marginalization in the church, I remember what I call "Safety Pin Sunday." The week after Donald Trump's election in 2016, I was working as the education director at a small, moderate congregation in New Jersey. There had been a movement among white liberals to start wearing safety pins on their shirts to indicate that they were a safe and supportive person to marginalized folks who felt terror at the prospect of violence and loss of rights under the new administration. In what many would tearfully describe as a grand gesture of support, people in my congregation grabbed safety pins, explained their meaning, and passed them around to the many folks eager to don them. Meanwhile, I fled to the empty chapel, lay down on the floor, and tried not to sob since I soon had to be "on" for twenty-five enthusiastic, safety-pin-clad kiddos. The church was generally moderate and open-minded. Yet, from conversations I had with more conservative parents and, confidentially, with a few trusted allies, I was nearly certain that if I came out to the congregation, it would mean the loss of my job and the income I needed to support myself during the final years of my doctoral program.

This is what marginalization *feels* like in churches. Holding back our full selves. Protecting ourselves from the violence of rejection. Avoiding pushback because we've had enough—and nothing changes. I have lost count of the times I have had to hold my tongue in church-related settings because they were not ready for the discomfort that full, transformative liberation requires of people privileged by the marginalization of others.

You might be thinking, *This isn't me. This is not my church*. It is. I hate to break it to you, but it is you; it is your church. Because it is us: you and me and our church. Marginalization in the church reflects marginalization in society. Even the most progressive and diverse congregation is racist, sexist, cisheteronormative, classist, and ableist because it is embedded in systems of patriarchal, queer and transphobic White supremacy.[3]

Marginalization and the Mythical Norm

In her essay "Age, Race, Class, and Sex," Audre Lorde emphasizes how a "mythical norm" divides people and enables their oppression. "In america, this norm is usually defined as white, thin, male, young, heterosexual, christian, and financially secure. It is within this mythical norm that the trappings of power reside within this society."[4] This norm is *mythical*, Lorde writes, because no one perfectly fits the ideal in every possible way. Yet, because the "trappings of power" reside within this norm, we consciously *and unconsciously* shape our decisions based on it. When people deviate from the mythical norm, we see them as *different* because, usually, they will *never* fit this norm.

At its core, marginalization happens when a person, based on at least one identity factor, is considered *not normal*. Let's summon an imaginary church leadership meeting at a predominantly white church where the membership is largely straight and cisgender. While discussing how to attract new members, one leader says, "How do we bring *different* people into the church? How do we *attract diversity?*" The desire for congregations to become less monochromatic is not, itself, bad (to be clear). But when *difference* and *diversity* is something "we" need, who is the we?

The issue is that the *mythical norm* embeds itself in these statements. People who are part of a privileged population consider themselves to be the *normal* group to whom "different people" need to be added. This assumption erases the history of how that population *became* normal. We

---

3. In their podcast *Keeping It 101*, Megan Goodwin and Ilyse Morgenstein Fuerst discuss the Islamophobic perception that "Islam oppresses women" and observe: "Muslims don't oppress women. The patriarchy oppresses women, and as many folks have pointed out, patriarchal systems exist across cultures, communities, religions, and races." Here, Jimmy extends their perceptive point. Goodwin and Fuerst, "What Does It Mean to Be 'Religious'?," *Keeping it 101: A Killjoy's Guide to Religion*, ep. 105, March 10, 2020, https://tinyurl.com/mvu8ucua.

4. Audre Lorde, *Sister Outsider: Essays and Speeches* (Crossing Press, 1984), 116.

all theoretically accept that all humans are different from one another. In practice, normal people are never *different*.

Our sense of *normal* is defined by power. When (as above) privileged populations talk about others as "different," Lorde points out that they have mistakenly used "different" when they actually mean "deviant." LGBTQIA2S+ people are "different" because they are *deviant* according to the mythical norm that is cishet. BIPOC people are "different" because they are *deviant* according to the mythical norm that is white.[5] Abled people refer to disabled folks as "differently abled" because they deviate from how bodies and minds are "supposed" to work. The "normal" people in these scenarios are uncomfortable with *naming* the difference with any specificity. We recognize that marginalization has made these folks deviant and that calling humans "deviant" is bad. Instead of confronting our thought disparities, "normal" people cover over them and remain comfortable in the power and privilege held through their sense of mythical normativity.

Marginalization happens because only some of us are actually considered "different." That difference might, in this context, be framed as a strength—but in reality, the fact that we *deviate* from the "norm" means we have less power. Our difference is tokenized because only we are different. The people who deign to include us do not consider themselves to be *different*. Embracing human differences means that people with privilege must get (un)comfortable with the terms that they have learned signal marginality and deviance. Like what Jemisin imagines in Um-Helat, Lorde imagines *redefining difference* in ways that consider *all people different* and that names and embraces the specific ways we differ.

The mythical norm requires us all to meet an unmeetable standard, and many of us will try our whole lives to be completely "normal." These standards don't just apply to race, sexuality, ability, or other parts of our identity typically discussed in relation to marginalization and oppression. The mythical norm directs us all to act in certain ways; it demands women to marry and have children, guides men away from mental health resources,

---

5. On the limitations of terms like "BIPOC," see Shereen Marisol Meraji, Natalie Escobar, and Kumari Devarajan, "Is It Time to Say R.I.P. to 'POC'?," *NPR*, September 30, 2020, https://tinyurl.com/4tbr3hpp.

and forces individuals to only act in ways deemed socially acceptable. Now may be the time to ask, how does the mythical norm affect you?

The mythical norm is baked into all aspects of society, including our churches. We often hear about religious trauma preventing young adults from coming back to church. Many have grown up with religion feeling like a threat rather than a community. Those who have never been part of the church are often hesitant to explore a community they observe holding bigoted views or that appears resistant to change. Christian ministry often speaks of "transforming" individuals. This implies that something is wrong and they need to change. Similar to the way Christianity has invaded and colonized countries, outreach can feel like someone telling you to change your life or beliefs because you are not okay as you are. Why would someone want to participate in a community that doesn't welcome their whole selves?

Another mistake churches make is believing that in order to have more diversity they *must* go outward. While indeed we need to open our doors, restructure our leadership, and redefine difference, the church would also be wise to look inward. We forget that our differences are often hidden. Oftentimes the same voices get prioritized, even if there are others in the room. What voices are already among us that we are ignoring or shutting down? The inability to be authentically ourselves contributes to the marginalization we seek to end.

THE JOURNEY FROM MARGINALIZATION TO LIBERATION

To move from marginalization to liberation requires intentional changes—personally, organizationally, and systemically. *Intersectionality* and *inclusion* are two concepts that may inform our next steps, yet it's not a straight path. As we map out the work ahead, it will be important to look for pitfalls and to be courageously curious about the risks we must take to experience liberation in our communities.

Intersectionality Exposes Oppressive Systems

Intersectionality dismantles divide-and-conquer tactics. Oppression perpetuates through oppressive structures that seek to divide and then conquer marginalized populations. This "divide and conquer" approach has remained an effective tactic of people in power since antiquity. Lorde observes, "Those of us who stand outside that power often identify one way in which we are different, and we assume that to be the primary cause of all oppression, forgetting other distortions around difference, some of which we ourselves may be practicing."[6] This single-issue approach to oppression misses how different oppressions intersect and interact. By dividing oppressed populations, the mythical norm prevails even though most people deviate from it in at least one way.

Legal theorist and critical race scholar Kimberlé Crenshaw gives an example of how this divide-and-conquer strategy works in practice, specifically perpetuating the oppression of Black women.[7] In 1976, Emma Degraffenreid filed an employment discrimination lawsuit against General Motors, alleging their hiring practices violated equal employment laws because the company did not hire Black women. Though it was clear that GM systemically disfavored Black women in hiring, the court ruled against Degraffenreid. Equal employment law separately banned gender discrimination and racial discrimination from hiring practices. Therefore, according to the court, as long as GM hired Black men and white women, it was not in violation of equal opportunity law *even though* Black women were never hired. Crenshaw argues this demonstrates the limits of a single-issue focus to marginalization and liberation.[8]

Crenshaw coined the term "intersectionality" as a theory and praxis that can address the overlapping societal oppressions that she saw exemplified in Degraffenreid's case. Crenshaw shows how *oppressions intersect*. Racism and sexism cannot be treated independently because they intertwine. The marginalization that results is greater than the sum of its single-issue parts.[9] Crenshaw's legal theory builds off the work of Audre Lorde as well as the Combahee River Collective, a group of radical Black feminists who worked collectively against marginalization in

---

6. Lorde, *Sister Outsider*, 116.
7. Kimberlé Crenshaw, "Demarginalizing the Intersection of Race and Sex: A Black Feminist Critique of Antidiscrimination Doctrine, Feminist Theory, and Antiracist Politics," *University of Chicago Legal Forum* 139 (1989): 139–67.
8. Crenshaw, "Demarginalizing the Intersection," 141–42.
9. Crenshaw, "Demarginalizing the Intersection," 140.

the 1970s. They wrote, "If black women were free, it would mean that everyone else would have to be free since our freedom would necessitate the destruction of all the systems of oppression."[10] A system based on the mythical norm always privileges cishet abled white men with the most benefits. Dismantling this systemic norm means starting from the perspectives of the folks who sit in the crossfire of multiple, intersecting marginalizations.

As we think about marginalization in the church, we have to carefully consider the multiple identities we each hold, and how that can lead to further marginalization. If we fail to recognize intersectionality, we fail to see the entirety of a person; their full range of experience and identity. Only through full recognition—and the understanding that we may never know every component of a person—can we create policies and practices that actively fight marginalization.

Limits and Benefits of Inclusion

I (Jimmy) have experienced many congregations (and society at large) to assume that inclusion is the solution to marginalization. If the church and society cast certain people out and keep many people at the bottom, then *including marginalized populations* brings them into the church and gives them more power and agency. The belief: when everyone is included, the church thrives.

Inclusion *is* significantly better than exclusion. Christian congregations and denominations have formally banned BIPOC and LGBTQIA2S+ people from entry, and they have (and still have) policies that prohibit women and LGBTQIA2S+ folks from ordained ministry and leadership. Even without formal policies, many congregations essentially exclude BIPOC, LGBTQIA2S+, poor, or disabled people through hostile treatment that makes it clear they are unwelcome. Congregations and denominations should actively work to eliminate these exclusions and become places that actively include marginalized populations among their membership and leadership.

10. "(1977) The Combahee River Collective Statement," Black Past, accessed December 9, 2024, https://tinyurl.com/2672ea9d.

That said, the church has a history of abusive inclusion. Christianity and churches *cannot include everyone.* The missionary emphasis of colonizing Christianity transforms an inclusive church into a mandate: "make disciples of all nations" (Matt. 28:19). Inclusion focuses on bringing people into the pews. It assumes Christian identity as normative and dominant. This continues the colonizing legacies of Christianity. It ignores how, for the church, "inclusion" has historically assumed an ideology of conversion. Beyond colonization, this ideology purports to "include" Jewish people when it appropriates their texts and traditions and presumes to label as "better" Christian interpretations of these traditions.[11] Everyone is included even if they do not want to be.

Inclusion is one of those words that's both lauded and challenged. As a new teacher, I (Abby) am responsible for cultivating a healthy learning environment for my students, and valuing inclusion in the microcosm of my classroom is crucial. Cornerstone to this healthy learning environment is building trust. Trust leaves room for vulnerability, and vulnerability is a must for learning and attempting new things. It is inevitably challenging because the students themselves are very different. Some come from different cultures, where always being quiet is seen as the right etiquette; some have been told that the education system won't serve them; and everyone comes with their own set of beliefs, shaped by the teachers before, their home environment, and so much more.

The church, like a classroom, is a microcosm of people that must learn how to be together toward everyone's shared flourishing. How can our leaders lay the groundwork for practices that don't allow for marginalization or prejudice to run rampant but still allow for vulnerability and growth? Inclusion isn't about perfection, but it is about effort. There is no cookie-cutter approach, and each community and each situation will require thoughtful and intentional responses as Jimmy's own classroom story below illustrates.

Inclusion is not the same thing as ending marginalization. In six years of teaching introduction to biblical studies at a Lutheran college that pro-

---

11. This is what scholars call "supersessionism." For some helpful discussions, see Amy-Jill Levine and Marc Zvi Brettler, *The Jewish Annotated New Testament*, 2nd ed. (Oxford University Press, 2017).

fessed inclusive values, I (Jimmy) have often been made to feel *guilty* and *ashamed* for alienating "conservative" students. My reading assignments include a vast array of different authors, many of whom I do not agree with. However, none of them are cishet white men. And none of them argue that the Bible condones hateful oppression that puts some people's humanity up for debate.

My students are not required to agree with these readings. In fact, they are encouraged to disagree with them. My only rule, as stated in the syllabus, is: "Hateful or discriminatory speech of any kind will NEVER be tolerated in this class." Midway through one semester, I checked in with a section where discussion was especially difficult, and several students expressed that they felt like they could not contribute because what they had to say was "too controversial" and that they feared repercussions. After class, another student wrote to me about a different experience of hearing this conversation. They shared how frustrated they were hearing this because it sounded like these students wanted to be able to express hateful views about them, how terrifying it was to feel like their classmates harbored this hatred toward them and wanted my permission to express it.

The problem with inclusion is that people in the mythical norm refuse to recognize that inclusion is impossible without genuine change. It won't work if we refuse to exclude certain ideas and mind-sets—*and the people who refuse to abandon them*—from our midst. Congregations frequently want to include marginalized populations while avoiding conversations and changes that would alienate their current membership.

Another pitfall of inclusion I (Abby) have experienced in the church is when we attempt to apply inclusion in our efforts of helping others; we must resist the urge to think everyone *needs* our assistance. One misguided service project with my youth group in an impoverished neighborhood in Detroit was enough to wake me up to the damage we can do when we make assumptions about others' needs. Inclusion cannot be an effort to broadly sweep everyone into our box, making promises of salvation or happiness. Instead, our efforts must be focused on where they are wanted, and what, exactly, is wanted. If we are called to build a home, it is not the time to preach our beliefs. We show our inclusionary practices by acting on them and accepting that others do not need to share our beliefs to be part of our community.

Indeed, everyone does not need to be part of our community. We might extend Jemisin's "paradox of tolerance": a community should never be toxically exclusive *and* a community can never include everyone. Everyone should experience community; but different people can experience community and sanctuary in different ways and in different places.

Ultimately, inclusion is far from the end goal, and it's fair to critique the efforts we've seen—from halfhearted reviewing of expectations, to condemning current events, to long leadership meetings that are focused on talking, not on doing. It requires attention to leadership that can cast a vision, take accountability when mistakes are made, and demonstrate willingness to learn from those mistakes.

For me (Abby), inclusion exists in a gray area, in a place that I'm not yet ready to dismiss. When I think of inclusion, I think of an invitation, of a hand outstretched, eager for camaraderie and community. Sometimes this hand is shaky and sometimes it doesn't know quite where it's going. But it's there, and it's trying. When inclusion fails, it's not a sign to rescind the invitation or just let go, but a sign to reevaluate and grow.

The Necessity of Intersectionality for Systemic Change

Inclusion is a starting point, but, in our view, it ultimately hinders an intersectional approach to ending marginalization. Crenshaw's work on intersectionality warns against inclusion-based strategies that bring Black women and other multiple-marginalized populations into already established institutions: "These problems of exclusion cannot be solved simply by including Black women within an already established analytical structure."[12] Inclusion does not eliminate the *systems* that excluded marginalized populations in the first place.

Crenshaw illustrates the intersectional nature of oppression using a metaphor of a house with a basement and a main floor. Her basement metaphor exemplifies the limits of inclusion. To paraphrase her illustration:

> Imagine a house with a basement and a main floor, where everyone desires to be on the main floor. At the start, everyone on the main

---

12. Crenshaw, "Demarginalizing the Intersection," 140.

floor reflects Lorde's mythical norm: the people with the most privilege in society, based on every category of human difference. Anyone who deviates from the mythical norm in any way is left in the (very deep) basement. There is a small opening to the main floor that the folks in the basement can look up and see, but it is too high to reach. So, the folks in the basement stand on each other's shoulders so that some folks are able to pull themselves through. The order they stand in reflects how close they are to the mythical norm: the folks who only deviate in one way are at the top, those who deviate in multiple ways are at the bottom—bearing the weight of the group on their backs. As folks near the top climb through, they join the main floor—and they do not reach down to help anyone else. Eventually, it is only the multiple-marginalized folks who remain in the basement, and the main floor is still too high for them to reach.[13]

Inclusion focuses on bringing people to the center (or the main floor) and misses the people who are most marginalized. It leaves the building's structure in place, which creates the spatial conditions that limit who can reach the (supposedly better) main floor. Lorde writes, *"For the master's tools will never dismantle the master's house. They may allow us to temporarily beat him at his own game, but they will never enable us to bring about genuine change."*[14]

An emphasis on inclusion usually winds up contradicting the liberative goals of intersectionality. Churches can hang Pride flags when they would never consider an out LGBTQIA2S+ candidate to be their head pastor. Neighborhoods can visibly support Black Lives Matter and still talk about how "unsafe" they feel when they see Black people on their sidewalks. Companies can still hire women in prominent roles and pay them less than they would have paid a man. Pastors can work closely with their neighboring rabbi and still preach sermons that urge their congregations "not to be a Pharisee." We include "different" people and still consider them deviant: *they* are different; *we* are normal. In other

---

13. Crenshaw, "Demarginalizing the Intersection," 151–52.
14. Lorde, *Sister Outsider*, 112.

words, institutions can become inclusive without destroying the mythical norm that shapes our social, political, and religious institutions.

Efforts at inclusion tend to assume that marginalized populations can be integrated into the mythical norm. We see this in Crenshaw's basement example: the assumption is that it is better for everyone to be on the top floor—where the mythical norm resides—than to be in the basement with the most marginalized people. Why does everyone need to reach up to the top floor? The fact that the basement receives less support and is considered less desirable is an *effect* of the structural norms that prioritize the top floor to begin with. Inclusion alone cannot address the structures that reinforce the mythical norm that perpetuates marginalization.

LIBERATION MEANS DECENTERING

Our starting point for liberation matters. Crenshaw concluded the article in which she coined the term "intersectionality" by writing: "It seems that placing those who are currently marginalized in the center is the most effective way to resist efforts to compartmentalize experiences and undermine potential collective action."[15] Inclusion starts at the center and draws marginalized people into it. Crenshaw demands the opposite: beginning with the most marginalized.

Liberation starts with the basement: this *flips* how folks tend to imagine inclusion (at least, folks with privilege). Crenshaw coined *intersectionality* as a *new* analytic structure. What happens if we give more value to the basement—and move away from assuming everyone should be (or should want to be) on the top floor? If the basement and the main floor are too divided and exclusive, what happens if we change the structure, instead trying to include everyone in the only space we have made livable?

Lorde demands we embrace difference. We need to admit and cherish the ways we differ. This must go far deeper than paying lip service in sermons or slogans on social media or church marquees. Embracing difference requires us "to recognize those differences, and to examine

15. Crenshaw, "Demarginalizing the Intersection," 167.

Beyond Marginalization, Intersectionality, and Inclusion to Reach Liberation

the distortions which result from our misnaming them and their effects upon human behavior and expectation."[16] *Naming* difference means talking about difference—*and the imbalances of privilege and power that have been built upon certain human differences.* It means that when a Black person says, "This beloved hymn is racist," white people cannot gaslight them by saying, "You're reading into it the wrong way." To be clear: "the wrong way" in this example really means *not the white way.*

IMAGINING SANCTUARY TO FOSTER LIBERATION

Abby imagined the church in terms of a sanctuary. I (Jimmy) want to ask our readers: What does "sanctuary" feel like to you?

I suspect most of us share our experience of sanctuary within our church contexts. We experience sanctuary in the church as it is (even as we imagine what the church could and should become). But, as Abby pointed out, many marginalized folks—especially young adults—do *not* feel sanctuary in churches. Our efforts to liberate the church from marginalization often look for ways to create that sanctuary feeling for more people, bringing them that feeling within the church walls. This seeks to include marginalized folks into our sense of what sanctuary can be.

When marginalized people don't feel sanctuary in church, we keep creating it elsewhere: in dance clubs, on the streets, in protests and community gatherings, in our stories, music, and art. For the church, liberation means recognizing that sanctuary happens far beyond our sanctuaries. And our sanctuaries were not designed to create these other experiences of sanctuary. Starting with the experiences of the most marginalized means challenging our norms. We have to transform our expectations of sanctuary and be open to other ways of doing it. We have to be willing to close our sanctuary doors sometimes (or forever). Liberation decenters the church.

Liberation means the church can only ever be *one among many spaces of sanctuary.* Liberation means the church no longer gets to be the most powerful, wealthy, and influential space of sanctuary. (This privileged position comes from its shape that fits the mythical norm.) We cannot

---

16. Lorde, *Sister Outsider*, 115.

offer a firm solution to how an expanded, liberated meaning of sanctuary could transform the church because it will require more of us—and others "beyond the walls"—to creatively imagine and enact this liberation. We can point to ways that we can see marginalization, confront our privileged history, and resist harmful and limited notions of inclusion. And we can suggest concrete ways to start dreaming together in community.

+++

As we consider our role in liberation, I (Abby) am brought back to my classroom, to a minor event that showcased the power of the individual within a community. When I first started teaching, I taught in a classroom that wasn't my own. I came in midyear and had to quickly lay out my standards and expectations. The transition was challenging, especially when I realized the students had far more power than me. One of the most contested routines had been the seating chart. To many young children, friends are everything, and a simple seating assignment can feel like a cruel punishment. I remember distinctly one student who refused to move to her spot. She would joke around, distract her friends and herself, but refused to move. When she told me no, I was at a complete loss. What was next, I had wondered. Would it all be downhill from here? I knew that if she got too upset, she wouldn't be able to focus for the rest of class, and I knew that if she didn't move, it would be her peers who would suffer. I wanted to give up—that's always easier—but I didn't, especially when it was her best friend who told her she should do what was asked. Suddenly, the whole dynamic changed. Now, it wasn't me, a new teacher, asking her to move, but a friend, saying they would catch up later, once the lesson had wrapped up.

The event showcased the power peers have with each other, and that a community isn't strong because of its leaders, but because of the values that are slowly being shared and spread. Liberation is a community effort, yet most members feel their role is minor. Who is a leader if not someone who steps up? Stepping up, in many cases, can also look like stepping down; creating room for others around you. Wherever you are in the spectrum of power and privilege, there is a space for you to contribute.

Beyond Marginalization, Intersectionality, and Inclusion to Reach Liberation

TAKING STEPS TOWARD LIBERATION

Liberatory practices must start as an active decision to challenge your own biases and narratives that have been treated as truth. Like my (Abby's) classroom, our congregations and communities will need to practice trust and vulnerability and be open to taking risks to learn new things.

While there's no one road map—every community and their needs will look different—here are some possible beginning steps.

- Read with fervor from various authors. Read memoirs about sex work, books about slavery, Afrofuturism, lived experiences of poverty and disability, and anything else. Read alongside members of your congregation. Discuss. Wonder. Books are both mirrors—reflections of who we are, and windows—the opportunity to explore other cultures and ways of being. Books can be one of the best ways to begin conversations and increase empathy.
- Remain reflective. If you say bias doesn't exist in your church, you are most certainly wrong. Make peace with the idea that we are all imperfect people and that we *all*—even the scholars and the advocates—have work to do.
- Create a multitude of opportunities for leadership. Does the same person plan the potluck every year? Can you always count on the pastor to take the pulpit? Invite others to step in—even if only for one event or one sermon. As your mind opens to what a sermon, a brunch, or a Sunday school class could look like, new ideas and possibilities will emerge.
- Embed accountability into everything. Make it okay to be wrong, to be called out, to be checked. Instead of shying away from these conversations, embrace them so much you forget they were ever taboo.
- Give. Give your time, your money, your energy, your kindness. Give anything you can spare, and when you can spare nothing, hope that someone else may have some extra room in their own heart.
- Do not let humans ruin your relationship with God. Recognize that church is a community of people coming together for God, but it cannot replace your relationship with her. When you are disheartened, broken, or distressed, remember that a relationship with God does not

require a particular church or community. It is okay to leave if you are no longer safe.
- Keep hope close to your chest. In a dark, often despairing world, do not give up on change.

Remember that as a leader or congregant your role is vital. A liberated church isn't just for the people that we notice are different from ourselves. A liberated church is for all of us, for the parts of us that we have hidden away or neglected, and for the youth and children and people of all ages who love the church and need the church. We can open the doors, re-create sanctuary, and set the table for all instead of the few.

I (Jimmy) cannot, in good faith, give practical suggestions for liberation because liberation will never be practical. The most practical advice I can give is: seek out, listen to, and properly compensate marginalized voices who have long been writing about and demanding justice. Find people who aren't "big names" on the topic—*and pay them*. Listen to *many different perspectives* from people who, on the surface, might seem similar. Get comfortable with our contradictions—as Abby and I have had to do with the disagreeing differences you see in this chapter. Most importantly, when you start to sense what justice can feel like, act on those instincts—especially the ones that feel "right" at the same time they seem least practical and most impossible.

Embrace *decentering*. "Decentering," as an orientation or method, comes out of feminist and womanist theology, especially as an approach to the Bible. Scholars like Mitzi Smith and Elisabeth Schüssler Fiorenza show us what is possible when we decenter "heroic" figures (such as Jesus or Paul) from our focus.[17] This decentering directs attention to queer, enslaved wo/men in and around these stories—both as characters and as folks who heard them.[18] When we decenter Jesus, we lose a figure whose

---

17. See, for example, Elisabeth Schüssler Fiorenza, *Wisdom Ways: Introducing Feminist Biblical Interpretation* (Westminster John Knox, 2001); Schüssler Fiorenza, *Rhetoric and Ethic: The Politics of Biblical Interpretation* (Fortress, 1994); Schüssler Fiorenza, *The Power of the Word: Scripture and the Rhetoric of Empire* (Fortress, 2007); Mitzi J. Smith, *Womanist Sass and Back Talk: Social (In)Justice, Intersectionality, and Biblical Interpretation* (Cascade, 2018); and Mitzi J. Smith and Yung Suk Kim, *Toward Decentering the New Testament: A Reintroduction* (Cascade, 2018).

18. Though I am far from the only scholar to do this (building on the work of

centrality has made centuries of theological meaning. This means sometimes Jesus and Paul were wrong, and the folks they argued with were right (e.g., the Syro-Phoenician woman in Mark 7:24-30). But we gain many more people and their differences: Jesus and Paul become *some among many* folks who desired God's justice and worked, imperfectly, toward enacting liberation.

When discussing liberation in your church or other Christian spaces, pay attention to how central "the church" (whether as a particular building, denomination, or wider institution) is to justice and liberation. Above, I wrote: "Liberation means the church can only ever be *one among many spaces of sanctuary*." This statement enacts a decentering approach to liberation. Christianity still stands at the center of a White-supremacist cisheteropatriarchal culture that the church built through centuries of colonization, enslavement, oppression, and domination. Liberation cannot start from these central spaces: it must be led by the most marginalized. It must start with different perspectives. Decentering means we can listen to and work for liberation, but most of us cannot be the ones who lead it.[19] The citations in this chapter—of authors who write nonfiction and fiction—are all good voices to listen to.

Many church conversations yoke the church's survival to liberation. *If we figure out how to do justice, our church will thrive*. Again, this keeps the church too central: if we are working to make sure the church survives or grows, then we are still invested in the norm, the way things have always been.

But also, I think this is false. I think these conversations are not invested in true liberation or genuine change. A fear of failure motivates them—a fear of the church's utter failure. We are more afraid the church may collapse than we fear the ongoing failure of enacting liberation. Genuine change might mean risking church failure. Liberation decenters the people with power: that is a promise and a threat. Losing "our church" or

---

Schüssler Fiorenza, Smith, and others), I demonstrate this decentering (and cite many other examples of this work) in my book on the queer wo/men around Paul's letter to the Romans: Jimmy Hoke, *Feminism, Queerness, Affect, and Romans: Under God?* (SBL Press, 2021).

19. Charlie Jane Anders's young-adult "heroic" characters grapple with this at the end of the final novel in her *Unstoppable* space trilogy: Anders, *Promises Stronger Than Darkness* (Tor, 2023).

"the church" or its centrality feels like the end of the world. The institutional church has always been a part of the world we know. But the world we know is also the world where marginalization flourishes. We need to seek liberation from the world we know, and that means the end of the world.[20] In *Black on Both Sides*, C. Riley Snorton writes, "Perhaps black and trans lives' mattering in this way would end the world, but worlds end all the time. . . . Even so and as yet, there is still life."[21]

We (Abby and Jimmy) want to end with hope. José Esteban Muñoz describes hope as "a backward glance that enacts a future vision."[22] It is easy to become cynical after years of enduring disappointment from people and institutions who claim to care about liberation while benefiting from and perpetuating marginalization. We want to recognize and honor both Jimmy's years of experience as a thought leader and Abby's current experiences as a young adult in the church. We also want to name that cynicism and hope are not always opposites: our critique and anger hope for change by refusing to be happy with the way things are.[23]

In the song "Sanctuary," there is another line repeated: "With thanksgiving, I'll be a living sanctuary for You." We can be a living sanctuary, breathing life and hope into the world and the spaces we occupy. We can be a living sanctuary for ourselves, for God, and for each other. We can burn what we need to and build what we must. We can liberate the church and then, one day, the world.

---

20. See "Destruction and Re-Creation," chapter 3 in this volume, for further exploration of how worlds, including but not limited to the environmental world, have been ending all the time as the result of marginalization and injustice.

21. C. Riley Snorton, *Black on Both Sides: A Racial History of Trans Identity* (University of Minnesota Press, 2017), 198.

22. José Esteban Muñoz, *Cruising Utopia: The Then and There of Queer Futurity* (New York University Press, 2009), 4.

23. See Sara Ahmed, *The Promise of Happiness* (Duke University Press, 2014).

8

SEX IS A GIFT

The Bigger Gift Is Talking About It

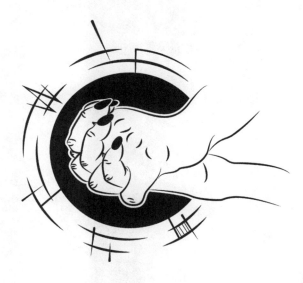

Rev. Madeline Burbank
Kara Haug

OUR INVITATION

When you bring up sex and religion, people get uncomfortable. How are your shoulders right now? Are they tense? You can imagine the reactions of people at parties when they meet Kara, a sexuality health educator, and her husband, a pastor. People awkwardly smile and retreat from the interaction, not fully knowing how to proceed. Kara and her husband are the epitome of what makes everyone uncomfortable—sex and religion. Sometimes Madeline gets polite questions about being a pastor who's a young woman, and furthermore openly queer, but initial surprise ("that's allowed?") often gets in the way of deeper curiosity ("what do you enjoy?"). Here's an opportunity to go deeper.

In this chapter, we'll share both of our perspectives with the goal of painting a future for the church rooted in the radical intimacy made known to us through Jesus. A future in which we can name grief and exploitation, map pathways to healing and learning, and transform the way we frame sex and intimacy. We'll explore our path to this future using three main questions: Why is sex hard to talk about? What needs to change? Where do we go from here?

You are invited to wonder and explore in ways that previously seemed unthinkable. We all deserve nice things—pleasure, healing, and open access to information. When students ask why sex education class is important, Kara tells them, "Because you deserve it. You deserve to know about your body, and to have good and healthy relationships." But even when we embrace such goodness and importance, this subject can be difficult, so let's start there.

Sex Is a Gift

WHY IS THIS HARD? A SEX EDUCATOR'S PERSPECTIVE

"Nothing about this is okay," I (Kara) thought, as I turned my minivan onto a street with manicured lawns, large homes, and the smell of Glade plug-ins. I was a foster home licensor dropping off a thirteen-year-old girl at her new placement. It took me a week to find her a place to live, two hours away from everything she knew. She and her other sibling were in foster care because they were raped by family members and lived in extreme poverty. Many would consider this new placement a win, but I saw in her eyes, these signs of upper-class suburbia were signs that she didn't belong. This was the message she received at her previous placement, including at her former foster mom's church. There she was told what a "good girl" was—a girl who didn't have sex before she was married. All she heard was that she was bad, that she didn't belong.

It was through this experience and countless others, that I became a sex educator. Too many of us simply hear, "Sex before marriage is a sin." "Sex is bad. Don't think about it." "Sex is a gift, save it for the one you love." But many of us experience a form of sex before marriage and often not by our own choosing. When this happens, we assume our default is that we are bad and unlovable. Others experience sexual intimacy by their own choosing before marriage in a way to explore human connection. Does this really make them bad or unpure? Is seeking a form of connection a terrible thing?

This story of abuse is not an isolated story. Too many of our children grow up in foster care due to sexual abuse. Every sixty-eight seconds, an American is sexually assaulted.[1] There is a good chance you were one of them. I was too. It wasn't until the age of thirty-two that I finally said the words out loud that I had experienced sexual assault. I was twelve and twenty-one. I wasn't able to say the words because I didn't want to be another statistic. My grandmother and mother were a statistic, and I desperately didn't want to live the repercussions of their reality. I didn't want the experience of being violated to shape my entire being as I have

---

1. Keep in mind that this statistic is based off of what is reported. There are many assaults that go unreported. "Every 68 Seconds, an American Is Sexually Assaulted," RAINN, accessed December 16, 2024, https://tinyurl.com/z7xehrxc.

seen it shape so many others. But here I am. Here I am learning that it does indeed shape who we are, but we have the ability to learn and change how it affects us moving forward.

As a sex educator I have heard countless statements like:

> "I did everything they told me to. I was good. I followed the rules, so why do I feel miserable in my marriage?"
> "I keep having miscarriages, and no one wants to talk about it with me."
> "I had an abortion before grad school. The condom broke."
> "What if the affair was the only way I found myself?"
> "Boys get abused too. I am one of those boys. No one seems to care about us."
> "Sex for me has only been about punishment. Pleasure has never been a factor, so now I choose to not have it."
> "We were both virgins, but we got an STI (sexually transmitted infection). Why don't we talk about this?"

We all have secrets that crystallize into shame that live behind the veil of grief.[2] Many of us carry grief with us, afraid to feel it. Our shame and grief become a gift basket of generational shame stories around sex that we keep indulging in, even though the contents in that gift basket expired long ago. If you took the contents out of that gift basket, most of the labels on the items read "silence," "misinformation," "this is the only way," or "your hard is too hard for me." We consume these items daily, feeding the idea that we are not worthy or good enough to receive love. Without opportunities to process our shame and grief, we pack up the basket and hand it over to the next generation.

Sadly, the church has often fed its flock shame, silence, and misinformation around sex, likely contributing to church decline. As we have gained more understanding of sexuality and started to talk about how it affects us, people see the contradictions in the messages received at

---

2. Many of our secrets are rooted in experience born from grief. Or we have thoughts that we don't share because we have been told that they won't be accepted, and we then feel bad. Because we hold these so tightly within, what is born is shame. Wanting to belong is a human desire and if that is going to be jeopardized, we hide a bit of who we fully are.

church. What has been served up in a binary understanding of good/bad, virgin/slut, pure/sinful, clean/defiled has created a feast full of illusion and harm that has been set at Christ's table. A harvest of shame around our bodies was not the eternal meal that Christ prepared.

The more I learn, the more I grieve for the little girl, the adolescent, the college girl, the wife, and the mom. We experience pain from our past losses when we start to learn more about what healthy relationships look like, how our bodies really function, and how so many of the rules we follow were constructed from past shame stories. We recognize that maybe we didn't need to feel the fear we had as our bodies changed from puberty, parenting, illness, disability, or aging and how those changes affected our relationships. Christ invites us to a table of conversation and connection of the most intimate kind. At this table we can gain tools to navigate our hard emotions. We can ask honest questions about our bodies and our bodies' limitations. We can talk about our desire or why it doesn't equate to the desire of others. According to Brené Brown, "Shame derives its power from being unspeakable."[3] Silence equals shame, and it's time to let go of silence.

When I lead workshops and open the door to a nourishing and brave space where we can talk about sexuality and how we experience it, there are many who say, "me too." Many share our grief over the inadequate education we received on this topic, the loss of body autonomy, the choices we made based on our wounded child, and the missed opportunities of stating our needs. When we learn how to talk about these things, they change. We change. We stop feeding one another a feast that doesn't provide.

Think about what it was like as a child when your questions to caregivers or adults were ignored. Maybe you did something you were proud of and wanted to show them, but nobody paid attention. Being ignored hurts us in a way where it feels like we don't really matter and what we have to say doesn't hold any value.

Now think about your sexuality. Often, our relationship with our sexuality has been brushed aside or flattened; it's either right or wrong.

---

3. Brené Brown, *Daring Greatly: How the Courage to Be Vulnerable Transforms the Way We Live, Love, Parent, and Lead* (Penguin Books, 2015), 67.

Our sexuality has been ignored, it's hurting, and we are grieving. When a part of us, like our sexuality, isn't nurtured or acknowledged, we try to find other ways to fill that need. Some of us might have turned to magazines or the Internet to look for answers. Maybe we talked to peers, which is sometimes helpful, sometimes not. Some may have turned to a substance, used people, or withdrawn, turning inward, left alone with despair. Many of us don't feel good enough—in our bodies, our relationships, or our expressions—to deserve the love and deep connections that God imagined for us. This is why when we talk about sex in church spaces, walls go up, tempers flare, and people shut down.

Our story doesn't need to be one where we continually pass down pain from grief, trauma, and shame. We can find a new way, but we must be willing to face our grief and learn from it. Grief and love are unassuming and unexpected lovers. Their partnership is strong. By entering into conversation with our grief, we give ourselves permission to seek out education, we learn to include others in what we discover, and we find that we are more alike than we imagined. We start to tear off the labels of "silence," "misinformation," "this is the only way," and "your hard is too hard for me." We find the courage to embrace both love and grief. This is what it means to commune together. Christ's table offers a true feast and a place for belonging for bodies beautifully made.

WHY IS THIS HARD? A PASTOR'S PERSPECTIVE

Jesus's invitation to communion extends to all people, not just those who check certain boxes. As a pastor, I (Madeline) believe this to be essential. But it's difficult to embody such radical love and welcome in our contexts, due to ideological contradictions and competing models of belonging. We're navigating oppression and its legacies, which claw onto people with external obstacles and internal shame. Shame ultimately aggravates our fear of not belonging, which is synonymous with death for social creatures.

Our contexts were seeded by illusions of purity and white supremacy culture, and shame spirals into feeling bad for having too much sex, or not enough, or maybe just the wrong kind of sex. We worry about wasting our time, or causing irreparable harm, or failing our partners, or disappointing our families, or betraying ourselves, or single-handedly stumbling into new ways to sin. But no one is alone in wrestling with such shame, and it's usually misguided.

Belonging and identity are overarching themes in Scripture. People of faith are wrestling with questions like "Where did we come from? Where are we going? And who are we called to be?" The Christian Bible is a collection of over sixty texts—compilations of rules, genealogies, poetry, narratives, and letters—written thousands of years ago, shared through cascading translations and interpretations. Throughout the Bible, we see how the ways humans record and interpret God's word is always shaped by cultural context, systemic oppression, and glimmers of hope.

With such variety, Scripture is more like a sacred library than a life manual. But authorities still point to the Bible as if it presents one cohesive sexual ethic that perfectly translates to today. Gilded ideas like biblical literalism, inerrancy, and univocality all reject diverse perspectives and mask individual attempts to inflate one's own credibility. "Don't look at me; I'm just repeating the inerrant word of God! If you honor the Bible, you must trust what I'm saying!" In reality, we all interpret Scripture through the lens of our personal contexts and beliefs (authors of this book included!), so we get to embrace the messiness of biblical interpretation, and encourage critical thinking.

The Center for Media Literacy provides great guiding questions, whether you are critically reading a social media post or a biblical passage: (1) Who created this message? (2) Which techniques are used to attract my attention? (3) How might different people interpret this message? (4) Which lifestyles, values, and points of view are represented—or missing? (5) Why is this message being sent?[4] The *why* can be expanded with contextual curiosity about *who benefits* if the message has its intended impact, and who is harmed? This tool kit helps make sense of why mainstream discussions of Christianity focus on sexual morality instead of economic responsibility to liquidate riches and address poverty.

So, who benefits from messages that prioritize sexual purity and abstinence? Biblical discourses about sex, food, and bodies touch on

---

4. Jeff Share, Tessa Jolls, and Elizabeth Thoman, *Five Key Questions That Can Change the World* (Center for Media Literacy, 2007).

such intimate parts of our lives, it's like they provide direct lines of human influence and control. Historically, group identities were delineated through "us versus them" norms about these intimate parts of our lives. Members belong because they "eat correctly" (whether that's following the family recipe or avoiding whole food groups) and "practice intimacy" (whether that's serial dating or arranged marriage), and outsiders aren't just *different*, they *live wrong*. People are who they are because of who they are not—identity rooted in contrast that requires constant maintenance and inevitable anxiety. Most people don't live in uninterrupted conformity, and diverse life experiences bloom even within subgroups.

That's the revolutionary aspect of Christianity and the early church! Jesus touches the untouchable, teaches the disciples to serve the public, and smashes through distinctions like ethnicity and class and gender that try to divide them. Jewish followers and gentile converts ate together, whether they were keeping kosher or eating food sacrificed to idols. Circumcision status no longer mattered; having a penis at all shouldn't matter!

In popular imagination, Christian dogma is focused on temptation as a threat, bodies as mere vessels, and sex as solely reproductive. In a world of slavery and militarized violence, this interpretation of Christianity contributes to purity and superiority being sought over wholeness and reconciliation. It's hard to comfortably address sex and intimacy when *this* is our backdrop!

So, what else can we reexamine to make things easier to address? The Ten Commandments aren't exactly a *Cosmopolitan* list of relationship tips. Amid specifics about adultery and coveting, women are objectified alongside houses and donkeys, and slavery goes uncondemned. But with nuanced interpretation, the enduring guidance is to "Love God with your whole self, and love your neighbor as yourself."[5] Living as people of faith requires us to strive for mutually supportive relationships.

But it's not easy to find relationship goals reflected in biblical sex. Sex-related scenarios are usually recorded in Scripture for being unusual or uncomfortable. Sometimes they double as a lesson in "what *not* to do,"

---

5. As indicated in Jesus's teaching on the Greatest Commandment, Matt. 22:36–40.

but generally they provide supporting evidence for the bigger drama. King David assaults Bathsheba, which highlights his selfish arrogance and lack of accountability. Onan uses the withdrawal method to prevent Tamar from getting pregnant, denying a secure future for his late brother's widow but having sex anyway, shirking family responsibility until there are deadly consequences. Sarah convinces Abraham that together they can use Hagar to solve their fertility issues, trying to take control instead of trying to trust God's promises.

Even if contemporary Christians have different contexts and sexual priorities, these stories resonate, experiencing or witnessing assault, abuse, harassment, exploitation, lies, manipulation, and betrayal. It happens outright maliciously, but also insidiously, sometimes in a creeping series of mistakes. The closer we get to people, physically and emotionally, the easier it is to cause serious harm. But vulnerability and connection are also essential to intimacy, even in acts as simple as saying hello to the neighbors. So how do we maximize love and minimize suffering?

Principles like fidelity or lifestyles like abstinence are marketed to have mediating effects to protect people from suffering or causing harm. But historically, fidelity and abstinent purity (specifically women's virginity) are more motivated by clear paternal lineage than honest emotional intimacy. Men like Abraham and Jacob fathering children with multiple women isn't portrayed as a double standard, because pro-fertility patriarchy is the standard of their context. Even today, post-#MeToo Movement, cheating gets more daily attention while sexual abuse is disproportionately swept under the rug, because cheating threatens the status quo and abuse is the status quo.

Our current beliefs primarily shape our interpretations of faith stories, and vice versa, but usually in the reverse order that people expect. Politicians, pastors, relatives, even our own internal critics continue to co-opt the Bible to justify abuse, fearmonger, and consolidate power. Exploitation is not unique to one religion, but Christianity has a particular role in the growth and maintenance of oppressive power structures.[6]

---

6. See also chapter 6 in this volume, "Why Are You So Angry?"

Sexual harm and chronic shame reinforce these systems in ways that silence us, isolate us from each other, alienate us from our bodies, and consolidate power in unscrupulous hands. Faith has been weaponized by intersecting forces of oppression, mingling with grief and making it difficult to address healthier sex.

We need to be intentional about challenging our beliefs and complicating our readings, and can uncover greater wisdom by doing this in community. Sharing and comparing also help us notice that the Bible is full of contradictions and stays in conversation with itself, often highlighting characters whose accomplishments challenge "Bible-based" prejudice. These heroes are almost always "sexual outsiders" (eunuchs, foreigners, widows, sex workers, women in general) who subvert expectations and champion God's work from within their social location (not "despite" their identity). Their marginalized identity is still a place they have power.

One of these biblical heroes is Rahab, a Canaanite sex worker who ensures victory for the Israelites by sheltering Joshua's spies before the fall of Jericho. Rahab is charming, cunning, and fiercely protective of her loved ones. Her sex-related power is not sinister or glamorous; it's simply a fact of her social location, which she heroically uses to help the Israelites and trick the patrol officers. The story frames Rahab's faithfulness as a foreigner to be subversive, more so than her sexuality. Rahab's story reminds us to read in the margins and tear down the king's walls.

It's not all war and espionage. People also enjoyed happy, fulfilling relationships in biblical contexts. I wish we had a play-by-play dialogue of a flirty exchange between a Galilean couple, just as much as I wish we had a detailed menu of what everyone ate at the Last Supper. But such information is unremarkable to the people living in it, and we regularly assume shared knowledge to more efficiently communicate.

There are many questions left unanswered, but there is a wide canvas to explore different themes and possibilities. People have weaponized Scripture to justify slavery and colonial violence, but the gospel magnifies the wisdom of the poor and liberation of the oppressed. Even for practiced medical practitioners, loving parents, ministry leaders, and well-meaning mentors, we're reaching inside ourselves for helpful information that's been stored alongside wounds and damaging ideologies. We're tangled in both forces of healing and forces of exploitation.

Grief and love can be intimate lovers, as Kara highlights, and in my experience the greatest adversary to love is exploitation. Exploitation distorts relationships between beings who would otherwise be collaborators. Whether we are attempting to interpret the narrative of Scripture or our own narratives, it will serve us well to interrogate where exploitation shows up and pay close attention to where love shows up. Any version of a story rooted in exploitation serves the systems of hierarchy and disrupts the stories God intends for creation, rooted in love.

Understandably, some people set faith aside in order to heal. Churches can be too focused on trying to win those people back, and in doing so we disregard those who highlight faith as part of their healing, and we neglect those pained by fear of sin, as so many have been discouraged from thinking critically about anything related to God. If we're worried about helping God with lost sheep, let's focus on the wandering path under our own feet. Let God be God, who created us to *be*, just be, together.

Jesus demonstrates that all are welcome in eternal belonging, renewed through forgiveness and reconciliation. The Holy Spirit leads us in expressions of that faith. Our Creator is actively equipping us with faith to trust that we are good enough.

WHAT NEEDS TO CHANGE?

There is a long list of responses to this question. We offer just a few important initial steps and trust that as you or your congregation take them, you will discover new paths to take toward healthy and whole approaches to radical intimacy.

Ditch the Shame, Embrace Curiosity!

When I (Madeline) was in ninth grade, at a "sex ed retreat" for my church youth group, the volunteer nurse read an anonymous question with stern disapproval. "'Why do vaginas smell like fish?'" She crumpled the paper. "Well, I sure hope this question came from a girl, because none of you boys should be in contact with that." Her tone dripped with disgust and discomfort, a reaction that went beyond concern about the risks of teen sex.

Regardless of sexual activity, this peer group had been making jokes about "fishy beavers" for years. We were fourteen and fifteen, navigating increasingly complex social interactions, eager for approval, and terrified of rejection. This intense pressure swelled alongside growing messages that young bodies were disgusting, disappointing, or drawing the wrong kind of attention.

I boiled with indignation, thinking about how people might avoid asking questions, scared away by the nurse's response. I had never felt so antagonistic toward a teacher, besides my growing animosity with the pastors who organized this whole thing. It had been promoted as relaxed and educational, instead of the ominous "abstinence only" content typical for churches, but the information given was still shrouded in shame.

Years later, people are having the same (or worse!) experiences; hurt, neglected, admonished, or misinformed. And those of us who want to provide better experiences run into reactionary pushback, our own discomfort, and simple fear of saying the wrong thing. At this retreat, how much did the nurse's own pain from body anxiety and misogyny amplify her reaction? Our best intentions are crammed against damaging ideologies and old wounds.

If we're eager to heal and reorganize ourselves but rush through to avoid conflict, we risk re-creating the same cycles. We can't distance ourselves from past harm and pretend it doesn't impact people anymore. We need to open up! I find guidance in the liturgical practice of confession and forgiveness, and in South Africa's Truth and Reconciliation Commission; being explicit about harm, and outlining what will be done for healing.

God brings us grace that surpasses all understanding, and the ultimate commandment to love. Our responsibility toward mutual care harmonizes with bodily autonomy and the goodness of desire. Whether flirting with a crush or shopping for sex toys, no one needs to hold back in shame. Christian faith ideally celebrates reconciliation, freedom, and love. The liberated church will deconstruct sexual ethics focused on fertility, fear, and control.

There is no individual duty to reproduce, no salvation in virginity, no entitlement to others' bodies. Fruitfulness is fulfilled in the cornucopia of ways to participate in being pro-creation. Protect the environment, let kids explore, honor unfamiliar perspectives, help parents be the best parents they can be.

We need to create a church that values consent, pleasure, and mutual well-being. This is a collective undertaking; it is about starting therapy journeys, braving dinner table conversations, critically consuming media, letting go of harmful and normalized scripts, supporting comprehensive sex education (for young and old), valuing public health, creating environments that support self-esteem and genuine curiosity.

When we lead with curiosity, we can disentangle assumptions about life paths and preferences. Participate in family support as a community priority. Contribute material resources, child care, and other labor so that all parents have what they need to do their best, whatever their relationship status. Get involved in youth support, from regular volunteering to spontaneous conversations that honor their wisdom, reinforce their courage, and celebrate their curiosity.

Increased age and independence prompts a shift in guardians becoming guides. Sexually active young people deserve guidance without surveillance. Restrictions meant to prevent sexual activity are more likely to inhibit safer sex behaviors. Without options to have sex in a safe, controlled environment, people are more likely to rely on the comparative privacy of vehicles, public parks, and house parties. Without access to birth control or condoms, people have an increased chance of unplanned pregnancies or STIs.

Everyone needs to be able to access condoms, lubricant, sex toys, and contraceptives, with or without the involvement of parents and trusted advocates. Everyone, of all ages, deserves comprehensive education about sex and bodies throughout their lives. The demographic that has been reaching out to me (Kara) the most recently are those forty-five and above. And there are many in their eighties who want more education and are learning more than ever about their bodies. Everything we need to change for community healing goes on to promote personal healing, and vice versa.

Deconstruction and Debunking Binaries

The church is stuck in a pattern of disturbing silence, misinformation, or blatant shame. It is causing irrefutable harm.[7] One in three Americans is suffering from religious trauma. Centers that specialize in religious trauma are prevalent nationwide. Mental health professionals are now equating religious trauma and distress generated by the purity movement to the similar experiences of those who have been sexually abused. Most people I (Kara) work with talk about the incongruencies between real life and messages from their faith communities. They share how much deconstruction is required in adulthood. How are we promised the love of God in committed partnerships while simultaneously being told that the love we have to give in the form of sex is sinful, dirty, and a gift? This doesn't make sense. This message also leaves people out—those who never marry, who are not in hetero relationships, who can't or don't want to have children, and who may not experience sexual attraction or expression.

God's story starts with our creation in a garden filled with a multitude of species. Often our imagination stops there. God created us alongside so many other wonderful and odd creatures, all unique in their own right; we are included in this as well. There is no such thing as just male or female as evidenced by the existence of intersex folk and the forty variations in which that can happen. We are not binary, though our mind likes to make things binary to better understand them.

Think about the phrase often associated with matrimony, "one flesh." We say this to signify two becoming one. But as I (Kara) have learned more about science and sexuality, I do not equate one flesh with marriage, but with community. We are born into a community. When you apply paint to the placenta, it looks like the tree of life. When you take a deeper look into some of the structures in our bodies like lungs, the mammary

---

7. Darren M. Slade et al., "Percentage of U.S. Adults Suffering from Religious Trauma: A Sociological Study," *Socio-Historical Examination of Religion and Ministry* 5, no. 1 (2023): 1–28.

glands, our veins, we resemble the root system of trees and plants.[8] As part of this diversity, community, connectedness, and mending, there is growing openness and forever-evolving language about diverse genders, orientations, relationship structures, and community needs. Consider LGBTQIA2S+ identities (Lesbian, Gay, Bisexual, Transgender, Queer, Intersex, Asexual, Two Spirit, and beyond) being named in church spaces and celebrated in Christian leadership. Invitation and celebration go beyond tolerance. Universal welcome is only authentic when we are told we belong *because* of who we are, not "despite our differences."

We all start out the same in the womb; we are one flesh. God made us to be connected not to just each other but to the ecosystems that we live in. We need one another and are a part of one another. This is why for me (Kara), gender, orientation, and sexes are no longer a mystery but a continuation of the fulfillment of the web of diversity that connects us to God. I am she, he, they, them, us, and we. I am all of these things, and so are you. This is why as a church body we need to learn how to talk about sex and our lived experiences with grace, compassion, and curiosity. We are wired for connection, and our sexuality is an integral part of that.

We experience diversity within our relationships that goes beyond gender and overlaps with endless variety in domestic living. Consider how all sorts of people are navigating single living, cohabitation, polyamory, dating, divorce, coparenting, single parenting, no kids, intergenerational housing, bereavement, roommates, caregiving for/as disabled adults, and countless other contexts that go unacknowledged or even stigmatized in their home church settings. We can better serve our community by using more expansive language, resisting assumptions and invasive questions, and intentionally representing diversity in our display images, resources, and public stories.

But what does this all mean in the life of the church? When I (Madeline) visit congregations, I notice when women are only pictured as caregivers or partners. I'm troubled when a church's art displays the stark violence of the crucifixion but never the wholeness of naked bodies. I'm

---

8. For more on how trees communicate and are connected to each other, see Peter Wohlleben, *The Hidden Life of Trees: What They Feel, How They Communicate—Discoveries from a Secret World*, trans. Jane Billinghurst (Greystone Books, 2016).

even more frustrated when a space comfortably features artistic nudity but lacks signage about public and private options for breast feeding. I wonder whose needs go unmet when free pantries provide everything from food to diapers, but not tampons or condoms. I feel like evaporating when someone asks if I have a boyfriend in an effort to get to know me.

Beyond assumptions about default heterosexuality, many young people navigate contexts where marriage is a prerequisite for being treated as a fully realized, mature adult. Married couples face invasive questions about fertility and family planning, whether or not they've shared interest in having children. Expectant (and even experienced!) parents get unsolicited advice about pregnancy and parenting. People with disabilities and elders are made to feel invisible, or dehumanized as an outlet for others to project their own anxiety about age and disabling conditions.

Since childhood, we have been instructed to color within the lines and have been given a narrow script on how to operate in this life that resembles those bold block lines. It is not always inherent to stay within those lines; our natural tendency is to explore, squiggle, connect, and live beyond in a space that is expansive. We are molded into following a story that quite frankly has been made up to suit the need for control. Expansive living for some could be quite scary; not fitting into lines could feel dangerous. We are not saying everyone needs to do that, but choosing to continue a story that has caused many harm is not a story we wish to continue. We invite you to open a box of crayons and rewrite yours and be as fluid as you want. We deeply believe that part of Jesus's invitation into radical intimacy is to embrace the fluidity of all creation much like the waters we're made in.

Take the Risks to Reclaim Our Connection to One Another

I (Kara) teach a class for sixth graders called "Wired for Connection." I introduce the concept of secure attachment and how our brains are wired to connect. We discuss how the first experience of attachment happens when we breast- or bottle-feed. In that moment we release oxytocin, which is the chemical in our brain that promotes bonding. (Oxytocin is also released when we experience sexual intimacy.) We need touch and connection to thrive as humans. Our society got a collective taste of what losing this feels like during the pandemic. This contributes to why social media is so addictive—it plays off our need for connection. As we scroll and receive likes, our bodies release another chemical called dopamine—the "happy chemical." Why do I tell you this? Because from the womb we are wired for connection.

God took on flesh through a womb. The womb is a powerful and sacred place. The womb is the only place that full immersion in water offers us life—echoing a call to baptism. The womb is warm, it is embodied, it becomes a protective home. The womb can also, in a moment, change. It can become unstable. The waters could subside and retreat, the organ could get tangled, the growth could cease. God took a risk to be with us, to know us in a way that beforehand God was not able to touch.

The womb God chose was that of a young unwed girl. Mary, in her devotion to God, took a risk too. To be pregnant and unwed was social destruction. God could have chosen a married woman to be the vessel in which they came into this world, but God didn't.[9] Think about our reactions to teenage pregnancies today. I remember when a woman in one of my churches approached the unwed teenage girl with whom we were throwing a baby shower and said, "How do you feel now that you ruined your life?" I wonder if this woman would have said the same to Mary? I looked at the hurt in the girl's eyes and then promptly asked the woman to leave. Being born through the womb by a teenage girl was Jesus's first act of breaking societal norms to invite us into radical intimacy.

What sets us up for disconnection is looking for who we "are better than." We have based our entire society on who is in and who is out. Who is moral and who is not. Our need to win and be better infiltrates our sports, grades, corporations, access to health, safety, and more. This tendency is a barrier to experiencing abundance in our connections with one

---

9. There is an element of cocreating, Mary agreed. God told of the Holy Spirit descending upon her. Have you ever had a "religious experience" that you felt through your whole body? There is an element of pleasure there. God wanted a tangible experience and one where maybe the most unassuming can surprise us the most.

another. Constant comparison minimizes another person and, in turn, minimizes ourselves. We lose the ability to experience intimacy.

Life starts with risks, with knowing that nothing is ever truly guaranteed, but we choose to risk for the chance of connection. So did God. This is the point. We start in the womb with the risk of never fully becoming; we also learn how to enter a tomb with the risk of becoming something more and shedding what no longer works for us. Jesus's example is powerful. He came through a womb and was laid to rest, finding new life in a tomb. Sometimes for new life to emerge we need to let things lay to rest. Sometimes for connection to happen we take a risk to change what we always knew, because oftentimes what we have always known isn't the whole story.

When it comes to the topic of sex and sexuality, we as a church community need to enter the tomb. We need to lay some things to rest. The tomb is hard, cold, uncomfortable, and dark, but this environment forces us to acknowledge what we are hiding from. The challenge is to emerge from the tomb practicing and living into what we have learned inside. The tomb is a place where we are invited to listen. For the church to change, it needs to listen to the stories of its people. We each hold complex stories and emotions around sexuality that don't always have a holding space in church because of the fear of judgment. Jesus taught us through story, but Jesus also taught us through listening.

When we take the time to enter the tomb and make room for stillness to process our grief, learn and deconstruct our miseducation, and then risk to emerge, new options become available to us. This can feel scary, but living with shame and silence is hurting us and those we care about. Choosing to enter and experience the world through a womb and become one of us demonstrated God's deep intentionality and vulnerability. The beginning of radical intimacy. To experience intimacy with anyone always involves a risk of rejection, abandonment, and betrayal. Any attempt to connect to another and to the validation of self is a risk worth taking. Inevitably there will be some gain: a lesson, friend, lover, confidant, or a moment of deeper knowing. In relationships we will get hurt and we will hurt others. But with vulnerability and intentionality we can learn from our mistakes and minimize harm for the future. The church has caused harm in relationships, and it is past the time that we learn about this harm and how to repair relationships toward healing.

WHERE DO WE GO FROM HERE?

One of my (Kara's) favorite experiences as a youth was lying on the grass with a friend, looking up at the stars. The stillness of the night surprised us—it made us more vulnerable. My body would quietly shake with small vibrations—it felt like our souls were merging. This is what I believe intimacy is, when we invite another into a corner of our inner world to walk around and share in amusement. Intimacy is also when we invite another into our bodies. To feel the flesh of another and embody their inner world of desire and longings. This is what I imagine God had in mind for us—a deep connection.

I have with my best friend one of the most intimate relationships I have ever experienced. She is someone who sees all of me, even the parts that I keep hidden from others. The beautiful part is that she loves me anyway. She holds compassion for me even when I have made choices that harmed others. Her way of caring embodies for me what I believe the grace of God is like. She has said words to me like, "I see you are lost right now. Please come back to yourself." "You are okay, but try to do that differently next time." "It's okay to forgive yourself." "I love you, you are a good person."

This, her, is my vision for what I hope the church can become. We can learn how to better support one another, knowing that we are all messy and beautiful humans. We open our minds and release judgment. With healthy boundaries, we can experience a new sense of freedom and love when "Your hard isn't too hard for me" becomes a new reality.

God desires for us a radical intimacy. God was born through a womb, took on flesh to sit with us, to offer us his body and blood. How incredibly intimate and, if I dare say, erotic. The root word of "erotic" is *eros*, which is love, and more simply a desire and passionate kind of love. Some think that eros holds an aspect of deep knowing. In "Uses of the Erotic," Audre Lorde argues that "The erotic is a measure between the beginnings of our sense of self and the chaos of our strongest feelings. It is an internal sense of satisfaction to which, once we have experienced it, we know we can aspire. For having experienced the fullness of this depth of feeling and recognizing its power, in honour and self-respect we can require no less of ourselves."[10]

There is a passion that God has for us. This passion was shown through Jesus's ministry when he ate with us, washed our feet, shared moments of awe, and broke the rules that didn't serve us well. There is a deep, erotic, passionate sense of knowing, even through "the chaos of our strongest feeling," when God invites us into these spaces. In these spaces we meet God in erotic, intimate, vulnerable ways; and God meets us.

This is the feast of "Take and eat." This is the remembering of us. Rather than meeting parishioners at the door with judgment, a rule book, or a guarded self who passes down shame, how might we invite people to this kind of table instead? What could it look like if we made efforts to care for the entirety of the persons among us, including their sexuality? It might look like . . .

- A dinner ministry put on by retirees for single moms who are trying to do everything.
- A dedicated group to talk about the lack of touch that an elderly person experiences following the death of their longtime partner.
- A monthly babysitting night for parents of young children so they can invest in their relationship.
- A monthly potluck for singles in the community so they can have a family meal.
- A resource room to turn to for those experiencing domestic violence, suicidal thoughts, and addiction. Also resources on where to access health care for the uninsured, nonprofits helping with housing insecurity, safe spaces for LGBTQIA2S+ communities, etc.
- Healthy relationship classes for all ages that focus on coping skills, communication, consent, boundaries, rejection, and more.
- A consultation group on how to make church spaces and experiences available to folks with varying abilities.
- Educational classes around how to date in your older age, finances for newly divorced, learning how to recognize your needs and wants, un-

10. Audre Lorde, *Sister Outsider: Essays and Speeches* (Crossing Press, 2007), 54.

derstanding gender identity and orientation, how to talk to kids about their bodies, etc.
- A group dedicated to grief related to infertility, miscarriage, or the death of a child.
- A group dedicated to caregivers who spend their days thinking about the needs of others where they can gather and remember they are their own individual.

We all carry pain, grief, and trauma, especially around our bodies. Many are leaving the church because they don't experience love there. We are aching with the need for true body-shaking intimacy, for mutual relationships that see the wholeness of each person. Neuroscientist Bruce Perry, who studies the brain and trauma, tells us that "relationships are the agents of change and the most powerful therapy is human love."[11] If as a church community we decided to brave the interactions with grief, open our minds to learning and deconstruction, and care for the woundedness in one another, we can heal. When we find our whole selves being valued, we recognize God's promise of deep connection, experiencing love.

Our bodies were built for connection, and part of that connection is pleasure. There is an organ with ten thousand–plus nerve endings that is proof to that, which serves no other function (nod to the clitoris). However, not all pleasure needs to be a sexual experience. I experience pleasure through dancing, music, seeing the sun hit a flower, eating brownies right out of the oven. We deserve these good things, and our neighbor does too.

Pleasure reminds us that there was a time, a place, before all the harm. The writer and activist adrienne maree brown reminds us of this place: "I touch my own skin, and it tells me that before there was any harm, there was a miracle."[12] When we touch our own skin, may we

---

11. Bruce D. Perry and Maia Szalavitz, *The Boy Who Was Raised as a Dog: And Other Stories from a Child Psychiatrist's Notebook* (Basic Books, 2006), 61.

12. adrienne m. brown, *Pleasure Activism: The Politics of Feeling Good* (AK Press, 2019), n.p.

remind ourselves of this sacred miracle. God invites us into the miracle of radical intimacy.

When have you felt most seen? For me it's been when I can tell the story of the real me. Not the shiny, polished me, but the me who gets scared, who makes mistakes, who manipulates, and who desperately tries to feel loved—and all of those were met with compassion. These moments when we feel seen remind us that we indeed are lovable and valuable. That we possess this gift, this miracle of pleasure. A gift of deep connection and radical intimacy that doesn't need to be earned but is freely given.

MADE FOR RADICAL INTIMACY

Lifting the veil of grief and facing our shame isn't an easy task, but it is worthwhile. We can let go of our shame and break the silence. Moving forward will include creating spaces that welcome ingenuity, messy community and conversations, and beautiful imperfection. This also requires an understanding about boundaries that are healthy and affirming, so we can work to not inflict further harm.

Radical intimacy is fun, courageous, vulnerable, consensual, and compassionate. It promotes pleasurable reconciliation and directs sexual behavior to adapt within diverse communities dedicated to mutual well-being. At its core, radical intimacy is about connection, not just what we do with our body parts but how we connect and align the most vulnerable parts of our lives: sharing breath, asking for help, building our futures, doing God's will for the good of all. The good of all necessitates diversity, which includes the extensive variety of human desires, activities, and relationships. Not everyone will have sex or want touch, so while intimacy is fundamental to human well-being, it doesn't have to be sexual to be fulfilling. Someone's primary expression of intimacy might be shaking hands in church, or petting a cat, or fantasizing with a friend about future travel plans. Making connections and feeling belonging through intimacy is crucial, varied, and necessary. Intimacy will continue to be experienced as a source of shame, but intimacy is also a pathway to healing.

Sex Is a Gift

As a sex educator and theologian, we often play the role of opening the window of wonder to look through and seek something new. We invite you to continue to peer through that window and discover. We give you permission to ask the questions, to feel the real emotions, and to explore in a new way to heal, mend, and rebuild the intimate parts of yourself. Let's take a risk together and embody a community that is built not on shame, but one that is built knowing that we all are deserving of pleasure, love, and connection. Let's act on and remind ourselves that we are indeed a miracle.

9

GATHER AT THE TABLE

A Call for Communities Marked by Love and Belonging

Amar D. Peterman
Nicholas Tangen

OUR INVITATION

The church is one of many locations that young Christians are formed in. Youth groups, Bible studies, Sunday sermons, mission trips, and more all play a key role in how young people perceive the role religion plays in both their personal experience and the broader world. We (Amar and Nicholas) write these words following decades of being formed by the various Christian communities that have been a part of our stories. The theme of this chapter—community—is something we hold dear. For me (Amar), community is a central and indispensable part of the Christian life because, in its beauty and complexity, Christ is made known. For me (Nicholas), community has a geography (the land, the streets, and the public spaces shared by neighbors) and community has a center (the presence and saving love of Jesus shared and expressed in the relationships among neighbors).

Many have endeavored to show that faith is always formed by the places we inhabit and the people placed around us. However, we often fail to name explicitly what this formation is toward. In other words, the emphasis we place on Christian formation means little unless we can identify what this formation is leading to.

The hopeful vision of formation that we propose in this chapter imagines the local church as a community joined together and marked by the centrality of Jesus Christ. Community, as we understand it, is the context within which every person is formed and where identity, culture, and religion are shaped. Social bonds and the practices related to relationality and neighboring also significantly contribute to the common good in associations, neighborhoods, and larger contexts by building trust, mutuality, and shared stories. In what follows, we propose that Christian community, as a divine reality that all are invited to participate in, is markedly different because it is grounded and centered in the person of Jesus and the story of God's ongoing activity in the world among multitudes of particular peoples, places, and experiences. We believe that it is the deep longing of Christian young adults to participate in this kind of community.

The Christian community we describe here is named in the story of Scripture and the person of Jesus. It is manifest in house churches, local gatherings, and communities that participated in eucharistic fellowship across lines of difference. However, the Christian New Testament is far from an instruction manual for building a church. For all the moments the early church shared in a common life by selling their possessions, distributing wealth among the communities, breaking bread together, and praising God (Acts 2:44–47; 4:32–37), there also loomed the conditional "but," like in Acts 5, "But a man named Ananias . . ." (v. 1).[1]

Today, many Christian young adults are longing for worshiping communities that truly love them and allow them to lead with authenticity. In this chapter we argue that this deep longing is true *and* that attending to this longing is an act of Christian faithfulness, not a strategy for church growth or cultural capital. To be sure, this is not about marketing community to young adults in order to bring them into a community and culture that was not designed for them; rather, it is about the qualities of authentic community that are most important to young adults following Jesus. Leaning into this realistic reading of the early church, this chapter offers an invitation for the church to reflect on the nature of our positional unity as a divine reality amid the polarization we see in the world today. We aim to offer a compelling vision for the church as a Christian community named by Jesus Christ and marked by the active work of the Holy Spirit that is birthed out of the imaginations of young people and articulated *by* and *for* young people.

---

1. Eric D. Barreto, "Acts of/and Imagination: The Bible and Community," in *Poetic Living: Theological Education, Culture, and Pastoral Ministry*, ed. Jacqueline E. Lapsley and Neal D. Presa (Cascade, 2023), 9–14. Ananias and his wife, Sapphira, both members of the early church, sell a piece of property and fail to distribute all the proceeds to the apostles and the rest of the community, in opposition to the communitarian ethic of the church. This episode reveals the immediate challenges faced by the emerging Christian community to sustain faithful and mutual participation in a collective vision.

A Call for Communities Marked by Love and Belonging

> As we gather at your table, as we listen to your word,
> help us know, O God, your presence; let our hearts and minds
>   be stirred.
> Nourish us with sacred story till we claim it as our own;
> teach us through this holy banquet how to make Love's vict'ry
>   known.[2]

DIAGNOSING THE PROBLEM

I (Amar) grew up in a large, evangelical megachurch in Wisconsin. Although I was raised in a Christian home, I didn't embrace the Christian faith until I began attending the church's youth group as a teenager. I quickly found myself deeply invested in this community. I'd lead worship for one youth group, preach at another the next day, and then lead a Bible study the next. On Sunday, I'd arrive early to brew coffee for the church café, rehearse with the church band, and faithfully sit in my front-row chair, head down in the front row taking (and retaking) diligent notes from the preacher. Driven by an evangelical fervor, I gave all I could to this community because I found a deep sense of meaning and achievement on a cosmic scale. I believed that, by committing myself to this work, I could change the lives of those who sat in the sanctuary—whether they be weekly congregants, high school students, visiting missionaries, or new attendees.

Through all of this, however, I felt a deep unbelonging in this community as a young, Asian American leader.[3] Despite their eagerness to volunteer my time to various positions, the leaders on staff exhibited little willingness to meet when I had questions about theology, leadership, or relationships. I was given a pulpit for the Wednesday night service but was rarely taught how to teach. I led the church band for Tuesday youth group but was never mentored by the church leadership. I volunteered at the church welcome desk but rarely felt welcome in this worshiping community. I took notes during every Sunday, and yet each sermon of-

---

2. Carl P. Daw Jr., "As We Gather at Your Table," in *Evangelical Lutheran Worship*, pew edition (Augsburg Fortress, 2006), no. 522.

3. Amar D. Peterman, "Navigating a White Evangelical World in This Brown, Indian Body," *Sojourners*, June 16, 2021.

fered little about my lived experience as an Asian American in predominantly white spaces.

This experience is not phenomenal. Today, young people across the Christian tradition are filled with a Spirit-given passion to serve the church that often goes unrecognized and unappreciated by church elders and leadership.[4] However, before we can address the question of community within the church, we must first understand the broader context in which our churches minister.

In *A Secular Age*, Charles Taylor diagnoses the cultural landscape of our society as increasingly apathetic about religion and religious practice.[5] For Taylor, our modern secular age emerges from patterns of disenchantment, a deepened sense of interiority and a sharpened distinction between the inner and outer world, and an increased individuality.[6]

In this age of secularity, religious life becomes one possibility among many where one might discover belonging, moral and spiritual wisdom, and understanding. The personal commitment one makes to this frame is grounded in individual authenticity and the sense that community, religious or otherwise, is consistent with one's sense of self. Young adults formed within this secular age are evaluating if the church might be a place where they might flourish.

This secular age functions differently from the cultural moments within which many of our churches were formed. Therefore, these questions of authenticity and creativity are often met with suspicion or disregard by dominant culture churches who have formed a culture of being within a framework that sees secularity as something to war against. In these contexts, young people and groups on the margins are asked

---

4. See John Gramlich, "Young Americans Are Less Trusting of Other People—and Key Institutions—Than Their Elders," Pew Research Center, August 6, 2019, https://tinyurl.com/yf6e6ey8; "Finding Community as a Young Adult," Christian Reformed Church, March 22, 2023, https://tinyurl.com/ry8yavje.

5. Charles Taylor, *A Secular Age* (Harvard University Press, 2018).

6. Charles Taylor explains that "the social orders we live in are not grounded cosmically, prior to us, there as it were, waiting for us to take up our allotted place; rather society is made by individuals, or at least for individuals, and their place in it should reflect the reasons why they joined in the first place, or why God appointed this form of common existence for them." Taylor, *A Secular Age*, 540.

to assimilate—in essence, to deny—their own sense of authenticity as a prerequisite to belonging. Not only that, but young people often encounter a culture and practice within churches that look radically different from the Jesus they encounter in Scripture, a failure of authenticity that undercuts any desire for shared community.

One final piece of our current cultural moment important to name is the "loneliness epidemic" facing Americans across generations but hitting young adults particularly hard.[7] In a recent study at Making Caring Common, an organization promoting care and the common good among children and adolescents, 61 percent of those between the ages of eighteen and twenty-five reported high levels of loneliness.[8] Similar numbers exist for the presence of anxiety-related disorders among young adults who are experiencing isolation and division in all facets of their lives—work, family, education, social media, friendships, and more.[9]

This isolation and division is not simply a social and political inconvenience but a public health crisis. In an advisory released in 2023 titled "Our Epidemic of Loneliness and Isolation," US Surgeon General Dr. Vivek H. Murthy writes, "Loneliness is far more than just a bad feeling—it harms both individual and societal health. It is associated with a greater risk of cardiovascular disease, dementia, stroke, depression, anxiety, and premature death. . . . And the harmful consequences of a society that lacks social connection can be felt in our schools, workplaces, and civic organizations, where performance, productivity, and engagement are diminished."[10]

The local church has an incredible opportunity to address this epidemic because the impact of authentic community where people are able

---

7. Emma Goldberg, "Teens in Covid Isolation: 'I Felt like I Was Suffocating,'" *New York Times*, November 12, 2020, updated October 5, 2021, https://tinyurl.com/yt5m76bt.

8. Richard Weissbourd et al., "Loneliness in America: How the Pandemic Has Deepened an Epidemic of Loneliness and What We Can Do About It," Making Caring Common Project, Harvard Graduate School of Education, February, 2021, https://tinyurl.com/yjum6u9s.

9. See "Our Epidemic of Loneliness and Isolation," U.S. Surgeon General's Advisory on the Healing Effects of Social Connection and Community, 2023, https://tinyurl.com/46j626r3.

10. "Our Epidemic of Loneliness and Isolation," 4.

to find safety, belonging, and connection is immense not only for spiritual or religious practice but for the physical and psychological health of individuals and societies. Human beings are communal creatures, learning and becoming selves in and through the connections of family, neighborhood, and associations. Community is an essential component of the common good and human flourishing, and the church—called to community as the body of Christ—has a responsibility to attend to those practices that build healthy communities for the sake of the world.

Rather than relegating young adults to administrative work, or overlooking them entirely, the church ought to recognize the wisdom, experience, and insight young Christians today have in engaging this secular age. We do not need to tear down the churches and institutions that were built to address the issues of a different social moment, but we do need innovation and creativity to address the problems that plague our society today. This has long been the legacy of the church.

CHURCH AS A COMMUNITY JOINED TOGETHER AND MARKED BY THE CENTRALITY OF JESUS CHRIST

There are countless communities that exist in any given place. The first that might come to mind are those shaped by ethnicity, culture, religion, politics, or sports. You may also think of geography: neighborhoods, cities, towns, and villages. But there are even more shared communities within these larger categories: book groups, civic committees, offices, sports leagues, coffee shops, gyms, and libraries are all communities too. In the past several decades, dedicated online communities have served similar purposes, whether it be a Facebook group, Discord chat, Twitter (X) hashtag, or Reddit forum.

With all these communities available to us, Christians must be able to name what makes their tradition distinct. Indeed, young people are asking what the church might possess that no other community does. Christian leaders must have an answer to the question of why young people should choose to invest their time in a Christian community rather than the hundred other communities vying for their attention.

We unequivocally believe that the Christian church has compelling and meaningful answers to these challenging questions. As a community decisively marked by the centrality of the Scriptures and the person of Jesus Christ, the power of the Holy Spirit is present particularly as we gather every Sunday to hear God's word, confess our sins, and draw near to the Lord's Table to participate in the body and blood of Christ that has made possible our redemption. As a community, these liturgies unite us in a common life that cannot be mass-produced or flippantly replicated.

This is because the formative power of Christian community is found in our encounter with Jesus Christ—in worship and in the bodies and lives of our neighbor. As Paul writes in Ephesians, through this encounter with Christ, "You are citizens with the saints and also members of the household of God. . . . In him the whole structure is joined together and grows into a holy temple in the Lord" (2:19, 21). In this way, the local church functions as a context wherein Christ acts upon the individual and the assembly, forming them into the embodied presence of Christ for the world. A community that centers Christ is in fact called to decenter itself turning toward our neighbor to embody the love of Christ.[11]

Drawing from God's presence and work among Israel in the Hebrew Bible, Christ forms the church in and through the small simple practices of daily life together, a pattern emphasized in the Gospels and throughout the New Testament letters.[12] Community life for the disciples during Jesus's earthly ministry included radical practices of table fellowship, hospitality, prayer, and storytelling.[13] The miracle stories largely happen within the context of a community's regular life and practice. Christ's presence transforms a small meal into an abundant feast that feeds thousands.[14] The Scriptures transform simple stories about farming and labor into liberating parables illustrating God's grace and justice.[15] The formation of Christian community—which welcomed even those on the fur-

---

11. Chapter 7, "Liberating the Sanctuary," expands on the idea of a decentered church.
12. We often call this "liturgy"—the work of the people. See Matthew Kaemingk and Cory B. Willson, *Work and Worship: Reconnecting Our Labor and Liturgy* (Baker Academic, 2020).
13. For examples of this, see Matt. 6:5–21; 13; 14:13–21; Mark 4:1–34; 14:12–25; Luke 10:38–42; 14:7–14; 19:1–10; 22:1–33; 24:13–35; John 2:1–12; 6:1–15; 13:1–20; 21:1–14.
14. See Matt. 14:13–21; Mark 6:30–44; and Luke 9:10–17.
15. See Kaemingk and Willson, *Work and Worship*.

thest margins—was so radical that it rose to the level of criminal offense in the eyes of the dominant culture.

The New Testament witness, including the Pauline Epistles' emphasis on navigating interpersonal conflict, leadership, food and fellowship, and generosity, reveals that the gospel is a community-shaping—and a *world*-shaping—reality. It is a freedom we are invited to participate in together for the sake of each community member and the world.[16] The formation Christ provides takes place in and through the small simple practices of social connection and mutuality, including the very messy and complicated challenges that emerge from community life.

Recognizing the centrality of the church, theologians throughout Christian history have sought to nourish, contextualize, equip, and guide believers through the complex realities of life. Nearly all of those great medieval mothers (Julian of Norwich, Teresa of Ávila, Hildegard of Bingen, Catherine of Siena) and church fathers (Augustine, Athanasius, Irenaeus, Cyprian) we read today were first and foremost pastors and leaders in the church writing to their congregations, guarding them against false teachings and malpractice. Even as the theological academy grew, many of the great theologians we know today were intimately concerned with the life and witness of the church.

Feminist theologian and eminent professor at Yale Divinity School Letty Russell echoes and expands the centrality of Jesus Christ in community practice in her examination of the church titled *Church in the Round: Feminist Interpretation of the Church*. "I describe the church as a community of Christ, bought with a price, where everyone is welcome. It is a *community of Christ* because Christ's presence, through the power of the Spirit, constitutes people as a community gathered in Christ's name. This community is *bought with a price* because the struggle of Jesus to overcome the structures of sin and death constitutes both the source of new life in the community and its own mandate to continue the same struggle for life on behalf of others."[17]

---

16. See Miroslav Volf and Matthew Croasmun, *For the Life of the World: Theology That Makes a Difference* (Baker Books, 2019).

17. Letty M. Russell, *Church in the Round: Feminist Interpretation of the Church* (Westminster John Knox, 1993), 14. Hereafter, page references from this work will be given in the text.

A Call for Communities Marked by Love and Belonging

Russell, like many young adults today, struggled to maintain her relationship with the church, where she encountered a sense of alienation and inhospitality. She imagined a feminist interpretation of the church that would "affirm the full humanity of *all* women and men" (11), rooted in the saving grace of God in Jesus and gathered around the welcome table. Her interpretation of Christian community as hospitality rejected shallow uniformity, cheap understandings of election, and the boundedness of community that often results in marginalization and oppression (173).

Russell's central metaphor for the church, the table, emphasizes the saving love of God in Christ as the invitation for "the rejected ones of society . . . to share the feast of God's new household" (25). This imagery challenges us to interpret Christian community as a practice of life together with Christ as the host, where the whole of our lives is transformed into a radical act of hospitality and fellowship. "The church finds its own identity as a sign of Christ's work in the bringing of God's household by being a community of faith and witness, a community of struggle for the poor and oppressed, and a community of hope in the fulfillment of God's New Creation" (136). This understanding of ecclesiological identity rooted in radical hospitality and solidarity with the poor and oppressed is also highlighted in the work of Howard Thurman, a Black preacher and activist in the United States. Like Russell, Thurman's ecclesiology was born out of the trials and suffering his community faced. In *Footprints of a Dream*, Thurman unequivocally rejects the segregated reality of the American church and, in return, articulates a vision of the church that welcomes all people across lines of difference.[18] It is the task of the Christian, he argues, to participate in "the movement of the Spirit of God in the hearts of men . . . [that] calls them to act against the spirit of their times or causes them to anticipate a spirit which is yet in the making."[19]

The Black theological tradition also holds a wealth of resources for us.[20] In his well-known book *Jesus and the Disinherited*, Thurman fur-

---

18. Howard Thurman, *Footprints of a Dream: The Story of the Church for the Fellowship of All Peoples* (Wipf & Stock, [1959] 2009).

19. Thurman, *Footprints of a Dream*, 7.

20. As an introduction to this tradition, we recommend the work of James H. Cone, Ida B. Wells, Fannie Lou Hamer, Martin Luther King Jr., Willie James Jennings, and Cornel West. For a historical and hermeneutical view of the tradition,

thers this task by writing to disenfranchised and disinherited communities about the flourishing found in the "religion of Jesus." Jesus, Thurman argues, offers marginalized communities a way to not only survive but live abundantly while their backs are "against the wall." In doing so, Thurman pushes against the segregationist spirit of his time by locating the embodied Jesus among the oppressed, not the powerful and elite. Jesus, Thurman believed, is found among the outcasts and the ones who are told they do not belong.[21]

TURNING TO TODAY

Although we have selected only a handful of biblical passages and modern Christian theologians who are influential in our conception of the church, the desire to be a part of Christian community exists across the generations, and for much of history the local church has provided opportunities for all ages to participate in this life together. However, the very human impulses for control, power, and homogeneity have also left many Jesus followers wondering if Christian community as they have encountered it has any interest or ability in making space for them. In the United States, this has been true for people of color and Indigenous Christians, the LGBTQIA2S+ communities, and, increasingly, young adults.

There are also doubts, born of experience, that the incarnate Christ is still understood as the center and animating force of Christian com-

---

see Lisa M. Bowens, *African American Readings of Paul: Reception, Resistance, and Transformation* (Eerdmans, 2020).

21. This theme is also present in many Latin@ theologies. While we do not have space to include them here, we recommend the work of Justo González, *Mañana: Christian Theology from a Hispanic Perspective* (Abingdon, 1990); Ada María Isasi-Díaz, *En la Lucha / In the Struggle: Elaborating a Mujerista Theology*, tenth anniversary ed. (Fortress, 2004); Fernando Segovia, *The Farewell of the Word: The Johannine Call to Abide* (Fortress, 1991); and Eric D. Barreto, *Exploring the Bible* (Fortress, 2016). See also the recent work of Asian American theologians like Soong-Chan Rah, *The Next Evangelicalism: Freeing the Church from Western Cultural Captivity* (InterVarsity Press, 2009); Daniel D. Lee, *Doing Asian American Theology: A Contextual Framework for Faith and Practice* (InterVarsity Press, 2022); Jonathan Tran, *Asian Americans and the Spirit of Racial Capitalism* (Oxford University Press, 2021); and Kwok Pui Lan, *Postcolonial Imagination and Feminist Theology* (Westminster John Knox, 2005).

munity. Christianity's reputation in the United States is largely based on what it opposes, on who it excludes, and on which political party can best leverage religious language for influence and power. Young adults see a church that looks less and less like Jesus, which is often perceived as inauthentic, judgmental, and ideological. This church deepens division and increases the loneliness and isolation that young adults face on a daily basis. And anxious reactions to a declining church have too often encouraged churches to focus more on programming and marketing their existing culture in their efforts to reach young adults, rather than on the essential building blocks of Christian community and discipleship that looks and acts like Jesus.

Churches interested in building authentic relationships with young adults ought to remember Dietrich Bonhoeffer's insight that "Christian community is not an ideal we have to realize, but rather a reality created by God in Christ in which we may participate."[22] It is not the church's task to develop or manufacture the ideal Christian community as a product that they distribute to young adults. Rather, it is the church's call to embrace the courageously curious posture of listening and awareness, and to make space at the table for the Christ present in their young adult neighbor, to join them at the various "tables" each chapter in this book has set. It is the church's call to practice discernment and to pay attention to where Christ is already at work, extending authentic welcome and resisting patterns of judgment, cultural hubris, and exclusion.

> Turn our worship into witness in the sacrament of life;
> send us forth to love and serve you, bringing peace where
>   there is strife.
> Give us, Christ, your great compassion to forgive as you
>   forgave;
> may we still behold your image in the world you died to save.[23]

---

22. Dietrich Bonhoeffer, *Life Together*, Dietrich Bonhoeffer Works, vol. 5, ed. Gerhard Ludwig Müller, Albrecht Schönherr, and Geffrey B. Kelly, trans. Daniel W. Bloesch (Fortress, 2005), 38.

23. Carl P. Daw Jr., "As We Gather at Your Table," in *Evangelical Lutheran Worship*, pew edition (Augsburg Fortress, 2006), no. 522.

WHAT DOES CHRISTIAN COMMUNITY LOOK LIKE?

What do young adults have to teach the church, and how might the church open itself to the renewing and transforming power of the Holy Spirit? We suggest an imagination of Christian community that is *incarnational, sacramental, contextual, and relational*, rooted in Christ and committed to the flourishing of the common good. This imagination has the power to transform local congregations and communities, and throughout history has proven to have the capacity to transform entire nations. The Peaceful Revolution, which brought an end to the repressive communist regime in East Germany, is a powerful example that helps us imagine the qualities of Christian community we desire.

Incarnational

The Peaceful Revolution was a largely youth-led and church-supported movement embodying the justice-making love of God. The prayer gatherings that formed the base of the movement were established to cast a vision for a new reality in East Germany and to practice the kind of community solidarity young adults had been demanding of the church throughout the 1970s and 1980s. Ultimately, they were advocating for a reunited Germany and for democracy.

In 1989, the movement building for decades spilled out onto the streets, toppling an oppressive government and casting an image of a church embodying the call of Christ to confront sin and death in the public square. Reflecting on the Peaceful Revolution, Dirk Lange, the assistant general secretary for ecumenical relations at the Lutheran World Federation, writes: "Finally, in summer and fall 1989, the prayers erupted into the streets, especially in Leipzig, in what came to be known as the *Montagsdemonstrationen*. . . . In summer 1989, there already were seven thousand people attending, then twenty thousand, then seventy thousand, then three hundred thousand, then over half a million people. Of course, these numbers are like the numbers in Acts—difficult to estimate—but there were many, many people. Obviously, the church could not contain the worshippers, and they poured out into the streets with their candles in hand."[24]

Christian community is an incarnational reality, acting as the very presence of Christ in the world. The incarnation remains a radical proposition; the God of creation takes on flesh in the person of Jesus Christ, enters into the human experience, and liberates the cosmos in his life, death, and resurrection. Christianity is a fundamentally embodied reality, and the life together for Christian community takes place in the dynamic exchange between bodies. In other words, as a worshiping community centered around the eternal and enfleshed person of Jesus Christ, we believe that our bodies matter decisively because they are a sacred gift from God and the vehicle of our gospel proclamation in the world. Again from Lange: "They were like a liturgical procession moving with solemnity, not toward some high altar, some mythical center of meaning, but moving sometimes with song, sometimes silently, always with determination into the world."[25]

Many dominant culture churches in the United States struggle to embrace, or even acknowledge, this incarnational principle in their practice of community life. Faith is understood as a psychological or emotional phenomenon, and, even more, the body is often seen as dangerous and sinful, or at least of secondary concern. This theological posture has been used to justify homophobia, misogyny, ableism, slavery, and an irresponsible quietism. If churches can distance themselves from the reality of God's presence in the body of the neighbor, and relegate God to the safety and inefficacy of a faraway heaven, then they will not be responsible for the concrete and material needs of their community.

Young adults have been on the front lines of an incarnational struggle in the church for years, and many churches and denominations are facing calls from their young people to recognize and affirm the diversity of bodies and embodied experience as sacred. This includes calls for racial and gender justice within church structures and systems, a longing

---

24. Dirk G. Lange, *Today Everything Is Different: An Adventure in Prayer and Action* (Fortress, 2021), 26–27.

25. Lange, *Everything Is Different*, 26–27.

for the church to act as the body of Christ in the streets and the public square, and a demand that Christ's invitation to new life and liberation be extended to all people regardless of race, class, gender, or sexual orientation. The chapters in this book have offered these kinds of invitations. As the medical and psychiatric worlds deepen their understanding of the mind-body connection, the language and practice of embodiment have been increasingly called for by young adults in their communities. Resmaa Menakem, a psychologist and embodied antiracism teacher, says, "Our bodies have a form of knowledge that is different from our cognitive brains. . . . The body is where we fear, hope, and react; where we constrict and release; and where we reflexively fight, flee, or freeze."[26] For Resmaa and other somatic teachers, the work of justice and equity, the work of community, is embodied.

Authentic communities that hold space for young adults must reassert their foundationally incarnational presence. Christ is not present as the psychology or the imagination of associated minds, but as the physical bodies of the assembled community, in worship, at the table, and in the public square. Young adults, who may be more comfortable and familiar with an embodied theology and ethic, can share this wisdom and experience as a part of the ongoing formation of authentic Christian community that takes bodies, place, and presence seriously.

Sacramental

Authentic Christian community is also sacramental. That is, our participation in the community of God mirrors the divine reality of God's incarnate and communal dwelling with us (John 1:14). To say that Christian community is a "sacramental" reality is to name the ongoing dialectic between the ordinary and theological: our ordinary communing as believers and the divine reality of our unity in Christ (John 17:21-23).[27] This is what a life marked by the sacramental looks like: finding spaces

---

26. Resmaa Menakem, *My Grandmother's Hands: Racialized Trauma and the Pathway to Mending Our Hearts and Bodies* (Central Recovery, 2017), 5.

27. Jonathan Tran, "Linguistic Theology: Completing Postliberalism's Linguistic Task," *Modern Theology* 33, no. 1 (January 2017).

A Call for Communities Marked by Love and Belonging

where the ordinary, mundane things of life are instilled with a greater sacred significance of liberation and love, which, in return, point us to divine realities that we are invited to participate in.[28]

Lange, reflecting again on the clandestine prayer groups that animated the Peaceful Revolution, writes:

> The vigil candle, then, not only represented the light of Christ shining in the darkness; it became a symbol for peace. . . . The small vigil candle became a sign for peaceful manifestation, peaceful resistance, for, as one pastor explained, when you set out in the chilly October evening with lighted candles to face the soldiers, you have no hands for weapons. One hand holds the candle and the other shields the flickering light from the autumn wind . . . it was this liturgical procession—a kairos moment or, as Luther would have called it, a gospel shower—that brought down an oppressive political, economic, and social system.[29]

The vigil candle was not simply a tool for providing light but a sacramental object giving language and imagination to the new world and the kind of Christian community that the young people in East Germany were calling for. The collective light of the half a million marchers illuminated the possibility for revolution and the presence of Christ in the midst of the struggle.

To imagine Christian community as a sacramental reality is also to live attuned to an earth that is filled with heaven.[30] As we envision what the future of the American church might be, a sacramental vision constructively aims to mirror the divine reality of God as we understand the world around us as sacred and worthy of our love and attention.[31]

For the Christian, the sacramental life is marked by the common participation in the sacraments among the people of God. This shared practice is our communion, our shared bond that reminds us of our unity

---

28. Amar D. Peterman, "Adoption Is Sacramental," *Sojourners*, May 11, 2023.
29. Lange, *Everything Is Different*, 27–28.
30. Aaron Damiani, *Earth Filled with Heaven: Finding Life in Liturgy, Sacraments, and Other Ancient Practices of the Church* (Moody Publishers, 2022).
31. Norman Wirzba, *This Sacred Life: Humanity's Place in a Wounded World* (Cambridge University Press, 2019).

in Christ as those who have died to ourselves, been raised in Christ's resurrection, and now are nourished spiritually by Christ's body and blood at the Lord's Table.[32]

Relational

The Peaceful Revolution in East Germany began as small collections of citizens and neighbors gathering for intentional time of prayer, lament, and check-ins about friends who had been arrested by the Stasi (the secret police). Over time, the relationships built at kitchen tables, in living rooms, and on the floors of church sanctuaries grew into a movement for transformation. When this network of relationships finally stepped beyond the walls of their churches and their homes, it had built enough justice-making social capital to topple the repressive government of the German Democratic Republic (GDR).[33] It was the connections and the relationships built amid these prayer meetings, grounded in the reality of Christ's presence in prayer and the word of God, that made the Peaceful Revolution possible.

The relationships and connections we form in our communities play a vital role in shaping how we engage with those around us. When the only meaningful relationships we hold are between those who look, think, act, and believe what we do, a fear of the "other" can quickly form. While this is as true for Christian community as it is for any other, years of insular, instrumentalized religion have atrophied many churches' ability to build authentic and mutual relationships outside of their existing ideological, doctrinal, and social networks. This means that when a young person or a neighbor walks into a church for the first time, they are often seen and treated as a category rather than as a unique and beloved human being. They become objects of the church's own survival anxiety.

Authentic Christian community sees young people not as a desperately needed demographic but as people called to follow Jesus in and through their own unique gifts and strengths. This is a relational com-

---

32. John Zizioulas, *Being as Communion* (St. Vladimir's Seminary Press, 1985).
33. Lange, *Everything Is Different*, 24.

munity that values curiosity, intimacy, and vulnerability, that is interested in the neighbor for the neighbor's sake and for the sake of Christ. This community understands that they will only go as far as their relationships allow them to.

In the book *Better Together*, Robert Putnam and Lewis Feldstein outline stories of communities with high levels of social capital, which "refers to social networks, norms of reciprocity, mutual assistance, and trustworthiness."[34] The stories they tell and the research they conduct show that social capital, the deep relatedness of people within a community, contributes to the overall health and well-being, not only of the immediate community members, but also of bystanders and neighbors. When young people call for the church to embrace social justice and the common good, they are not calling for programming and charity but for the church to build higher levels of accountable and justice-making social capital, in and through mutual and authentic relationships.

Confronting the epidemic of loneliness and isolation in America will require attention to authentic relationships and the practices that build social capital. The most powerful act a community can do is to foster a place and a network of deep belonging, where young adults know that they belong because of who they are, not because of what they can do for the church. People feel seen when they are known, when community members are curious about their lives and notice when they are gone. Isolation is confronted and overcome in networks of relationships where people can share and develop their gifts and strengths for the well-being of the whole, when they can contribute to something larger than themselves. This is Paul's vision of the body of Christ in 1 Corinthians, where each member of the body contributes to the whole and is supported through their relationship to the other members.

Contextual

While churches and faith communities across the world stood in solidarity with the prayer meetings and revolutionaries in the Peaceful Revolu-

---

34. Lewis Feldstein and Robert Putnam, *Better Together: Restoring the American Community* (Simon & Schuster, 2003), 2.

tion, it was essential that transformation emerged from the communities embedded in their particular context in East Germany. The citizens and neighbors who met to pray and build community knew that they bore responsibility for their own city and country, and it was their investment in the particularity of place that ensured that the movement achieved its vision for a free German nation.

Furthermore, the particularity of cities like Leipzig and Dresden, and the cultural exchange that happened within churches during the late 1980s, allowed for the movement and the community to be infused with their own unique qualities. One congregation in Leipzig opened its doors to local artists, musicians, and authors who had been censored by the state, providing a venue for important and particular cultural influence, especially from the society's margins, on the burgeoning movement.[35]

Christian formation always happens within the context of one's social location. Our beliefs, actions, habits, and conception of the world are all formed by the people, ideas, systems, patterns, and physical places we are located within. While the church serves as just one of many contexts in which this formation happens, it holds incredible potential to nurture and shape the lives of young people to constructively engage in the world around them. This begins by naming and recognizing the diversity of our experiences and locations as a gift from God.

The Scriptures are filled with stories of God's people drawing from their lived experience and the locations in which God had placed them to make sense of the world and their place within it. Paul does this writing as a Jewish convert and a Roman citizen, Jeremiah laments as an Israelite observing his community's destruction, King David writes psalms of joy during Israel's prosperity under his reign, and the gospel writers each draw from their view and experience of Christ's life to write an account bearing witness to what they've heard and seen. This means that local worshiping communities that are located across region, culture, language, experience, and ideology all can embrace their particular contexts as a gift from God and as a place where God is fully present.

However, under the premise of missionary action or becoming "one in Christ," dominant-culture Christians have historically equated appeals to

---

35. Lange, *Everything Is Different*, 26.

A Call for Communities Marked by Love and Belonging

unity with assimilation.[36] Rather than understanding the particular culture, language, norms, and expressions of worship as a majority culture as one expression out of many, these often majority-white churches fuse together their social imagination with a Christian one, deeming such to be the "normal" or "standard" Christian practice.[37] To assert that particularity matters, then, is to reject this project and instead view diversity and difference as a gift from God, not a hindrance to our unity.[38]

In total, *incarnation, sacrament, relationship, and context* collectively uplift the embodied, experiential life of the Christian. We see this in the ministry of Jesus and examples of Scriptures as both embrace place, time, and context as resources to see God at work in our world.[39] While God is certainly all of the "omni-"s we ascribe (omnipotent, omnipresent, etc.), God has also made Godself known to us through the concrete, incarnate person of Jesus, who was placed in a context to enact his earthly ministry. Jesus did not speak in abstract life lessons that could transcend time. He used the vernacular and context of his community to reveal a divine message through both word and deed.

We, too, must do the same as we negotiate how the spaces we are placed in form both us and young adults today. Are young people in our churches being challenged and equipped to engage in the reality (and, we must remember, *gift*) of difference and diversity in our world where different cultures, identities, beliefs, and values must find common good and a shared vision of flourishing? Or, are churches forming young people in a single vision of what Christian faith looks like where anything that diverges from this vision is seen as less faithful or even heretical?

---

36. Willie James Jennings, *The Christian Imagination: Theology and the Origins of Race* (Yale University Press, 2010).

37. For examples of this, see Andrew Whitehead, *American Idolatry: How Christian Nationalism Betrays the Gospel and Threatens the Church* (Brazos, 2023); Daniel G. Hummel, *The Rise and Fall of Dispensationalism: How the Evangelical Battle over the End Times Shaped a Nation* (Eerdmans, 2023).

38. Eric D. Barreto, "Negotiating Difference: Theology and Ethnicity in the Acts of the Apostles," in *Soundings in Cultural Criticism: Perspectives and Methods in Culture, Power, and Identity in the New Testament*, ed. Francisco Lozada Jr. and Greg Carey (Fortress, 2013).

39. James K. A. Smith, *How to Inhabit Time: Understanding the Past, Facing the Future, Living Faithfully Now* (Brazos, 2022).

FAITH FORMATION TOWARD A COMMON GOOD

We have intentionally focused on what faith is being formed *toward*. In offering a constructive vision of Christian community, we want to move from ideas and theory to action and impact. We believe that recognizing localized common goods is an indispensable part of this project.

While the "common good" is often framed as a universal discussion, we must first engage this concept on a local level. If we cannot agree on a common good for our family, our congregation, or our city, how will we ever find a truly *common* good for our entire nation? When we frame the common good as "what is good for the most number of people," we quickly find that any notion of the common good will favor the majority—Christians, white communities, traditional nuclear families, and the like—at the expense of minority communities.

To be sure, the task of defining a common good is too great for one chapter to accomplish, let alone one section of this present chapter. However, by emphasizing a local vision of shared goods, we believe that crucial to the task of achieving anything we may call "good" in our church communities requires us to be in conversation across lines of difference with young people leading the way. In what follows, we offer two examples of this.

Gather: A Young Adult Ministry in the Twin Cities

In 2018, three clergy leaders in my (Nick's) network launched Gather, a ministry with young adults in Minneapolis and St. Paul focused on building connections through the simple relational practices of community: table fellowship, worship, and convening. "We just thought that sometimes church is best when it's at its simplest," said Deacon Stephanie Anderson.[40]

The three clergy leaders who launched Gather each work closely with young adults in their context.[41] They each were aware of pockets of young

---

40. Deacon Stephanie Anderson, interview by Nicholas Tangen, Minneapolis, June 29, 2023. Subsequent Anderson quotations are from this interview.

41. The three founders of Gather are Deacon Stephanie at Augustana Lutheran

adults who had formative experiences of church as young people, but had languished in their connection to church since. Initially, the community gathered quarterly with a table set for contemplative worship and prayer, and a shared meal. However, because the response to this simple gathering was overwhelming, it soon became a monthly gathering.

Deacon Stephanie said there were a few qualities that Gather has embraced that seem to find meaning with the young adults who come together. First was a loud and clear welcome for LGBTQIA2S+ siblings. "I can't imagine the courage it takes for young adults who are marginalized in other parts of their life to show up, and to trust that you will find a place that is genuinely curious about you and affirming of you," she said. "I had some young adults tell me that they know they are loved in their congregation, but aren't sure if it's because of who they are, or in spite of who they are."

A second quality is the contemplative worship experience, which encourages playfulness and embodied practice. One memorable sermon included a body movement practice and slow breath work, with time to reflect on Scripture and to pray. "Contemplative practice feels ancient, and it kind of strips away what has felt like generations of manipulative spiritual practice," said Deacon Stephanie. "There is something about the earthy vibe that just feels like the realest expression of church."

This desire for realness, for authenticity, is the third quality that Stephanie said is core to Gather's mission. "The young adults who come to Gather don't show up to worship to feel happy, they are coming to feel something real. They are coming in search of something true, and we're trying to find out what that is together." Authenticity at Gather is a willingness to make space for young adults to bring their full person to the table. No one is asked to keep their identity, the full expression of their emotional lives, or their doubts at the door. The community builds trust by setting this table of radical welcome.

Church in St. Paul and Pastor Jen Nagel at University Lutheran Church of Hope, congregations closely connected to the University of Minnesota's Lutheran Campus Ministry (LCM), and Pastor Kate Rauer Welton, who serves as the LCM pastor.

Good Road Network: A Learning Laboratory for Young Adults

I (Amar) love the theological academy and the questions and conversations that it holds. I especially love the classroom because of the discussion and environment generated by peers pursuing understanding and wisdom. In my last semester of seminary education, the uneasy realization that I would no longer have immediate, daily access to the conversations that brought me great joy weighed heavily on my soul. In return, I decided to create this space myself. Gathering a few seminary friends together, we committed to meeting virtually once a month to continue asking good questions and encouraging one another as we moved across the world to the places God called us.

I quickly found that the vision of these gatherings resonated deeply across leaders in the church who craved a similar space for fellowship, conversation, and encouragement. Soon after, the Good Road Network (GRN) was officially formed in June 2022 as a learning laboratory of young Christian leaders who feel a call to build bridges, seek justice, make peace, and educate the church.

In the time since, the GRN has grown into a national network of young leaders who gather through various digital platforms to network, learn from world-renowned scholars, foster relationships, and leverage our collective knowledge to address the pressing issues in our communities. Beyond the growth and achievements made, what has made the GRN a meaningful place for young leaders is its reminder that they are not alone in their calling.

What makes opportunities like the Good Road Network and Gather appealing? It is recognizing and embracing the empowerment of young people and awareness of their formation. This is very similar to the strategy of many asset-based community organizers who value supporting and developing leaders, rather than spotlighting themselves. Like these organizers, it is the task of church leaders today to support, equip, and admonish young leaders to share their story and frame their unique gifts in a larger movement toward a common good. When we set the example of a table, rather than a main stage, we actively participate in forming young adults in love and belonging.

A Call for Communities Marked by Love and Belonging

> Gracious Spirit, help us summon other guests to share
>   that feast
> where triumphant Love will welcome those who had been last
>   and least.
> There no more will envy blind us nor will pride our
>   peace destroy,
> as we join with saints and angels to repeat the sounding joy.[42]

CREATING COMMUNITIES MARKED BY LOVE AND BELONGING

Christian community that makes space for young adults will be grounded in an encounter with Jesus Christ and marked by love and belonging. Young adults are seeking a community that is authentic and honest, embodied and relational, contextual and particular. They are in search of a community that takes Jesus seriously and practices the kind of radical welcome that Christ models and calls the church to practice.

To participate in this kind of community, the church must begin by listening. "The first service one owes to others in the community involves listening to them. Just as our love for God begins with listening to God's Word, the beginning of love for other Christians is learning to listen to them."[43] Rather than marketing programs that attend to the needs we assume young adults have, or demanding assimilation into an existing culture and practice, we can begin by setting a welcome table and getting curious about our neighbor. We can listen for where Jesus is at work in the lives of young adults, and where we are called to celebrate, adapt, and accompany their own sense of vocation.

Authentic relationships cannot be artificially manufactured. They take time, devotion, and a commitment to knowing another person fully. If we desire to see the fruit of such connection, Christian communities must nurture the seedbed of community for deep and mutual relationships to form. Americans across generations are stretched thin and overwhelmed. We live within a culture that measures value

---

42. Daw, "As We Gather at Your Table."
43. Bonhoeffer, *Life Together*, 98.

by productivity. But Christian community can act as a balm from that pressure, and create the space for deep connection, belonging, and solidarity. When Christian community embraces a practice of listening and relationality, they will discover that young adults bring unique and powerful gifts to contribute to the well-being of the whole. This asset-based approach ensures that young adults are not seen as categories, as needs, or as objects of church survival.

Within this community, the church must also embrace the call to share power and to build up the leadership of young adults. Young people in our churches want to lead, teach, and organize but are often passed over for leadership roles or asked to lead in roles that were not created with their gifts, strengths, and experiences in mind. If the church has faith enough to trust that Christ is at work in the unique lives of young adults and the communities they belong to, then they must be willing to support their leadership, especially when it challenges existing culture and norms.

Christians are called to community and formed in and through Christ being present in the faces and the bodies of community members. In a world awash with an epidemic of loneliness and isolation, and a culture that asks young adults to go it alone, this call to a shared life together with Christ at the center represents a radical alternative. And when we remember that this community is not ours to create in our own image, but that of Christ, who invites us to participate, we can free ourselves from the hypervigilance that comes with the church's oft-rumored death. Instead, we can embrace the gifts and strengths that have undergirded communities for centuries, learn from young adults and adapt to the unique and particular invitation in this moment, and live together as Christian communities for the sake of the world.

10

BEYOND THE WALLS

The Church's Call to Be in the World

Kayla Zopfi
Dr. Jeremy Paul Myers

OUR INVITATION

We begin with a hypothetical story of a congregation that could very easily be your congregation. The First Church of the Neighborhood was preparing to celebrate their 100th anniversary in one year. Over the last thirty years they had seen their worship attendance and church membership steadily decline. They wanted their anniversary to be a moment to celebrate the past but also a springboard into the future. Because of this, the congregation committed to becoming more engaged with both young adults and their surrounding neighborhood. They launched what they called a "100 Conversations" campaign to engage their immediate neighbors and young adults in the larger community in 100 conversations over the following year, with the sole purpose of hearing the life stories, hopes, dreams, and concerns of their neighbors. They knew it would be a big challenge, but they also knew they needed—and wanted—to do something radically different. They dove in.

They started by meeting with and learning from a variety of young adults living in their community. Of the few young adults already active in the congregation, one worked at a local cybersecurity firm that had committed to hiring a young workforce. She began hosting dinners where members of the congregation could meet her coworkers. Other members had connections with young adults involved with the Jesuit Volunteer Corps, Teach for America, and AmeriCorps. These young adults were active in community organizing, helping run a community garden program, and another program registering neighbors to vote. The congregation realized that these young adults had some expertise the congregation was lacking—the ability to organize and train people to listen to the neighborhood. So, the congregation paid them stipends to help lead the work of engaging the neighborhood. The town was also home to a community college. A few members got permission to serve free coffee and cinnamon rolls on campus every Wednesday morning. Each week they asked the students a thought-provoking question as they handed them coffee and treats. It was slow at first, without much interaction. Slowly some students became regulars, good conversations started to happen, and real relationships were formed.

When the 100th anniversary rolled around, the congregation had completed its 100 conversations. In fact, they far surpassed that goal and lost count. The dinners with the young adults from the cybersecurity firm had expanded to include young professionals who were new to the area, and the dinners were held at a different person's home each month. Older members of the congregation were always guests at these dinners. The young adults who were paid to help lead the work devised a plan that resulted in at least three people from the congregation meeting every single person who lived within a three-block radius of the church, including one apartment building. They also helped the congregation become active tutors at the local elementary school, volunteers in registering voters, and key sponsors of the community garden, where they continued to meet their neighbors. A team of students from the community college took over the coffee-and-cinnamon-rolls project. It became known around campus as Wednesday Wonderings. You could always count on fresh cinnamon rolls, good coffee, and meaningful conversations. The congregation continued to show up and participate as well. The dean of students hired the Wednesday Wonderings organizers to be Peer Listeners, who helped keep her informed about the well-being of the student body. The dean contracted with the congregation to train these Peer Listeners and host a Peer Listening retreat each semester.

Their conversations resulted in a few new visitors to church from time to time, but there was no noticeable increase in worship attendance. However, the church felt as though they were finally living into their mission. They had become known around town as a valuable partner and community of people who really got things done. The relationships they had developed felt mutual and trustworthy. The young adults they had connected with had helped them lay a foundation of presence that would allow them to continue to evolve into bearers of the good news no matter what their neighbors might face. Their neighbors saw the congregation as a source of hope and goodness in the neighborhood. At 100 years old, they felt like they were just beginning.

OUR CALL BEYOND THE WALLS

Whenever we find ourselves at a crossroads like First Church of the Neighborhood, we get to choose how we respond to the challenge. We can react out of fear and anxiety, or we can respond from a place of hope and curiosity.[1] Every organization faces this choice when struggling to stay relevantly engaged with their constituents. Local congregations are not immune to this reality. Church membership and attendance have been declining for years, and the pandemic has only accelerated the decline in most congregations. In this chapter we will not be addressing this rapid decline—we all know those statistics. Nor is this a naïve attempt to ignore what is painful. Rather, this chapter explores an intentional choice to respond out of hope and compassion to our times. The current challenges congregations face are an opportunity to become what the church was always meant to be, public. This call to become a public church that exists beyond its walls is not the latest trend in innovation nor is it a last-ditch effort to save the church; it is, rather, a reminder to become what it has always been. As authors, we bring our own varied life and church experiences to a shared passion for seeing the church follow God's call into our neighborhoods. I (Kayla) am passionate about storytelling and equipping and empowering people to use their voices, especially in faith-based advocacy spaces. I am currently a Word and Service candidate through the Minneapolis Area Synod at Wartburg Theological Seminary. I (Jeremy) grew up the son of a Lutheran pastor who lived his theology in the public

---

1. You can read more about the impacts of anxiety in our church bodies in chapter 5 of this volume, "Health and Wholeness," and about the need for postures of curiosity in chapter 1, "What Else Could It Be? Courageous Curiosity and the Postures That Get Us There."

square. Standing on his shoulders, I have committed my life's work to articulating a vocational understanding of the human being and a public understanding of the church that keeps the neighbor as the location of God's revelation in our lives.

What Is a Public Church?

The phrase "public church" can mean many things to different people. The phrase is commonly used to express how denominations represent their worldview within the larger public dialogue about common life together. This often takes shape as a particular office within a denomination, and is primarily thought of as communications work. Some Christian denominations release social statements on current social issues such as climate change, the death penalty, human sexuality, etc. These statements present a theological framework that can be used to ground their constituents in public dialogue regarding these various issues. The work of being a public church is also often seen in denominationally-specific social service agencies who employ staff to provide direct service related to the organization's mission (care for creation, affordable housing, food insecurity, immigration, etc.). These agencies also often employ staff dedicated to lobbying or advocacy work around the issues related to their organization.

These expressions of the church are necessary and fruitful and do represent the public work of the church. Yet, another expression of public church that is less commonly practiced involves the slow, hard work of investing time and energy in building relationships. In this expression a local congregation or faith community becomes deeply connected and committed to its neighborhood and its neighbors, similar to what we saw with First Congregation of the Neighborhood. Their work begins by building relationships with their immediate neighbors, seeking to understand their lived realities and how the church might become good news to them or get involved in the good news already at work in the place where they are rooted. This approach offers public church as a model that prioritizes accompaniment over colonization. Community organizing, advocacy, lobbying, and service all have their place and purpose, but congregations should allow these practices to grow from the relationships they have with their neighbors—organizing, lobbying, and serving arm-in-arm in mutuality as neighbors.[2]

Why Must the Church Become Public?

It is vital that local congregations follow in First Church of the Neighborhood's footsteps and find contextually-specific ways to move beyond their walls for a few reasons. The first reason is straightforward and simple. People simply are not going to church at the same rate they had in the past. Many congregations struggle to offer services and keep staff employed as financial support has decreased. If a local congregation wants to share good news with their neighbors, they will need to go to their neighbors rather than waiting for their neighbors to attend church.

The second is related to how people learn and are formed in faith. We mistakenly assume participation in a faith leads to living one's faith in practical ways. This is not the case. There is significant agreement in the literature on effective education with all ages that highlights the importance of hands-on experiential methods for high-impact learning and transformation. So, if we want members of our congregations to move through their daily lives in ways that are informed by their faith and hope in God's promises, then we need to practice doing this together. A public church practices public relationships, public theological reflection, public discernment, and public proclamation together. By practicing this in a community, we learn how to do it as individuals in our daily lives.

A third reason for becoming a public church is to develop tangible ways to escape the "freeze mode" many of us encounter when worrying about the well-being of our communities and world. Freeze mode is one of four natural responses to stress and anxiety.[3] We freeze when we are not sure what our next action or response should be. It is a result of feel-

---

[2]. You can read more about this argument in Jeremy Myers, "The Vocation of the Local Congregation as Public Companion," in *Forming Leaders for the Public Church: Vocation in Twenty-First Century Societies*, ed. Samuel Yonas Deressa and Mary Sue Dreier (Lexington Books; Fortress Academic, 2023).

[3]. Read more about this in chapter 5, "Health and Wholeness."

ing threatened, or embarrassed, or worried about doing the wrong thing. The tangible work of getting to know our neighbors and working toward the common good with them not only helps us learn to live out our faith in daily life but also gives us practical hope.

A fourth, and significant, reason why congregations need to become public is to validate the ways young adults express their faith and values in the public square. You will not be hard-pressed to find examples of young adults leading the church beyond its walls. Many young adults affirm a sense of obligation to be ambassadors of social ministries for the church. Unfortunately, their approach—through organizing, advocacy, and policy change—often gets labeled as partisan or political and then dismissed by the congregation. Young adults are modeling that our health, happiness, and well-being are bound to each other's health, happiness, and well-being. We hope this chapter serves as an expression of gratitude to the young adults who are paving this path to the public square. Thank you for your patience and persistence, and for modeling the lessons and ethics you are learning as you go. It is becoming clear that this is where the church must head—whether we as individuals show up for it or not.

There are several reasons why young adults long to see the church become public. First, because *God is a public God*. The creative God of the universe is one who creates from within, and for the sake of, relationships. This is not a private God. Second, many *young adults live public lives* because of deeply held commitments to civic and social engagement. Lastly, this relational, public *God calls the local congregation to be a public church*. Faith in God is not an excuse to ignore the realities of this world in favor of the assumption that heaven is all that matters. Instead, it is our hope in God that frees us to live fully as public human beings with public lives in public communities.

GOD IS A PUBLIC GOD

This call to the church to become public is not a noisy gong or clanging cymbal. This is not the latest fad, nor is it a way to rebuild the church or increase attendance. Rather, it is simply true to who God is and how God has made us. This call to become a public church is rooted in four key theological claims about who God is and how God works in the world.

Relational God

The first claim is that the triune God of Christianity is a *relational God*. There is a breadth of biblical and theological scholarship from across the spectrum of languages and cultures that paints a picture of the triune God of Christianity as a relationship. Many have built upon this foundation of a relational God and laid out its implications for human life, ethics, and congregations. Identifying God as a relationship means God is dynamic rather than static, prefers dialogue rather than monologue, is open rather than closed, is engaged rather than passive, and is public rather than private. A relationship can no longer exist if one disengages and moves fully toward isolation. If God is essentially a relationship, then God must be an outwardly moving, engaging, dynamic, public God.

Relational Cosmos

A second claim fueling the call to become public is that this relational God has called into creation a *relational cosmos*. Creation is made in the image of this dynamic, engaging, public, relational God. Therefore, the entirety of the cosmos is also relational or interdependent. There is new research demonstrating proof of gravitational waves (NANOGrav) that have been present from the birth of the universe. The waves are generated from the interdependent reality of planets and black holes. Researchers are finding these waves in "every proton and neutron in every atom from the tip of your shoes to the top of your head . . . shifting, shuttling, and vibrating in a collective purr within which the entire history of the universe is implicated."[4] So, the relational and interdependent nature of our reality is not simply a feel-good story about caring for the

---

4. Adam Frank, "Scientists Found Ripples in Space and Time. And You Have to Buy Groceries," *Atlantic*, June 29, 2023, https://tinyurl.com/yemjkftz.

neighbor. We are actually caught up in an interdependent vibration with every other thing in our cosmos. Therefore, it would only make sense that we, as creatures vibrating with everything else in the universe, find ways to move into more intentional relationships, interdependence, and vibration with all of life in the public square. "Go outside, if you can, and watch the wind blow through the trees. . . . The endless comings and goings of galaxies, stars, and planets create a melding of songs that you are part of too."[5]

Incarnation

The third claim is that this relational creating God has chosen to enter into this creation. This is the *incarnation*. Not only does Christianity claim the creating God is a relationship who creates a relational cosmos, Christianity also claims that this God physically enters into this relational creation. Eugene Peterson, paraphrasing John 1:14 in *The Message*, writes, "The Word became flesh and blood, and moved into the neighborhood." The phrase "dwelt among us," which usually appears in translations of John 1:14, comes from the Greek word *eskenosen*, meaning literally "to pitch one's tent." So this relational, dynamic, creative force of the universe chooses to become public, to move into our neighborhood, and to camp with us.[6]

Vocation

Lastly, this relational, creative, incarnate God has now set us free to live our relational *vocations*. In the sixteenth century, Martin Luther used the word "vocation" to talk about how Christ calls us and frees us to live our lives for the sake of our neighbors in all the various roles we fill. Organized religion often has the opposite effect. It causes many to live their

---

5. Frank, "Scientists Found Ripples in Space and Time."
6. Chapter 2 in this volume, "Tokenism of Young Adults: Moving from Anxious Relationships Toward Cocreating Communities," ends with an invitation for elders to "make camp together" alongside young adults, cocreating the kinds of communities and places God desires for us.

lives in fear of judgment, either from God or from society. There can be a spiritual "keeping up with the Joneses" (or the Kardashians) that drives us to believe this life is either a test to prove to God that we are worthy of heaven, or a mad dash to accumulate enough physical possessions to prove to ourselves that God loves us. But the opposite is true. God's grace, freely shared with us through Christ, frees us *from* this religious rat race and frees us *for* our neighbors. We are free to serve our world for the world's sake, not for God's sake. God doesn't need our good works in heaven, but our neighbors need them here on earth.[7]

Many are longing for local congregations to move beyond their walls and become public churches—and our young adults are calling us to do this work. Being a public church is aligned with who God is and who God is inviting us to be. When a congregation sits back and assumes it is immune to the world's challenges, or not responsible for them, or powerless to change them, it sends a message that either the world outside the church does not matter or the church should not have anything to do with it. Young adults are not settling for either of these two perspectives. They want the church to live into the image of a relational God who is present with and for a relational cosmos that has been freed by the love of Christ for interdependence.

YOUNG ADULTS LIVE PUBLIC LIVES

Young adults believe in a public God, and they are not willing to wait for the church to become public. They are choosing to become deeply engaged in working for the common good in a variety of ways. Kristina Frugé, director of Congregational and Community Initiatives at Augsburg University and editor of this volume, has said (and I'm paraphrasing), "The church thinks young adults have left the church. But really, what has happened is the church has left the public spaces where young adults are choosing to live their faith on a daily basis. If the church were to reengage these public spaces, they would find themselves in relationship with young adults once again." The local congregation can learn much about public life through young adults.

7. Gustaf Wingren, *Luther on Vocation* (Wipf & Stock, 2004), 10.

As we saw in the story of First Church of the Neighborhood, young adults are leading experts on becoming civically engaged, or public. There is consensus within the research that young adults value civic engagement, and, as we have seen earlier, there is a precedent for Christian communities to become more publicly engaged together. We must understand the various roles young adults are playing in civic engagement in order to appreciate and learn alongside them. A 2020 study shows 61.2 percent of young adults (ages sixteen to twenty-nine) participated in discussing political, societal, or local issues with family or friends, 22.1 percent discussed the same with their neighbors, and 14.6 percent did so via social media. The study indicates that 30.3 percent of young adults had spent time volunteering, and 20.6 percent self-reported having done "something positive for their neighborhood or community."[8] Young adults are civically and politically literate and expect their church to be so as well.

Research also suggests young adults are far more civically engaged than older generations with issues like climate change and racism.[9] And the emergence of digital civic engagement will only increase their involvement by providing "a low-barrier-to-entry canvas for young people to create content that is potentially vastly scalable."[10] It is easy to see how young adults will continue to become more and more involved in civic engagement as more opportunities to do so present themselves and as the challenging realities facing our communities continue to cause damage.

It is clear that public civic engagement is growing in importance for young adults. They long to see a world that is more just and sustainable, and they want to be involved in making that world a reality. However, not all young adults have the same goals in mind. Every generation is differentiated and not a monoculture. In 2018 the Center for Information and Research on Civic Learning and Engagement gave us a snapshot of

---

8. Elan C. Hope, "Rethinking Civic Engagement: How Young Adults Participate in Politics and the Community," Brennan Center for Justice at New York University School of Law, February 16, 2022, https://tinyurl.com/5x75bejd.

9. Alec Tyson, Brian Kennedy, and Cary Funk, "Gen Z, Millennials Stand Out for Climate Change Activism, Social Media Engagement with Issue," Pew Research Center, May 26, 2021, https://tinyurl.com/34vnm75b.

10. Alexander Cho, Jasmina Byrne, and Zoë Pelter, "Digital Civic Engagement by Young People," UNICEF, February 2020, https://tinyurl.com/yc7sm5vj.

civic engagement among millennials in the following typology.[11] The left column names the different groups millennials might identify with in relation to civic engagement. The center column gives some descriptors of that group. The right column lists the percentage of millennials from this study who identify with that particular group.

Group	Description	% of millennials
Activist Egalitarians	Believe systematic inequalities affect society Value collective impact of civic participation Actively engage in conversations	39%
Disempowered Egalitarians	Believe equality will improve society Often feel underqualified to participate in civic life	8%
Participatory Libertarians	Believe society is fair and hard work brings success Value institutions and citizen participation	29%
Alienated Libertarians	Believe civic engagement and institutions add little value Support economic prosperity	5%
The Lost and Disengaged	Unsure about most political issues Little exposure to civic learning opportunities	18%

This typology does not include Gen Z. It was also completed prior to the pandemic and racial uprising of 2020. Both of these monumental events have certainly caused things to shift further. However, this ty-

11. "Millennials' Diverse Political Views: A Typology of the Rising Generation," Center for Information & Research on Civic Learning & Engagement, March 2018, https://tinyurl.com/vm7sr6p2.

pology is still a helpful tool for understanding how young adults might understand where they fit in the matrix of public civic engagement.

According to this data, approximately 68 percent of millennials value civic engagement (as Activist Egalitarians or Participatory Libertarians), while only 5 percent (Alienated Libertarians) do not value civic engagement. Close to 26 percent (Disempowered Egalitarians and the Lost and Disengaged) feel uncertain about how to engage civically. Regardless of where young adults fall on the political spectrum, the majority want to be engaged in a public civic life. If we believe faith can and should play a role in public life, then it is imperative that congregations find ways to walk into the public square as we all find ways to put our faith into action for the sake of the common good. It is neither uniform nor tidy, but it is necessary.

THE CHURCH IS CALLED TO BE PUBLIC

The local congregation is intended to be engaged in the daily public lives—the struggles, the celebrations, the monotony—of the community in which it is located. *Ecclesia* is a Greek word used to refer to the church in the New Testament. It was originally used to identify the assembly of those who were *called out* from among their peers to serve together politically in an advisory body similar to a city council. So, the *ecclesia* is an assembly of those who have been called out from among the larger community on its behalf. Members were called out not because they were special, or ordained, or blessed, or chosen by God. They were called out to represent the needs, concerns, and desires of their neighbors. Over time, the local congregation became those who were called out from their public lives to enact religious rituals behind closed doors that most of their neighbors would not recognize nor find useful or meaningful.

Kayla introduced me (Jeremy) to the term "Uno reverse." Of course I am familiar with the game Uno and its dreaded reverse card, but I am not hip enough to know it had become common parlance as a way of reflecting someone's insult back upon them. It is similar to "I'm rubber, you're glue. Whatever you say bounces off me and sticks back to you." So, we now jokingly use the term *"Ecclesia* Uno Reverse" to call local congregations out of their doors and back into their neighborhoods. After all, how can we be called on behalf of our neighbors when we don't even know our neighbors? When many congregations are not even demographically representative of their neighborhoods?

Many young adults put their hope in a God who shows up in ways that feel new and radical to many contemporary congregations. Their broadening understanding of God invites us all to interrogate what many of us have always thought about God and God's work in our world. This relational and public God creates a relational world, chooses to become public, enters into that space, and frees us to do the same. The grace and mercy of Jesus sets us free from the fear, anxiety, judgment, pride, privilege, self-righteousness, prejudice, and hatred that have held us in bondage for so long. This same creative, life-giving, liberating spirit is now manifest in each one of us. We are now free to work together in community with our neighbors on creating a more just and sustainable world for all.

When the church is reminded of the variety of the Spirit's gifts, we are told, "Each is given the manifestation of the Spirit for the common good" (1 Cor. 12:7). We are gathered by a relational God and freed by this relational God to use the variety of our gifts for the common good. This happens in the public square in relationships with our neighbors. The local congregation is not called *out from the neighborhood* to be an entity in and of itself. We are called *into the neighborhood* to be a public church, collaborating around our diverse gifts with our neighbors for the sake of the common good, to become good news with and for each other.

HOLY TRINITY AND EXODUS LENDING

First Church of the Neighborhood's story is aspirational. It provides us with a vision for what could actually be. If you reread it, you will find examples throughout of how God shows up as a public God, how young adults are living public lives, and how the local congregation realizes its call into the public square. Although it is hypothetical, it is inspired by examples of real congregations moving beyond their walls in their local contexts—encountering a public God, living public lives with young adults, and discovering their call to be public. Holy Trinity Lutheran Church in the Longfellow neighborhood of South Minneapolis is one of these examples.

Holy Trinity is rooted in three expressions: traditional worship, contemporary messages, and a call to social justice.[12] In the early 2010s, Holy Trinity wondered if they were fully utilizing the gifts of their members to serve their neighborhood. The congregation empowered a committee to reengage with Holy Trinity's immediate neighborhood.

Committee members eagerly approached this charge, anticipating to hear a certain set of issues arise from their conversations with local businesses and families. Holy Trinity is home to many community organizers with lifelong passions for justice and equity. So "picking" an issue would be no small task. They analyzed their staff capacity, the expertise of those in their congregation, the work already being done in their neighborhood, and new opportunities in order to determine where they could have the biggest impact. While in the throes of this process, they learned that another payday lender had opened a shop in their neighborhood. There were already a few such businesses in operation in the area, giving short-term, high-interest loans that often left users trapped in a debt cycle for months. These predatory practices rely on vulnerable communities who are facing financial hardship. These businesses simply exacerbate existing economic inequalities. The issue had found them.

Holy Trinity's unwavering commitment to their neighborhood led them to take on the payday lenders. They identified three potential routes to move forward: they could offer direct relief to those neighbors indebted to the payday lenders, they could engage local government to hold payday lenders accountable for their usurious conduct, or they could pioneer a code-of-conduct campaign to call their neighborhood businesses to commit to certain ethical and moral conduct. Holy Trinity identified the first two options as having the most potential impact based on their capacity and resources.

---

12. You can learn more at Holy Trinity Lutheran Church, https://tinyurl.com/3kwn83ce.

Holy Trinity felt God calling them to both serve neighbors *right now* by helping to alleviate their present suffering and work *toward the future* by uprooting the issue from its source so it would not continue to fester into the future. The clarity of this call led to two separate strategies: (1) direct relief through buying out their neighbors' payday loan debts and offering 0 percent APR (annual percentage rate) repayment, and (2) establishing a statewide coalition advocating for legislative reform against predatory lending practices called Minnesotans for Fair Lending (MFL). These two strategies became the foundation of Holy Trinity's new endeavor called Exodus Lending.[13]

The work was primarily stewarded by the congregation initially. After a handful of years of success, Exodus Lending grew to be self-sustaining. Holy Trinity and Exodus Lending were intentional about maintaining a partnership rooted in their shared mission. Exodus Lending, started by a local congregation to serve their specific neighborhood, has grown into a self-sustaining entity situated to serve more than just one neighborhood and has become a model for other communities across the country.

Holy Trinity felt compelled by their belief in God's vision for the world. They were eager to enact that vision in their immediate neighborhood, and, because they did not need permission from their municipality to proceed, they became public and did the work that was needed. The congregation felt and saw their neighbors' pain. They knew they had a responsibility and an opportunity to assess the capacities and gifts in their congregation in order to become God's good news with and for their neighbors.

WHERE DO WE GO FROM HERE?

Guilt and feelings of inadequacy for not doing enough can quickly cause us to freeze and keep us from trying new things. We hear stories like Holy Trinity's, and we struggle to imagine our congregations being able to pull off the same thing. It is difficult to take the first necessary step when trying to lean into change. But leaning into change is not about

---

13. You can learn more at Exodus Lending, https://tinyurl.com/33dphzje.

doing more or being perfect. It is about going slow and building relationships. We can all do that. We get to choose whether we react out of fear or curiosity. The principles of emergent strategy from adrienne maree brown might offer some consolation and encouragement as you begin this work. brown sees these as habits, patterns, and practices we must embrace to create a new way of living together.

1. Small is good, small is all. (The large is a reflection of the small.)
2. Change is constant. (Be like water.)
3. There is always enough time for the right work.
4. There is a conversation in the room that only these people at this moment can have. Find it.
5. Never a failure, always a lesson.
6. Trust the People. (If you trust the people, they become trustworthy.)
7. Move at the speed of trust. Focus on critical connections more than critical mass—build the resilience by building the relationships.
8. Less prep, more presence.
9. What you pay attention to grows.[14]

It is important to go about this work of becoming public with a sense of trust and patience and a commitment to relationships and listening. What follow are advice from some wise young adults currently doing this work and another story of a congregation who humbly stepped beyond their walls to begin meeting their neighbors.

Start Local, Find What Is Already Happening, Invite Others

The best way to start something new is to begin with what's directly in front of you. Aiden (he/him) is a twenty-eight-year-old hospice chaplain and writer with a religious studies BA and an MA from Princeton Theological Seminary. He is deeply committed to helping people understand their local communities, particularly their community's food source. "The biggest thing that a lot of people should begin with is getting to

---

14. adrienne maree brown, *Emergent Strategy: Shaping Change, Changing Worlds* (AK Press, 2017).

know the place that they live." The story of a place is the story of how we belong to our communities, to the network of relationships that makes our piece of society. Learn how your honeycrisp apples get to your grocery store every fall and whose hands picked them. Learn how water gets from the ground into your pipes. Learn about the architectural style your city or town hall building was built in. "It is theological information, it is knowledge of theological concern," he says. If we want to begin to understand how God is showing up in our location, then we first have to really know our location.

Sophia (she/they) is a twenty-five-year-old community organizer from the Midwest. She navigates economic justice issues with a background in political science and a global upbringing in Poland, Peru, and Qatar. She also advises a similar strategy of starting where you are at. "Follow the leaders." Support, uplift, fund, and join work that is already happening in your community. This is a manageable entry point for everyone, but especially for people who don't know where to begin. If the work you choose to do is informed by the hopes and dreams of your neighbors, then you will not be starting from scratch. There will already be others in your community doing that work. "Find a resource that already exists, go to an event you happen upon while scrolling Facebook too late at night," says Sophia. "You don't have to start from zero!"

Aiden and Sophia believe taking new endeavors one step at a time is the most faithful place to begin. Researching your neighborhood's history, learning about the systems that make life work (or not work) in that neighborhood, and actively seeking out new-to-you community events are all steps that can be taken immediately. These experiences will lead you down the path to becoming a public church, if you approach them with curiosity, honesty, and humility.

Grace Episcopal Church and a Big Front Porch

At the corner of Forty-Sixth Street and Colfax Avenue in South Minneapolis sits a little church that just started figuring out how to move beyond their walls one small step at a time. Grace Episcopal Church is a picturesque urban Episcopal church with a big red door situated where the East Harriet, King Field, Lynnhurst, and Tangletown neighborhoods of Minneapolis merge. It is a bustling residential neighborhood lined with old trees, restaurants, a hardware store, cafés, and other businesses. In 2019, Grace had a vision of all their neighbors streaming into their church through that big red door. They soon realized the vision was of the congregation streaming through that big red door out into the neighborhood. Uno reverse!

Fiona was a twenty-five-year-old young adult member of Grace at that time. She was part of a team working to lead the congregation out into the neighborhood. Fiona and her team spent a lot of time talking about talking with their neighbors. Which is always easier to do than actually talking with them. She knew they needed (1) a reason to strike up a conversation with their neighbors, and (2) a place to cross paths with their neighbors. But the local café where they had been hosting space to listen with neighbors was closing. So, the team at Grace began wondering how they could help the neighborhood replace that loss.

On a holiday visit back home in North Carolina, Fiona noticed how conducive her family's front porch was for meeting their neighbors. A lightbulb went on. Fiona realized her congregation needed a front porch. Their team began converting their congregation's front yard into a gathering place for their neighborhood. Adirondack chairs were purchased and placed in a circle. A picnic table was built and set under a sprawling linden tree. A Little Free Library and Little Free Food Pantry were planted along the sidewalk. Soon Grace Episcopal Church and their entire neighborhood had a new front porch.

Grace had found the place where they could cross paths with their neighbors, but what would be their reason for striking up a conversation? Fiona proclaimed, "Everything's better with ice cream!" That Sunday, Grace began serving ice cream to their neighbors in their front yard after church. The ice cream became a nonthreatening way to strike up conversations with their neighbors as they walked past the church on their way to the lake, or the store, or the bus, or their homes. The big red door had been opened. The congregation had moved through it into the neighborhood. Relationships began to form.

Grace quickly became known as the ice cream church, but the ice cream and the front porch were only vehicles for initiating conversations and relationships. Grace's front porch was established just before the COVID-19 pandemic stay-at-home orders during the spring of 2020. Since then, the congregation has had dozens of what it calls "neighbor moments." Sheila, the congregation's director of community involvement, was leaving church when she noticed six young adults sitting around the picnic table drinking beer. As she walked over they asked, "Are we in trouble?" She said, "No! Not at all! I'm just coming over to meet you." She learned that they were frequent users of Grace's front porch. They lived in an apartment building up the street and had no yard where they could gather together outside, a problem that many young adults in urban neighborhoods experience. Sheila also discovered that many neighbors who did not have yards would use Grace's front porch as a safe and inviting place to spend time. The neighbors would say the corner now exudes joy. Interfaith relationships with leaders and members from other faith communities in the neighborhood have been established over ice cream on the front porch. Local businesses and neighborhood groups now ask Grace to partner with them in their block parties and festivals. The local event center donated one of their large party tents to Grace because they are always doing things outside. A group of teenage girls from down the block joined in with the congregation of Grace one Saturday during the congregation's peace festival. The girls said, "You all are always doing cool stuff out here so we wanted to be a part of it."

One of these cool things is a regular peace walk through the neighborhood, during which the congregation walks the neighborhood and stops at certain places to pray for and give gratitude for the presence of peace. During one peace walk, the walkers stopped to pray at another Little Free Library in a neighbor's yard. The owner of the house came out to see what they were doing. He began visiting with the members of the congregation and joined them on their walk. He had lived in the neighborhood his whole life but had never stepped foot in their church. Now he is a member.

Fiona and the members of Grace are not naïve. "We know it's a continuous process. We never envisioned it as handing out ice cream a few times and suddenly knowing everyone in the neighborhood and then singing 'Kumbaya' together. We learn different things every year and we meet new people every year. That's our goal, to keep doing this so we keep meeting people so we keep learning new things." The front porch has become a place where people in the neighborhood feel safe and from where they can slip in and explore the sanctuary and the church. It has become a place where members of Grace feel safe and can slip out and encounter their neighbor. Fiona says, "It has removed the barrier of entering our church and it has transformed how we feel about our church. It has become an extension of our building and our ministry rather than just being a place we have to maintain." That big red door swings both ways pretty frequently these days.

YOUR SENDING

Both God and young adults are calling congregations to move beyond their walls, to become public churches. Public churches embedded in neighborhoods, connected to neighbors, and united with neighbors in the work that is necessary to bring about the healing and hope God desires for all living beings. We close with Kayla's story, hoping it and the many others on these pages will stir curiosity and confidence toward your next steps beyond the walls of your congregation.

I (Kayla) was baptized by the waters of the Moorhead Public Pool when I was nine years old, just old enough to be at the pool unsupervised by an adult. I would walk there every summer morning to find refuge with the other elementary schoolers who needed to escape home. I was reminded of my baptism when I was splashed by the garden hose as I watered my grandfather's 10 foot by 10 foot garden every summer weekend for years after my mom died—with well water from the ground at the intersection of Leech Lake, Red Lake, and White Earth Native Reservations. I was again reminded of my baptism as I let the cold water of Lake Superior turn my toes white, staring out at the majesty of the lake on a day trip to Duluth, Minnesota, with three of my stranger-turned-best-friend Lutheran Volunteer Corps housemates two months into our year of service.

I was confirmed by Pastor Emmy Kegler on Twitter when I was fourteen years old, realizing for the first time that my queerness was not an illness but a beloved piece of who I have been created to be. I was reminded of my confirmation the morning after the 2016 election, as

The Church's Call to Be in the World

I walked into first-period English, eyes puffy from a sleepless night mourning everything I thought my country stood for before I could even drive a car without an adult in the passenger seat. In the midst of a handful of male peers chanting "Trump 2020" under their breath as I walked to my seat, my teacher scooped her arm around me and walked me to her office. As God weeps and mourns with us, offering to be a confidant, so did Mrs. Koenig as she gave me the morning off of class to rest in her hideout.

The people who have nourished my faith challenge the church because almost none of them are from the church. I feel an overflowing sense of joy and peace when I recount the ways in which I have felt and watched the Holy Spirit work in my life, especially when the institution of the church could or would not meet me where I was. Almost all of my faith formation that occurred before I declared myself as a religion major in the spring of 2019 and applied to be on the Campus Ministry Commission as my entrance point back into a worshiping community happened outside of the church—beyond the walls.

There is so much fear for the future of our institution. Fear of secularism and pluralism is a wax coating around our walls. We seem to believe that if we seal ourselves from the outside, what's inside will stay exactly how it is, not understanding that the impact of this intended survival skill is in direct correlation to our own demise. The new breath of the Holy Spirit can do a lot, but only when we let ourselves out by inviting her in.

At every corner we see churches engaging in work they believe to be "beyond their walls"—mission trips to other countries, Feed My Starving Children events, pastors pushing the ELCA Good Gifts catalogue in their equity work for the year. This is still wax-coated engagement. When the only thing at stake in your actions is whether or not you feel good or bad at the end of the day, you are acting inside of your walls. Instead, what would it look like for congregations to wrestle with gentrification in their neighborhoods? To have congregational food pantries engage in policy advocacy that works to eliminate systemic poverty alongside their direct service work? To find avenues of public voice that unequivocally repudiate homophobia and work alongside queer organizations in our communities to repair harm?

Beyond the Walls

Work beyond our walls can feel scary and vulnerable, and it is seldom clean-cut or scripted. But that's how you know it's rooted in the message of the gospel. Beyond our walls we are invited into curiosity and invited into community with no motives other than love and authenticity. Beyond our walls is the fuller embodiment of the freedom we inherit through the grace of God and love of Christ.

11

RECLAIMING "ENOUGH"

Away from Scarcity Toward True Abundance

Catalina Morales Bahena
Dr. Cherice Bock

OUR INVITATION

Abundance and scarcity at first seem like opposites, but they are often two sides of the same coin: one group's abundance requires another group's scarcity. The true opposite of the scarcity/abundance dichotomy is "enough." When we seek abundance out of fear of scarcity, we tend to take more than we need and hoard what we have instead of sharing it with those who have a need. When we seek "enough" and focus on gratitude, when we share with one another what we have, everyone has enough, and there is a feeling of abundance in gratitude and care for one's community and oneself. This attitude of seeking "enough," sharing with others, and expressing gratitude is the type of community Jesus invited his followers to be.

We (Catalina and Cherice) have found the metaphor of dirt and soil a helpful way to wrestle with this topic, perhaps rooted in our own particular stories with the land we now call home. Soil is needed for us to live: it grows and nourishes everything we eat, grows trees that help us breathe, and enables the decomposition process—our bodies become soil again after we die. Soil teems with life. Microorganisms and fungi constantly participate in cycling nutrients to maintain enough oxygen, carbon dioxide, nitrogen, clean water, and other basic necessities for sustaining life—true abundance. Dirt, on the other hand, is what results when we use up the nutrients in the soil without giving the soil time to keep up. When we try to create constant abundance by overworking the soil, we end up with scarcity: we're left with only dirt.

Jesus said, "I came that they may have life, and have it abundantly" (John 10:10b). This concluding chapter prompts important questions for the church. *What does abundant life look like, here and now? Is it possible to live an abundant life that doesn't require scarcity somewhere else, or in the future? How might we create abundance through focusing on "enough," in our lives and communities?*

Some folks focus on the abundance that comes after death, focusing on the afterlife. Yet, Jesus set up a vision of his followers as a family that cares for each other, a new creation—an alternative to the Roman Empire. Young people in particular are seeking this new creation but struggle to see it manifest in their church. For generations, young people have tried to breathe new life into their church communities, and yet it feels like the church continues to try to grow new life out of depleted, undernourished dirt. We desire to see faith communities cultivating new growth in soil filled with abundant life.

It may be common in US culture today, when we think about abundance, to imagine building up wealth so we always have more than we need, and to always have access to more things: more food, more variety, faster products, faster ways to get around. But this way of thinking is actually causing scarcity. We're taking resources from people in other places, and we are collectively using more than the planet is producing.[1]

SETTLER COLONIALISM: ABUNDANCE TO SCARCITY

Both of us have been on journeys of learning about our ancestry, discerning our particular callings as followers of Jesus, and coming to terms with the harm and injustice caused—past and present—by the United States and the European nations that colonized the Americas, using up the abundant life that flourished here in just a few centuries. We know it is not sustainable—or faithful—for us as Christians to continue to operate under an abundance/scarcity dichotomy that is destroying our planet's ecosystems and that creates abundance for a few and scarcity for many. As authors, our families immigrated here at different times and for different reasons. Our stories shed light on the bigger story of the scarcity/abundance dichotomy that took root here.

---

1. In this volume see chapter 3, "Destruction and Re-Creation."

Away from Scarcity Toward True Abundance

Cherice's Story

I come from ancestors who came to the land we now call the United States of America as colonists from Europe. The ancestors I know the most about were members of the Religious Society of Friends (Quakers) from England. As white people moved to the New World, they marveled at the abundance of the land and saw it as a gift given to them by God—it was their "manifest destiny" to populate the land and use its resources. Colonists perceived the land as "empty," despite the people living here. They perceived the land as unused because it wasn't being put into agricultural production in ways they understood. More and more colonists arrived from Europe, and within a few generations, many of the abundant forests were chopped down and some animals became scarce due to the fur trade. Land that had been forest or prairie was put to agricultural use. Although I do not know the specific stories of my ancestors, I know the Quaker communities they lived in were agricultural communities. I can follow my ancestors back across the American frontier by noting which Friends communities they were in when they were buried. Several of my family lines go back from the town where I live, Newberg, Oregon, which was largely settled by Quakers in the late 1800s, through Friends cemeteries in Iowa, Indiana, Kansas, North Carolina, and Pennsylvania, with Quaker ancestors arriving from England in the early 1700s.

Why did these ancestors have to keep moving west? I'm sure they had individual reasons, but a major one for settlers in general was that they had exhausted the soil where they were: the farming tactics they were using were no longer as productive because they had used up the nutrients in the topsoil that take generations to form. Just like they had overtaxed the land and run out of space in England, they did the same thing in each community they created on Turtle Island,[2] until arriving at the West Coast with nowhere further to expand.

2. Many of the Indigenous people groups of what is now known as North America referred to the continent as Turtle Island (in their own languages) partially because of its shape: Mexico is the tail, Baja California and Florida are the back legs, the front legs are Alaska and Quebec, and the head is the land, islands, and ice leading up to the Arctic. Indigenous groups have different stories about Turtle Island, but some describe a great flood due to people fighting with one another, in many ways

Reclaiming "Enough"

My hometown, Newberg, was selected for Quakers to build a new community by William Hobson in the 1870s. He chose Newberg because of its healthy soil and comfortable climate: he called it "a garden of the Lord," a term he meant spiritually and physically.[3] Though my Quaker ancestors likely did not participate in wars forcing Indigenous people off their traditional lands, they did settle that land and founded and ran "Indian boarding schools"—institutions for forced assimilation of Indigenous people.[4]

My grandfather's parents, Glen and Fanny Beebe, were the first to homestead a 240-acre plot on the border of Oregon and Idaho starting in 1939. Land was doled out based on the Homestead Act of 1862. The Northern Paiute and Western Shoshone had been expelled from this land in eastern Oregon in the second half of the nineteenth century, but it had not been very usable for settlement due to its aridity. The land was vacant

---

similar to the flood in Genesis 7-8. Turtle Island was formed because there was no land, and the turtle offered to be the support for the new land. A version of the Haudenosaunee story is told by Robin Wall Kimmerer in her *Braiding Sweetgrass: Indigenous Wisdom, Scientific Knowledge, and the Teachings of Plants* (Milkweed, 2013).

3. Ralph K. Beebe, *A Garden of the Lord: A History of Oregon Yearly Meeting of Friends Church* (Barclay, 1968), 28. This history of Quakers in Oregon was written by my grandfather.

4. A comprehensive description of these schools can be found in David Wallace Adams, *Education for Extinction: American Indians and the Boarding School Experience, 1875-1928* (University Press of Kansas, 1995). Many of these schools were run by churches as a form of missionary outreach, and they were funded by the US government with a purpose of "civilizing" Indigenous people. Students were forcibly removed from their families and reservations and were usually not allowed to speak their languages, wear traditional clothing, or engage in their cultural practices. Many children died or experienced abuse; unmarked graves of children have been discovered at some former schools, but the complete number of deaths is unknown. See Bryan Newland, "Federal Indian Boarding School Initiative Investigative Report," United States Department of the Interior, May 2022, https://tinyurl.com/3zhcbkds. There is a growing body of research about the boarding schools run by specific denominations or church traditions, and readers are encouraged to look for resources about their own tradition. One such work from the Quaker tradition is Paula Palmer, "The Quaker Indian Boarding Schools: Facing Our History and Ourselves," in *Quakers and Native Americans*, ed. Ignacio Gallup-Diaz and Geoffrey Plank, European Expansion and Indigenous Response, vol. 30 (Brill, 2019), 293-311.

of human inhabitants by the time my great-grandparents came along. It was inexpensive to those who could show they had at least $2,000 in the bank and at least two years of successful farming experience, and who built a home on the land.[5] Glen and Fanny could meet these requirements, and they painstakingly cleared the land, disrupting the delicate high-desert ecosystem, planting cash crops and raising dairy cows.

In some ways, I look back in awe at my granny, who knew how to live off the land in ways that have not been passed down to me. In her letters, she talked about going out at dawn to shoot rabbits, then returning home to do all the household chores.[6] My mom remembers Granny going out back with an ax to butcher the Sunday chicken when they visited. My grandpa talked about the shelves of canned food Granny put up each year, a skill I had to relearn from my mother-in-law and Internet videos.

Granny saw the hand of God at work in her family's ability to get this homestead. She saw it as a blessing based on God's provision and her own and her husband's faithful work; a "bargain with God," she called it.[7] They experienced great hardship, and she often worried they would not have enough, but my grandpa remembers how Granny always set aside 10 percent of their net income for a tithe, no matter what, before paying any other bills. Additionally, they donated part of their land for the building of a Friends meetinghouse.[8] She sought to be a faithful woman. Still, knowing what I know about the damage to ecosystems and the destruction of the cultures of the Indigenous people groups that were forced to vacate that land, Granny's understanding of this land as a "blessing" for our family is problematic. Yet, her story and heritage are part of mine.

My Beebe great-grandparents saw themselves as coaxing abundance out of scarcity with the help of American ingenuity and the blessing of God. In an arid land where it was difficult to make things grow, in a place

---

5. Timothy A. Dick, *The Vale Project, Research of Historic Reclamation Projects* (Bureau of Reclamation History Program, 1993), 14–17.

6. My grandfather, Ralph Beebe, recorded some of his parents' correspondence in his 2015 self-published book, *The Ralph and Wanda Pierson Beebe Family*. This particular detail is from a letter she wrote in 1914. See p. 1.

7. Beebe, *Pierson Beebe Family*, 4.

8. Ridgeview Friends Church, built in 1941. Beebe, *Pierson Beebe Family*, 6.

where healthy soil was difficult to come by, and in a time when the country had just experienced the Great Depression and the Dust Bowl, they were able to create new farmland. Through massive feats of engineering, the land became dammed and irrigated, and through their own incredibly hard work, they put the irrigation to use and were able to farm.

But, as descendants of European settlers have come to realize in recent decades, this was a shortsighted understanding of abundance. It did not take into account the incredible ecosystem at work in the high desert, filled with biodiversity, each type of creature filling its niche. The river had been healthy and clean, home to salmon and other species. But dams built up and down the Snake River and the Columbia River into which it flows have made it increasingly difficult for salmon to make it home to spawn; the once-abundant fish population is now scarce, and agricultural runoff as well as emissions from "modern" human life are making it difficult for many species to thrive.[9]

My ancestors came to this country and saw abundance, but without understanding what they were doing or how to integrate into the community of life around them, they created scarcity.

Catalina's Story

My family's experience, like that of many other present-day immigrants, has been shaped by a false understanding of scarcity and abundance. When your humanity has been taken from you, for generations, it be-

---

9. Efforts are under way to remove five Snake River dams, and other dam removal projects have been or are in the process of seeing significant return of thriving ecosystems, such as the Elwha River in Washington, a network of waterways in Michigan under the care of the Pokagon tribe, and the Klamath River in Oregon. Elizabeth Castillo, "Elwha River Transformed 10 Years After Dam Removal," Oregon Public Broadcasting, August 2, 2022, https://tinyurl.com/yc38wcbs; Juliet Grable, "Scientists Are Tracking Ecological Changes as the Klamath River Dams Come Down," *High Country News*, May 1, 2024, https://tinyurl.com/mwa6vps8; "The Seven Generation River: Great Lakes Now," PBS Learning Media, accessed December 9, 2024, https://tinyurl.com/5n82hm78; "Why Remove the Four Lower Snake River Dams?," Save Our Wild Salmon, accessed December 9, 2024, https://tinyurl.com/22zws32w.

comes difficult to see abundance and beauty in what you have and in those around you. Out of fear, it becomes tempting to center your worth in the things you can possess and control. This mentality has infected all of us and has lasted far too long.

I migrated to this country when I was two years old with both of my parents. I have now been in this country for over thirty years. I still don't have a pathway to citizenship. For many immigrants today, this country is seen as the land of milk and honey, a place where one can possess all worldly needs if they make it here. The truth is that all of us in this country, documented or not, are benefiting from the overextraction of resources from the land. We have believed that we can take all the resources, without worrying about the future consequences. Empty, rotting houses sit all over Mexico as many immigrants come to this country with the plan to overwork for a few years, acquire more resources, and go back. Regretfully, many don't.

Fear is abundant in shaping a mind-set that prioritizes material possessions. Most people aren't horrible, money-hungry, evil hoarders. When you get curious about someone's story, you realize the truth is simple. They are scared they won't have what they need to survive and sustain their loved ones. This has become more prevalent in our society that keeps raising the cost of living and not the amount of money people are making. This fear is real and powerfully influential.

As an organizer, I experienced this firsthand when I led a large effort for the Sanctuary Movement in Minnesota.[10] The need for this advocacy was prompted by the election of Donald Trump in 2016, when the immigrant community feared being targeted by the policies of this new administration. Pastor Grant Stevensen, a fellow organizer, and I were the only staff leading this effort. As a team of two, we hosted forums for the purpose of recruiting Sanctuary churches that would commit to housing an undocumented immigrant or family that was in line to be deported.

---

10. The Sanctuary Movement in Minnesota was built after Donald Trump was elected president in 2016. It was composed of faith communities that related to ISAIAH, a nonprofit faith-based organizing group. Across the country, faith-based organizations built out their own networks with parishes inspired by the Sanctuary Movement of the 1980s.

We hosted multiple forums, some with over three hundred people in attendance. By the end of the year we had talked to well over a hundred parishes across the state, and over a thousand people, yet only a little over thirty congregations signed up, and of those, only ten became full Sanctuary parishes committed to hosting undocumented immigrants. The other twenty volunteered to support those being housed with things like supplies and legal and financial support.

As a "DACA-mented" immigrant myself, I knew the fears of those our Sanctuary Movement was advocating for. I also found myself needing to respond to the fears of congregations—majority-white middle-class or wealthy white communities—to push for the well-being of our undocumented neighbors. Throughout the discernment process with these faith communities I heard many fearful questions, like "What if Immigration & Customs Enforcement comes after our church? What if our 501(c)(3) status is taken away? How do we know if the people coming are good people? How do we know they are not going to cause us more problems? What if the people in our church stop coming? What if the diocese doesn't support us? What if our sustainers stop giving money to the church?" These are valid questions, but they are rooted in fear. There are other important questions also needing a response, ones rooted in relationship. It was up to Grant and me to engage people in these relationship-rooted questions.

Imagine leaving everything and everyone you know, hoping you will find good people to help you. For many immigrants and asylum seekers, by the time they get to a community to resettle, they have long since lost their possessions. They can only seek relationship and trust. We urged congregations to wonder, "How would it feel to leave your home and try to make a new one in a foreign place? What would it mean to love our immigrant neighbors? How would they know we love them? What risks might we take to participate in God's welcome to the stranger among us?"

I sat in the juxtaposition of questions rooted in relationship versus fear. Often those who had more worldly possessions feared more, and those who had literally only the clothes on their backs hoped more. That hope grew even bigger and stronger when new immigrants were received by their neighbors into a parish, were invited into their homes for a meal, or received hospitality through simple conversations that affirmed their humanity. I saw how being oriented toward relationship frees people to be generous with their resources and can overcome our fears. As a young adult, this was a time when the church was most alive and meaningful to me. It was scary but transformative to follow our faith together, to truly love our neighbors and share, to make sure everyone has enough. And as a young adult leader in the church, it was deeply influential. When I decided to launch the Sanctuary work, Pr. Grant was quick to collaborate and follow my lead. I was twenty-six at the time, and having him as a white male clergy in my corner and letting me lead, no questions asked, was empowering. This experience was formative as I witnessed firsthand what's possible when we prioritize relationships and fight through the fear that threatens them.

WORTH AND VALUE

Notions of worth and value—of humans, of creation, of our resources and our communities—are inherently shaped by the stories we adopt and what those stories teach us about abundance and scarcity. For a very long time, our society's compass has been orientated to stories of scarcity that have their roots in fear and anxiety.

Narratives of Scarcity

Cultural understandings of scarcity and abundance relate to how we try to get the things we need for survival like food and shelter. Our US context focuses on productivity, with the assumption that if our society is productive, together we'll create abundance, and those who participate in this productivity will be able to get their piece of this abundance. In this social framework, we must *earn* our place.

This creates fear and anxiety. Since it will be assumed that we're not working hard enough if we don't have enough money to take care of ourselves, we must always be in fear that an unexpected crisis will make us unproductive, or our job will become obsolete and we will no longer be able to afford rent or a mortgage. With a narrative of scarcity, we're taught to fear others, who are our competitors for the things we need for survival, creating winners and losers. If we win and find employment, someone else loses and is forced into a more desperate situation. We might feel bad for that person, but we can't feel too bad because we need to concentrate on taking care of ourselves. Even if we have enough food for today, we don't know what will happen tomorrow—so we need to hoard an overabundance because someday there might be scarcity.

Being successful in this system can foster the belief that one is more worthy: those who work hard get what they deserve. This leads to imagining that others should have worked harder, and they must be unworthy of success and deserve to be impoverished.

At the same time, the social expectation in the United States is based on the idea of unlimited growth: the economy must always be expanding, there must always be more productivity, more goods, more convenience, more speed. This keeps everyone seeking more and better, having to work harder to keep up, to prove we are worthy and deserving a place in society. It forces us to remain afraid and anxious.

It also ignores the limits of how much growth our planet can tolerate and how much waste the planet can handle. It ignores the needs of other species and ecosystems. Our planet is structured to produce an abundance of clean air, water, and biodiverse life growing out of the soil and returning to it. An ecosystem functions and teems with life because everyone is contributing to it and everyone receives what they need, then their bodies return nutrients to the ecosystem after they die, breaking down to form the building blocks for new life.

This cycling of nutrients, however, is currently out of joint. United States society thinks of productivity in a straight line rather than a circle. In this straight line, material resources are acquired through capital and labor, the materials are turned into something useful, these materials are consumed, and the waste is thrown away. Then, a new material must be created so it can also be consumed. This creates profit, as people must pay for the material they need to consume, and they must pay repeatedly every time that material is needed. Since we all need materials every day, this keeps us invested in the productivity system, offering our labor so we can pay to consume the things we need to survive.

In the United States, this can feel like abundance for those with economic security. We go to the grocery store and select any food we want, or a restaurant where someone can cook us food from any part of the globe. We can travel long distances with ease. Our homes can keep us comfortable in all but the most extreme conditions. Our waste is whisked away through sewer pipes and garbage trucks, and we do not have to think about it again.

This is a false perception of abundance. It leads to scarcity of usable resources and an abundance of trash that does not break down in an appropriate amount of time to be able to cycle back through the ecosystem.

Most Christians in the United States have bought into this understanding of our worthiness coming only from our productivity, and have bought into the idea that material wealth is a sign of blessing from God. This is despite the numerous places in the Bible where prophets and Jesus castigate those who are wealthy who do not share with others, and where the world's understanding of who is most important is turned upside down. In the Bible, people are good and made in God's image regardless of how productive they are; we are God's beloved children by grace, not by anything we do or don't do. We do not have to earn our right to be part of God's family, and all are included—particularly those the world's systems of power think are "least."

Narratives of Scarcity in the Church

The narrative of scarcity has seeped into every aspect of our lives, including our church communities. The church too has attempted to create a surplus of material possessions. Similar to the rich fool in Luke's Gospel, we have prioritized material wealth over relationship. Even with people's growing awareness of the sins of the church in the past, we continue to see privilege and possessions protected. This is evidenced by extravagant church buildings or successful campaigns to restore organs for decreasing crowds of worshipers while an affordable preschool in the same church is ordered to close because it isn't generating enough revenue. Even when the church building is not extravagant, we often are more anxious about keeping the lights on than addressing the needs of the human beings around us. The scarcity narrative drives many churches who are in decline to focus more on fear of survival, leaving little imagination for the relationships God continues to call the church to turn their attention toward.

This narrative of scarcity has also shaped the experience young adults have in their church homes, often experiencing disconnection due to the inability of our communities to be in real relationship with us. I (Catalina) can resonate with the experiences of many of my peers. We are often told others know best because of seniority, age, or titles. We are missing the relationships a church community might provide, because we experience ministry leaders who desire the presence and participation of young adults in their church but don't seem to value getting to know who we are as unique human beings.[11] Our presence serves to soothe the church's fear about current and future decline but ends up feeling tokenizing when our stories are dismissed or overlooked.[12]

This book seeks to reframe a scarcity-driven story—one that sees young adults as the solution to the church's anxiety about decline. Instead, imagine what could happen if we reoriented our anxiety about needing to attract young people to our churches and shifted *all* that energy toward investing in real relationships. Is it possible we might experience real abundance through relationships rather than clinging to the fear scarcity has cultivated?

Reorienting our compass to point toward relationship would shift the ground and open space for young adults to be contributing human beings, each valued as a unique child of God. Similar to the process of what it takes to have rich soil, when one's compass is relationship, you begin to learn how you can contribute to the abundance of the whole. Soil doesn't only thrive from your cultivation; it needs many elements to thrive. That is the beauty of a compass of relationship—it takes all of us together. It turns potential competitors for resources into neighbors caught up in each other's mutual flourishing.

MADE IN GOD'S IMAGE, FROM THE SOIL

"All are from the dust, and all turn to dust again," according to Ecclesiastes 3:20. Genesis 2:7 describes God forming the human being, *ha'adam*,

---

11. This is in contrast to what I experienced as a young organizer and leader with Pr. Grant and the Sanctuary movement, who invited, cheered on, and valued my gifts and leadership.

12. See in this volume chapter 2, "Tokenism of Young Adults."

out of the dust from the earth, *adamah*. The word for earth, soil, or land (*adamah*) is linguistically similar to the word for person (*adam*).

In the first part of Genesis 2, the first "earthling," as Wilda Gafney describes, is called *ha'adam*, the person. Adam becomes a name (without the initial *ha*, which in Hebrew is the definite article "the") after God separates *ha'adam* into *'ish* and *'isshah*, man and woman.[13] In Genesis 2:7, the first human being is simply an earth creature, a new being made of the soil of the land, into whom God breathes the breath of life. God makes the person out of the soil: out of that which is dead, broken-down organic matter, plus the land, which is teeming with the microscopic life of microorganisms. God makes life out of the ruins, you might say. In Scripture, humanity is understood to be formed from the land from a particular place, then given life through God's breath. Later, God promises to make Abram/Abraham's offspring like the dust of the earth, as numerous as the dust particles blowing in the wind (Gen. 13:16; 28:14).

In English, this wordplay works well: humanity is made from humus, and this should lead to humility—all we are is dust, and our bodies will again become particles of organic matter, ready to again become part of the land, new soil.[14] We're made from the life-breath of the Divine, enlivened soil interconnected with creation and Creator, conscious of the transcendent mystery of this tiny blue planet in the midst of a vast cosmos, in awe of this brief time and this beautiful place we get to call home.

The beauty and intricacy of life on this planet are mind-bogglingly abundant: a teaspoon of soil contains a billion bacteria, yards and yards of fungal filaments, and many other types of microorganisms.[15] These keep cycling the energy we receive from the sun and the nutrients and chemical compounds that keep life happening, breaking down and building up, keeping the stuff of life cycling with the rhythms of each season. From small particles of chemicals and dead organic matter, combined

---

13. Wilda C. Gafney, *Womanist Midrash: A Reintroduction to the Women of the Torah and the Throne*, e-book ed. (Westminster John Knox, 2017).

14. "Humus" is a word for soil. It is the organic part of the soil that is formed from decomposition of plants back into component parts that can be taken up to form new plants.

15. Lisa Howard, "Uncovering the Hidden Life of Soil: Microbes in Soil Are Essential for Life and May Help Mitigate Climate Change," *UC Davis News*, March 2, 2017, https://tinyurl.com/3fsyhz94.

with the place in which we live, we as humans get the chance to breathe the breath of God for a few short years, participating in this abundant, finite planetary community.

We cannot deny our role in the rhythms of our planet and how we all are better if we live into creation's interconnectedness. Like the narratives of scarcity, the truth about abundance is that it offers us an alternative story to root ourselves in. Right after we are born, we begin to form attachments to people and places. Many of us attach great significance to the land we call home. When I (Catalina) asked my mother where home was, she replied, "There has only been one place that actually felt like home to me." Right after I was born, my parents bought land for the first time. They moved in with nothing. They put together a shack with wood planks for walls, a steel roof, and the dirt was their floor. In one room, our entire family lived. She describes it as one of the happiest times of her life. She would wake up each morning to clean her little home, which included sweeping the floor and spraying the dirt with a bit of water.

Abundance in this story is really in the eyes of the beholder. My mother was happy because the dirt beneath her feet helped her remember where she came from. She had a deep connection to the potential of the dirt to become soil—soil like the land where she grew up, soil that taught her what it can provide and sustain if we develop a relationship with it. It's true that in that moment the dirt was not providing life for other species, but it was providing warmth and stability for our family, and for that it was tended to. More than thirty years later, that dirt became soil again because our family tended to the land in ways that helped bring healing to the ecosystem.

Unlike the dirt on the floor of my parents' first home, the soil from the farm of the wealthy fool in Luke 12 is very rich and provides this farmer with an abundant harvest. But he does not have enough storage so he wants to tear down his barns to build larger ones to store (and hoard) even more for himself. The impact of his decision to hold on to his abundant possessions and not put them into the market will limit the food supply to his community, likely drive up prices for smaller existing resources and harm those in the community who are already struggling the most. Jesus reminds the crowd in this story, "Life does not consist in

Away from Scarcity Toward True Abundance

the abundance of possessions" (Luke 12:15). That begs the question: What does life consist of then?

It seems Jesus is suggesting that a life rooted in trusting God can help us live with *enough*, and make sure others do as well. Abundance is not indulgence but enoughness. It is replacing greed with generosity, trusting that God will provide enough. This story demonstrates the harm that can be caused when we forget about this generous connection we have to each other.

My Indigenous ancestors passed on to me a belief that the smallest of things has dignity and worth. When I was nine years old, my mother and I made a trip to her place of birth, La Neblinas, Guerrero, Mexico. In her very small town, where life was and still is deeply dependent on your relationship with the earth and its animals, she was taught to have not only respect for them but also concern. My mother used to cry about everything, a trait I have inherited. Her parents told her that she was a lechecillo, that she had inherited his traits because every small thing made her cry. The lechecillo is a bush-like plant that has long stems bursting up from the ground that don't ever seem to brown, staying thin and green. The name comes from the word *leche* (milk) because it has a milk-like watery substance that runs through its stems. Depending on where in Mexico you come from, the lechecillo can look like an entirely different plant, but they all hold this milky nutrient in their stems, which will weep from the plant when its stems are damaged.

As my mother and I walked the same trail she walked with her parents as a little girl, we came to a lechecillo bush. She began to use her nail to scrape him, all while telling me the story of how her parents would call her lechecillo. When she finished scraping the lechecillo, tears of milk-like water came out of the bush. My circle of concern grew more than I could have imagined that day. That moment shaped my worldview forever and expanded my ability to see abundance and scarcity in one moment. My mother didn't refer to the lechecillo as an it or tell me it was leaking. She told me she had hurt him, just slightly, but still hurt him, and he had what any of us would consider a very common reaction to pain. The world around us is full of small reminders about our generous connection to one another.

MOVING TOWARD "ENOUGH"

We want to leave you with some ingredients that will help cultivate the literal and figurative soil in your context and turn the dirt back into something more ready to produce life abundantly. These practices are steps toward a true abundance, one defined by *enough*, and rooted in the trust of a God who has made us deeply connected to Godself and all that God has created.

Sabbath

Practicing the Sabbath can be a way to help us remember we have and are enough. It can help us reflect on the abundance that we have—and that we want to continue to cultivate. In the Bible, remembering and keeping the Sabbath is one of the Ten Commandments (Exod. 20:8-10). It is one of the things considered most important for God's followers. Those of us from Christian traditions in the United States tend to think of practicing Sabbath as synonymous with attending a church service on a Sunday morning, but the commandment is actually about a day of rest set aside for God. Jews practice Sabbath from sundown Friday to Saturday, the seventh day of the week, reflecting God's day of resting at the end of creation.

Early Christians practiced Sabbath in this way and added on meeting together on Sunday mornings to celebrate Jesus's resurrection—but this was not considered the Sabbath. Jesus said the Sabbath is made for humankind, not humankind for the Sabbath (Mark 2:27)—it is supposed to be a gift, not something we are enslaved to. God shows us an example by resting and celebrating on the seventh day after creating everything.[16] Producing more and more is not the ultimate goal; instead, we can reflect God as cocreators by recognizing that part of the point of creation or producing things is that we can take time to enjoy and experience, to reflect and rest.

God invites us into this gift of Sabbath. In the Bible, the day of rest each week was not just for the Israelites or a certain segment of the population, but was for everyone: all people in the community needed rest,

---

16. This is not to say that days in the creation story had to happen within literal twenty-four-hour periods.

every gender, even servants and foreigners. Exodus 23:10-13 specifically mentions rest for animals and the land on the Sabbath. This Sabbath concept is also applied every seven years, and again, after seven-times-seven-years, the Year of Jubilee is celebrated. The community is instructed to save enough food for six years so they can let the land lie fallow in the seventh year. This allows the people and the land to rest. Exodus 23:11 specifies that those who are poor can glean what grows on the land in that seventh year, and what they don't need, the animals can eat. In the Year of Jubilee, everyone takes a year off and the whole economy is reset. Debts are forgiven—everyone receives a fresh start. Land is returned to its original owners so it cannot be consolidated in the hands of a few. The land rests, the people rest and share what they have and celebrate, and everyone has enough. They realize the abundance of community and joy they share.

This way of living is hard to imagine today.[17] For many, it is impossible to take a day off each week and still be able to feed ourselves and our loved ones. Even if we can afford to take a day off, American culture ties our personal sense of worth so closely to our level of productivity that there is always more to do. If we are in a socioeconomic situation in which we can afford to rest, we may feel guilty for resting when we know others in our society cannot. It may feel countercultural to rest, but incorporating some aspect of Sabbath into our week can help break down our assumptions about scarcity and abundance, reminding us of what it looks like to have enough. We can practice gratitude and experience joy and rejuvenation, and we can bump into and take time to process feelings of inadequacy, questions around our own worthiness, and practice trust and boundary setting.

Sabbath is not meant to be practiced as individuals, but it is intended to be practiced together with one's community. Alone, it is very difficult to set aside a day to rest, and we cannot gain the communal benefits that come from ensuring the land has time to rest. Imagine a Sabbath-

---

17. We recommend the following to explore the ways in which practicing Sabbath is countercultural: Tricia Hersey, *Rest Is Resistance: A Manifesto* (Little, Brown, 2022); Walter Brueggemann, *Sabbath as Resistance: Saying No to the Culture of Now*, rev. ed. (Westminster John Knox, 2017).

practicing society that places a premium on rest, building communities in which everyone has enough so they can take time to rest. This vision of community requires immense trust and a willingness to share and collaborate. We have to be able to trust that God will provide. We have to trust each other, that if we don't have enough, others will help us out. We have to build a community strong enough that we can share our needs and our abundance and know that we will not be shamed or taken advantage of. This vision of community may seem out of reach, but it begins with us reclaiming Sabbath in our own lives and relationships.[18]

Gifting ourselves and one another Sabbath rest is perhaps one of the ways that we can begin to find our place back to who we have always been meant to be as a community. We are getting sick from all the stress of overworking, constantly trying to prove our place in this world. We have forgotten what it's like to live in tune with the seasons and the capacity of the land. Soil needs enough time and nutrients to replenish to be able to also give and be a home to other living beings. We need the same.

"Enough" Requires Boundaries

The perspective of an empire assumes that an abundance of goods and services must be sent to the center of the empire, and when resources run low, new colonies must be created in regions that have not yet been sucked dry. This mind-set requires an eternal frontier, with expansion continuing forever. This myth of unlimited growth is what underpins our current global economy: it must continue to grow to be healthy. We may think of this as abundance: we create abundance through continuing to expand, to search for more, to go faster. There are limits, however, because our planet cannot actually function in ways that support human life when it is depleted of resources, when species go extinct, and when the compounds in the air and water are not healthy for us. These natural limits let us know when we have arrived at "enough."

In the biblical tradition, the weekly Sabbath cycles, the years of rest, and Jubilee help to set boundaries for God's people. Rather than basing

---

18. Fellow author Jia Johnson describes in chapter 5 how she incorporated some of these values into her work environment to change its culture.

their personal and communal value on how much they have produced, a social system including Sabbath values people and other beings intrinsically, including a right to rest. Yes, more could be done on those days, but taking this day off reminds us individually and as a community that we do not actually need more. We have what we need, and we deserve to be able to enjoy our lives, our families and loved ones, and have a day to rest and be grateful. Sabbath provides needed boundaries for our well-being, our neighbors' well-being, and that land's well-being.

That said, I (Cherice) readily admit that it is incredibly difficult to just take a day off every week and not be productive. I personally bump up against what society expects of me: I feel I "should" be doing something useful, or I feel like I'm "wasting" time. Working for nonprofits and as an adjunct professor, I do not make a lot of money, so I do tend to need to work as much as possible to make ends meet—I can't afford to take a lot of time off to rest.

I suspect part of the barrier for me, and many others, is that practicing Sabbath will look different for different people. Rest will require different boundaries depending on who you are, what you love, and what brings you energy and joy. The parameters of when one can carve out time for rest will vary greatly, too, because of our different jobs and traditions. Sabbath should not be prescriptive or limited to certain rules. What does rest look like for you? What restores your energy and fills your cup? When can you carve out pauses for these things in your week? What habits can you cultivate that can help you protect the practices that help you pause and recognize the abundance you experience? We may not be able to completely dismantle the narratives of scarcity that shape our culture, but we can be more aware of when this fear-based mind-set is present. We can seek moments of Sabbath that help us reorient our lives to stories of real abundance, ones that value mutual flourishing.

RETURNING TO THE SOIL

I (Catalina) hope you hear the invitation on these pages to consider what these boundaries look like for you and your loved ones. As Cherice has pointed out, rest is a communal practice: you can become the first in your social group to begin to set this example. Humans are beings that do what we see more often than what we know is the right thing to do. Someone has to begin somewhere, then others will begin engaging in the now-radical practice of rest.

No one is immune to the harm that narratives of scarcity inflict on our lives and the lives of our neighbors. Sabbath, rest, recognizing there is enough and we are enough—this is holy and healing work. To practice rest and to create boundaries around this sacred need is the beginning of a journey that heals by helping us focus on trusting we will have enough, that we are enough on our own without having to earn our worth and value. This is essential in our faith communities. Seeking to foster healing is in the DNA of communities of faith. We see evidence of this in our sacred stories; the life, death, and resurrection of Jesus; and the God of creation who invites us into God's holy creative work. As we step into this healing journey, abundance begins to burst out like a new seed in fertile soil.

I (Catalina) have discovered that I am called to be a healer. This calling has allowed me a deeper clarity of our need to tend to our connectedness through relationships. When you decide to root yourself in fertile soil, you believe in the understanding that we need each other, not only to survive but to thrive. In the tree world, what's going on below the soil is deeply important to what happens above. The same is true of our human connections. It's the slow and steady work of relationship that keeps the trees—and us—alive for so long. Healthy forests embrace the day-to-day dangers together. They are actually a community and not just an individual, with not only trees but animals, insects, other plants, and fungal networks working together toward collective thriving. Unfortunately, many of us were planted in soil that was depleted and lacked care and life, told to survive as individuals rather than work together as communities. Yet even then many of us have done the work to replenish that same soil and have seen how seeking to root ourselves in relationship can change even the worst of circumstances.

Be curious about the dirt underneath your feet. Imagine the possibilities to create, to re-create, and to regenerate from what is already close to us, to revive the soil we are planted in. Let the questions, challenges, and ideas presented in this book take root, too. Be curious about the gifts and perspectives of others whose well-being is rooted in the same soil as you.

Away from Scarcity Toward True Abundance

Some of us have forgotten our generous connection to each other and the land, or were never taught what a relationship of care with others and creation could look like. We all experience hurt and grief, but this too is holy ground for healing. Tending this soil will require the investment of proper nutrients and care. It will require an intentional commitment for the long term. When soil is at its healthiest, it is a place where life can flourish. Healthy soil is the beginning of a web of life that withstands storms, droughts, and more. It is the beginning of many living organisms; it provides enough to allow for others to do the same.

It is our sincere hope that you and your community can find the big and small ways to cultivate the soil in your place, with the people, the plants, the critters, the microbes, and the rivers that are part of where you call home. We invite you to participate in abundance in the beautiful relationships all around you. Don't be afraid to make mistakes as you go, because there is also so much abundance in learning from them. Let this imagination of abundance be your guiding compass.

ACKNOWLEDGMENTS

Amanda mentions in the introduction that this book is the result of hundreds. She's not wrong. There is a long story with many chapters that ultimately brought forth the stories and chapters authored in this book. I'd like to offer a special thanks here to those who played crucial roles in the creation of this project. First and foremost, a special thank you to the twenty-two authors whose wisdom and stories are amplified on these pages. Thank you for the time, energy, and heart you contributed to help make this book possible and for your investment in the relationships of this special writing community that formed during its creation. To Lindsay Fertig-Johnson, thank you for sharing your gifts and for capturing the essence of this project, infusing it into images that speak to our hearts. To JD Mechelke, thank you for sharing the load of manuscript completion during a hectic summer and for your calm and kind reassurances along the way. And to our team of readers—Pr. Babette Chattman, Caleb Rollins, Rachel Farris, Pr. D. J. Chatelaine, and Ellen Weber—I am so appreciative for your insights, support, and encouragement.

To Amanda Vetsch, thank you for your reliability, your organizational skills, your creativity and for just being fun to partner with as you held together all the loose threads and big picture ideas to steward a project of this nature. To Rozella Haydée White and Jeremy Myers, you generously tended to our gathering of fifty young adults, facilitated a trustworthy space; your leadership not only gave birth to the themes for this book but provided a much-needed space of connection for all those who participated. Very importantly, to those participants from the No-

Acknowledgments

vember 2022 Envisioning Event at Augsburg—all fifty young adults and our keynote listeners—thank you, thank you, thank you! I hope you hear echoes of the stories, heartaches, and hopes you shared on these pages. And to the team at Eerdmans Publishing, thank you for the guidance, support, and stewardship you provided in developing our book project into a real book to share with the world.

I'd also like to acknowledge our Young Adult Initiative network, supported and funded through the Lilly Endowment. To the dozens of colleagues from seminaries, universities, and other nonprofit ministries across the country, thank you for the years of thoughtful conversation as we leaned into the complexities of our changing church, with a commitment to the well-being of the young adults in our networks and lives. Thank you for cheering on this book and (hopefully!) sharing it with your friends and ministry partners. A special thank you to Chanon Ross at the Lilly Endowment's Religion Department and to Kelly Minas, Wendy McCormick, and Sofia Cook at the Center for Congregations. All of you have been instrumental in fostering space for curiosity, learning, and connection for folks in the church who care about young adults. Thank you for the many resources—time, funds, conversations, connections—you all generously share.

And on a more personal note, I'd like to thank the folks who have been in my corner as I learned on the go about editing a book project with lots of moving parts. To my husband, Nick, who is my biggest fan and favorite human, thank you for all the support that made it possible for me to pore hours over these pages and get away to writing retreats and for tending to kids and life so I could get to work. And to my whole team at Augsburg—Ellen Weber, Amanda Vetsch, Geoffrey Gill, Brenna Zeimet, Jeremy Myers, and Gretchen Roeck—some of you have shared the responsibilities of this project with me (Ellen, Amanda, and Jeremy—heaps of thanks!), but you all have been incredible colleagues, offering to take on other work as this project demanded more time, checking in and cheering me on and reminding me to celebrate the accomplishments. Time to celebrate!

Kristina Frugé

CONTRIBUTORS

Shaya Aguilar was born and raised in Southern California. She has a BA in Psychology and Hispanic Studies and an MS in Ministry from Pepperdine University. Beyond the titles of friend, sister, and daughter, she has served as an assistant chaplain at Pepperdine and is currently working toward a PsyD in Clinical Psychology at Fuller Seminary. She is grateful to be able to study the intersection of theology and psychology and hopes to work as a clinician in the future. In her free time, she finds joy in exploring new hiking trails, cooking, and trying local coffee shops. She hopes to contribute to the dialogue that helps foster church communities that are known for being healing, hospitable and grace filled.

Rev. Talitha Amadea Aho is a Presbyterian pastor turned pediatric hospital chaplain, currently working at UCSF Benioff Children's Hospital in Oakland, California. Talitha is working to unplug her mind from the binary of natural/unnatural, to accept human responsibility for the caretaking of creation in a healthy way, and to laugh more. Her first book, *In Deep Waters: Spiritual Care for Young People in a Climate Crisis*, is about how we can take better care of one another in our climate grief, anger, despair, and confusion.

Catalina Morales Bahena is currently director of Learning for Faith in Action and resides in Minnesota. She is a proud DACA (Deferred Action for Childhood Arrivals) recipient and fierce advocate for immigration rights. Catalina conducted a TEDxUMN in 2018 about the struggles of undocumented immigrants called "Why We Need to Stop Talking About DACA & Start Talking About Immigrants." In 2019, she received the Immigrant of Distinction Award from American Immigration Lawyers Association for her work on Immigrant Sanctuary in Minnesota.

Dr. Cherice Bock (she/her) teaches, writes, and advocates at the intersection of religion and environment. Using her MDiv (Princeton Theological Seminary) and MS and PhD in environmental studies (Antioch University New England), Bock is adjunct professor of environmental studies at the University of Portland and works as climate policy manager at 350PDX. Her writing includes the book *Quakers, Ecology, & the Light* (Brill, 2023, with Christy Randazzo), articles and book chapters such as "Faith Communities as Hubs for Climate Resilience" (2022); "Watershed Discipleship," in *An Ecotopian Lexicon* (University of Minnesota Press, 2019); and "Scarcity vs. Abundance: Moving Beyond Dualism to 'Enough'" (2015). Bock lives with her family in Oregon on the land of the Kalapuya. Find her work at http://chericebock.com.

Rev. Madeline Burbank (she/her) brings experience as a Twin Cities artist, queer chaplain, and ordained pastor in the Evangelical Lutheran Church in America tradition. Madeline celebrates how God's divine love is reflected in ongoing cocreation and the diversity of human relationships. She believes everyone deserves pleasure, support, and art supplies. Her recent projects include visible mending and interfaith bridge building. As a trauma-informed educator, she emphasizes the importance of play, rituals, and embodied learning. As a white ministry organizer, Madeline highlights oppressed perspectives and intergenerational cooperation. Madeline's practice is shaped by crip theory, improv, antiracist advocacy, and the importance of art in mutual liberation. To recharge, Madeline enjoys tabletop role-playing games and lake-time with loved ones.

Lindsay Fertig-Johnson (she/her) is a Lutheran deaconess and candidate for ordination in the Evangelical Lutheran Church in America (ELCA). She serves as deputy director of the Festival Center, a hub for justice-driven organizations in Washington, DC, and is pursuing a Master of Divinity at Wartburg Theological Seminary. A published graphic artist and storyteller, Lindsay uses creativity as a spiritual practice and is committed to building inclusive spaces of healing and renewal for communities on the front lines of social change.

Kristina Frugé (she/her) has worked in ministry for twenty-five years and currently serves as the director of Congregational and Community Initiatives, where she leads the Riverside Innovation Hub at Augsburg University in Minneapolis, Minnesota. With an MA in Congregational Mission and Leadership from Luther Seminary, she has worked alongside dozens of congregations inviting them to be curious about their call to become vital neighbors in the ecosystem of their local neighborhoods. In all her work, she aims to animate the truth of our generous connection to one another, rooted in a belief that the Holy Spirit is activated in our relationships helping us to repair, problem-solve, love, and flourish. This includes her work as a mother, wife, friend, and neighbor in her South Minneapolis Longfellow neighborhood, where her family has lived for over twenty years.

Abby Grifno was born and raised in Austin, Texas, and now works as a high school English teacher. She loves to write about local culture and has work featured in *Bethesda Magazine*, the *Washington City Paper*, and more. As the daughter of an immigrant and living in a time of deep political turmoil, Abby has often thought critically about her role in the church and in the world. Ultimately, she believes that liberation is not a singular destination but a practice we can all take part in.

Kara Haug is an ASSECT Certified Sexuality Educator with a BA in Psychology from Hope College in Holland, Michigan, and has a master's in theological studies from Pacific Lutheran Theological Seminary in Berkeley, California, and a postgraduate certificate in Sexual Health Education and Counseling from the University of Michigan in Ann Arbor. As founder and partner of Reframing Our Stories, a sexuality health education business, her goal and passion is for people to have brave and caring conversations about their bodies, health and safety, and sexuality to enable self-awareness, growth, empathy, openness, and positive relationships. Kara is also an adjunct professor in Human Sexuality at Antioch University in Seattle. She lives in California with her husband and two kids.

Dr. Jimmy Hoke (they/he) researches and teaches about queer and trans folks in and around the Bible. They are the author of *Feminism, Queerness, Affect, and Romans: Under God*, which engages intersectional interpretive strategies to reread Paul's letter to the Romans. Dr. Hoke writes weekly commentaries for "Queering the Lectionary," an online project they created to help preachers and congregational leaders bring queer perspectives into worship spaces. Jimmy teaches courses in New Testament at United Theological Seminary of the Twin Cities and works with children and families at a Presbyterian congregation in St. Paul, where they are developing an LGBTQ-centered Sunday school curriculum for elementary-age learners. They are also a candidate for ordination in the Presbyterian Church (USA).

Sarah Brock Iverson is a physician assistant in Minnesota, where she has practiced in both Family Medicine and Obstetrics & Gynecology. She is passionate about patient education, women's health, and fostering habits that promote long-term health and wellness. Before becoming a PA, Sarah helped establish a high school science lab in Rwanda, cared for dementia patients in rural Minnesota, and was a storyteller for the Evangelical Lutheran Church in America Churchwide offices in Chicago. She enjoys running, cooking, traveling, and sailing on the Mississippi River with her husband, Andrew.

Jia Johnson is a mind-body coach, intuitive energy healer, shaman, creative educator, grief tender, and social justice entrepreneur. She is the founder and CEO of Freedom Dream Collective, LLC, a dynamic coaching and consulting firm dedicated to fostering the holistic well-being of mission-driven individuals, communities, and organizations. In recent years, she served as the founding director of the Solidarity Building Initiative for Liberative Carceral Education (SBI) at McCormick Theological Seminary, a higher-education-in-jail program. She served as an SBI adjunct, facilitating learning opportunities at the intersection of personal and social transformation at the Cook County Department of Corrections. Jia holds a master of arts in public ministry degree from Garrett-Evangelical Theological Seminary. She is a certified mind-body coach, shamanic Reiki practitioner, grief tender, and intuitive counselor and is training to be a meditation practitioner and *nusta paqo* (shaman) of the Apaz family lineage of the Qero Nation in Cusco, Peru.

Rev. Amber Kalina serves as a pastor of the Evangelical Lutheran Church in America in rural Minnesota. Even before ordination, Amber happily served in diverse ministry settings that provided space for play and creativity, such as Bible camp, campus ministries, a gap year program, and even a mission plant at a brewery. She loves encouraging members of the body of Christ to use their gifts and passions to serve God and neighbor. A Bible verse that guides her is "Keep alert, stand firm in your faith, be courageous, be strong. Let all that you do be done in love" (1 Cor. 16:13-14).

Rev. Dr. Eric H. F. Law is the founder of the Kaleidoscope Institute, which provides resources to equip leaders to create diverse and sustainable communities. He has been a consultant and trainer for over thirty-five years working with the Roman Catholic, Episcopal, United Methodist, Presbyterian, American Baptist, United Church of Christ, and Lutheran churches in the United States, Canada, Asia, Australia, and Europe. He served as the Congregation Development Missioner in the Anglican Diocese of New Westminster (1996-2000) and the Episcopal Diocese of Los Angeles (2001-2005). He is the author of over ten books, including *Fear Not: Living Grace and Truth in a Frightened World*, *Holy Currencies*, *The Wolf Shall Dwell with the Lamb*, and *Inclusion: Making Room for Grace*. He is an Episcopal priest, a composer of church music, a singer-songwriter, and a visual artist who uses arts to foster courageous introspections, gracious conversations, and transformative communities. Listen to his music at https://erichflaw.hearnow.com/ and see his art at https://www.interartions.com/.

Baird Linke is a pastor in the Evangelical Lutheran Church in America. He serves Our Savior's Lutheran Church in Bonner, Montana, and Lu-

Contributors

therans Restoring Creation. Baird's ministry centers on the promise of God's new creation revealed in worship, community, and the pursuit of justice and wholeness for the whole earth. He believes that young adults have a unique and essential perspective on what God is doing to offer the whole church.

JD Mechelke is a PhD student at Drew University in the division of Theological and Philosophical Studies in Religion and is adjunct faculty at Augsburg University in the Department of Religion and Philosophy. His research centers around political theology, temporality, and nomadic ecology in the Anthropocene. He holds an MA from Luther Seminary and a BA from Augsburg University. JD is a nomad in North America.

Dr. Jeremy Paul Myers currently serves as the Bernhard M. Christensen Professor of Religion and Vocation at Augsburg University, where he is also the executive director of the Christensen Center for Vocation. He is a rostered deacon in the Evangelical Lutheran Church in America. Myers researches and writes on a vocational understanding of young people and a public understanding of church. He resides in St. Paul, Minnesota.

Rev. Kristen Glass Perez is a college and university chaplain and has served at multiple institutions, including George Washington University, Northwestern University, Muhlenberg College, and Augustana College. Her direct experience is building and leading multireligious teams of chaplains and staff who work alongside students. Before working in college chaplaincy, Kristen was the founding director for Young Adult Ministry for the Churchwide Organization of the Evangelical Lutheran Church in America, the denomination in which she is also an ordained pastor, and a development editor for Augsburg Fortress Publishers. Kristen is a frequent keynote speaker, workshop leader, and author on themes related to college student success and economic hardship, vocation in the undergraduate experience, interreligious engagement, and young adult ministry.

Amar D. Peterman is an author and theologian working at the intersection of faith and public life. He holds an MDiv from Princeton Seminary, where he studied American religious history and public theology. He is also the founder of Scholarship for Religion and Society, LLC, a research and consulting firm working with some of the leading philanthropic and civic institutions, religious organizations, and faith leaders in America today. His first book, which focuses on the common good, faith formation, and love of neighbor, is forthcoming with Eerdmans.

Rev. Dr. Soong-Chan Rah is Robert Munger Professor of Evangelism and Church Renewal at Fuller Theological Seminary in Pasadena, California, and the author of *Prophetic Lament* (a commentary on the book of Lamentations from IVP Books, 2015); *The Next Evangelicalism* (IVP Books, 2009); *Many Colors* (Moody, 2010); and coauthor of *Return to Justice* (Brazos, 2016), *Forgive Us* (Zondervan, 2014), and *Unsettling Truths* (IVP Books, 2019). Soong-Chan received his BA in political science and history/sociology from Columbia University, his MDiv from Gordon-Conwell Theological Seminary, his ThM from Harvard University, his DMin from Gordon-Conwell Theological Seminary, and his ThD from Duke University. Rah is formerly the founding senior pastor of the Cambridge Community Fellowship Church (CCFC), a multiethnic, urban ministry-focused church committed to living out the values of racial reconciliation and social justice in the urban context.

Rev. Drew Stever currently serves as a pastor in Southern California and lives with his partner, three kids, and two dogs. In his free time, he is an amateur wood turner, bird watcher, and moseying enthusiast. When thinking about power, Rev. Drew looks to those who inspire him the most—drag queens, women and femmes, indigenous healers, and artists. When used correctly, power is the ability to imagine and create new, liberating worlds and inspire people to come along for the ride.

Nicholas Tangen is a writer, coach, and congregational organizer in Minneapolis, Minnesota. He is a graduate of United Theological Seminary and works as the assistant to the bishop for Faith and Neighboring at the Minneapolis Area Synod of the Evangelical Lutheran Church in America. His passion is writing and talking about Christian community, community engagement, and the common good. His work focuses on the life together, community development, spiritual practice, and the life of faith through a Lutheran theological lens.

Contributors

Amanda Vetsch calls Minneapolis, Minnesota, home. Amanda has helped build community through sharing her gifts of coaching, facilitating, and organizational leadership in a variety of contexts. This has included working on staff with the Riverside Innovation Hub, coaching high school volleyball athletes, serving with YAGM (Young Adults in Global Mission) in Rwanda, Africa, and in her current role where she organizes training and leadership development for folks in the energy industry. She studied the intersection of racism, antiracism, and the Evangelical Lutheran Church in America while completing an MA in justice and reconciliation at Luther Seminary. Amanda believes her life's purpose is to collaboratively sustain wholehearted and thriving communities.

Reesheda N. Graham Washington serves as the CEO and principal consultant of the Blackberry Collection. The Blackberry Collection comes alongside individuals, organizations, and companies, large and small, to realize the very best experiences personally and vocationally. As a twenty-year veteran educator and curriculum designer, Reesheda is a New Leaders-trained administrator who has led school leaders in their own professional development. Reesheda centers liberal arts and DEI practices in her development of leaders and strategy. Reesheda is one who finds great passion in ushering forth difficult conversations relationally and communally toward transformation for all, touching on subjects of equity, strategy, and development. In her spare time, Reesheda cooks, paints, writes, dabbles in world languages, and is a bit of a world traveler.

Kayla Zopfi (they/she) is a scholar of public church, is passionate about storytelling, and is always on the lookout for resurrection. Raised in a theologically conservative expression of Christianity, they joined the Evangelical Lutheran Church in America in college after experiencing a faith community rooted in Christ's commandment to love and serve your neighbor. Since then, Zopfi has immersed themself in Lutheran, ecumenical, and interfaith spaces, where they are vocationally called to help build and rebuild communities where all experience sufficiency, community, and love.

BIBLIOGRAPHY

Adams, David Wallace. *Education for Extinction: American Indians and the Boarding School Experience, 1875–1928*. University Press of Kansas, 1995.

Agamben, Giorgio. *The Time That Remains: A Commentary on the Letter to the Romans*. Translated by Patricia Dailey. Stanford University Press, 2005.

Ahmed, Sara. *The Promise of Happiness*. Duke University Press, 2014.

Albert, Simon, Javier X. Leon, Alistair R. Grinham, John A. Church, Badin R. Gibbes, and Colin D. Woodroffe. "Interactions Between Sea-Level Rise and Wave Exposure on Reef Island Dynamics in the Solomon Islands." *Environmental Research Letters* 11, no. 5 (May 6, 2016). DOI 10.1088/1748-9326/11/5/054011.

Anders, Charlie Jane. *Promises Stronger Than Darkness*. Tor, 2023.

Anderson, Bernhard. *Out of the Depths: The Psalms Speak for Us Today*. Westminster, 1983.

Anthropocene Working Group. *Newsletter of the Anthropocene Working Group 9*. December 2019.

———. "Working Group on the 'Anthropocene.'" Subcommission on Quaternary Stratigraphy. Accessed December 9, 2024. https://tinyurl.com/fh2tsu42.

Barreto, Eric D. "Acts of/and Imagination: The Bible and Community." In *Poetic Living: Theological Education, Culture, and Pastoral Ministry*, edited by Jacqueline E. Lapsley and Neal D. Presa, 9–13. Cascade, 2023.

———. *Exploring the Bible*. Fortress, 2016.

———. "Negotiating Difference: Theology and Ethnicity in the Acts of the Apostles." In *Soundings in Cultural Criticism: Perspectives and Methods*

in *Culture, Power, and Identity in the New Testament*, edited by Francisco Lozada Jr. and Greg Carey. Fortress, 2013.

Beal, Timothy. *When Time Is Short: Finding Our Way in the Anthropocene*. Beacon, 2022.

Beebe, Ralph K. *A Garden of the Lord: A History of Oregon Yearly Meeting of Friends Church*. Barclay, 1968.

———. *The Ralph and Wanda Pierson Beebe Family*. Self-published, 2015.

Bilgrami, Akeel. *Secularism, Identity, and Enchantment*. Harvard University Press, 2014.

Bolz-Weber, Nadia. *Pastrix: The Cranky Beautiful Faith of a Sinner & Saint*. Jericho Books, 2013.

Bonhoeffer, Dietrich. *Life Together*. Dietrich Bonhoeffer Works, vol. 5, edited by Gerhard Ludwig Müller, Albrecht Schönherr, and Geffrey B. Kelly, translated by Daniel W. Bloesch. Fortress, 2005.

Bowens, Lisa M. *African American Readings of Paul: Reception, Resistance, and Transformation*. Eerdmans, 2020.

Bowlby, John. *Attachment and Loss: Attachment*. Vol. 1. Basic Books, 1969.

Brewer, Judson. *Unwinding Anxiety: New Science Shows How to Break the Cycles of Worry and Fear to Heal Your Mind*. Avery, 2021.

Brockman, Terra. "A Church Returns Land to American Indians." *Christian Century* 137, no. 6 (March 11, 2020).

brown, adrienne maree. *Emergent Strategy: Shaping Change, Changing Worlds*. AK Press, 2017.

Brown, Brené. *Daring Greatly: How the Courage to Be Vulnerable Transforms the Way We Live, Love, Parent, and Lead*. Penguin Books, 2015.

Brueggemann, Walter. *Sabbath as Resistance: Saying No to the Culture of Now*. Rev. ed. Westminster John Knox, 2017.

Caputo, John D. *The Folly of God: A Theology of the Unconditional*. Polebridge, 2015.

———. *Hoping Against Hope: Confessions of a Postmodern Pilgrim*. Fortress, 2015.

Castillo, Elizabeth. "Elwha River Transformed 10 Years After Dam Removal." Oregon Public Broadcasting, August 2, 2022. https://tinyurl.com/yc38wcbs.

Cernero, J., B. D. Strawn, and A. D. Abernethy. "Embodied Grief and Primary Metaphor: Towards a New Paradigm for Integrative Bereavement Groups." *Journal of Psychology and Christianity* 36, no. 4 (Winter 2017): 325–33.

Cho, Alexander, Jasmina Byrne, and Zoë Pelter. "Digital Civic Engagement by Young People." UNICEF, February 2020. https://tinyurl.com/yc7sm5vj.

"The Costs of Correctional Mental Health." Array Behavioral Care. Accessed December 9, 2024. https://tinyurl.com/acecfrsj.

"COVID-19 Pandemic Triggers 25% Increase in Prevalence of Anxiety and Depression Worldwide." News release. World Health Organization, March 2, 2022. https://tinyurl.com/238npjwb.

Crenshaw, Kimberlé. "Demarginalizing the Intersection of Race and Sex: A Black Feminist Critique of Antidiscrimination Doctrine, Feminist Theory, and Antiracist Politics." *University of Chicago Legal Forum* 139 (1989): 139–67.

Damiani, Aaron. *Earth Filled with Heaven: Finding Life in Liturgy, Sacraments, and Other Ancient Practices of the Church*. Moody Publishers, 2022.

Dangendorf, Sönke, Noah Hendricks, Qiang Sun, John Klinck, Tal Ezer, Thomas Frederikse, Francisco M. Calafat, Thomas Wahl, and Torbjön E. Törnqvist. "Acceleration of U.S. Southeast and Gulf Coast Sea-Level Rise Amplified by Internal Climate Variability." *Nature Communications* 14, no. 1935 (April 10, 2023). https://doi.org/10.1038/s41467-023-37649-9.

Da Silva, Chantal, and Kurt Chirbas. "Southern Baptist Leaders Release Once-Secret List of Accused Abusers." *NBC News*, May 27, 2022. https://tinyurl.com/3s9wetzm.

Densmore, Frances. *Chippewa Customs*. Minnesota Historical Society Press, 1979.

Devine, Megan. *It's OK That You're Not OK: Meeting Grief and Loss in a Culture That Doesn't Understand*. Sounds True, 2017.

Dick, Timothy A. *The Vale Project, Research of Historic Reclamation Projects*. Bureau of Reclamation History Program, 1993.

Elmer, Jamie. "Understanding the Difference Between Mental Health and Mental Illness." *Healthline*, April 18, 2023. https://tinyurl.com/mp5mw23x.

Evangelical Lutheran Worship. Pew edition. Augsburg Fortress, 2006.

Feldstein, Lewis, and Robert Putnam. *Better Together: Restoring the American Community*. Simon & Schuster, 2003.

Frank, Adam. "Scientists Found Ripples in Space and Time. And You Have to Buy Groceries." *Atlantic*, June 29, 2023. https://tinyurl.com/yemjkftz.

Gafney, Wilda C. *Womanist Midrash: A Reintroduction to the Women of the Torah and the Throne*. E-book ed. Westminster John Knox, 2017.

Gibson, Ruby. *My Body, My Earth: The Practice of Somatic Archaeology*. iUniverse, 2008.

Gillihan, Seth. *Mindful Cognitive Behavioral Therapy: A Simple Path to Healing, Hope, and Peace*. HarperOne, 2022.

Gilroy, Paul. *The Black Atlantic: Modernity and Double Consciousness*. Verso, 1993.

Goldberg, Emma. "Teens in Covid Isolation: 'I Felt like I Was Suffocating.'" *New York Times*, November 12, 2020, updated October 5, 2021. https://tinyurl.com/yt5m76bt.

González, Justo. *Mañana: Christian Theology from a Hispanic Perspective*. Abingdon, 1990.

Goodwin, Megan, and Ilyse Morgenstein Fuerst. "What Does It Mean to Be 'Religious'?" *Keeping It 101: A Killjoy's Guide to Religion Podcast*. Episode 105, March 10, 2020. https://tinyurl.com/mvu8ucua.

Gorman, Amanda. *The Hill We Climb: An Inaugural Poem for the Country*. Viking, 2021.

"Gov. Justice: President Biden Must Tap into West Virginia's Rich Natural Resources to Make America Energy Independent Again." Press release. Office of the Governor, Jim Justice, March 11, 2022. https://tinyurl.com/ctj9pacr.

Grable, Juliet. "Scientists Are Tracking Ecological Changes as the Klamath River Dams Come Down." *High Country News*, May 1, 2024. https://tinyurl.com/mwa6vps8.

Graeber, David. *The Utopia of Rules: On Technology, Stupidity, and the Secret Joys of Bureaucracy*. Melville House, 2016.

Gramlich, John. "Young Americans Are Less Trusting of Other People—and Key Institutions—Than Their Elders." Pew Research Center, August 6, 2019. https://tinyurl.com/yf6e6ey8.

Gregory of Nyssa. *The Life of Moses*. Translation, introduction, and notes by Abraham J. Malherbe and Everett Ferguson. Paulist, 1978.

"The Gulf of Mexico Is Getting Warmer." NOAA, February 1, 2023. https://tinyurl.com/yeywphvc.

Hamilton, Clive. "Human Destiny in the Anthropocene." In *The Anthropocene and the Global Environmental Crisis: Rethinking Modernity in a New*

Epoch, edited by Clive Hamilton, Christophe Bonneuil, and François Gemenne. Routledge, 2015.

Hefner, Philip. "The Human Story: Created to Be a Creator." Lutheran Alliance for Faith, Science and Technology, December 16, 2013. https://tinyurl.com/78mb63d9.

Henry, Andre. "Why Therapy Isn't Enough, I Need a Revolution." *Medium*, June 14, 2023. https://tinyurl.com/yf5zyns6.

Henry, Gordon, Jr. "How Soon." In *The Failure of Certain Charms: And Other Disparate Signs of Life*. Salt Publishing, 2008.

Hersey, Tricia. *Rest Is Resistance: A Manifesto*. Little, Brown, 2022.

Hoegh-Guldberg, Ove, Daniela Jacob, and Michael Taylor. "Impacts of 1.5°C Global Warming on Natural and Human Systems." In *Global Warming of 1.5°C. An IPCC Special Report on the Impacts of Global Warming of 1.5°C Above Pre-industrial Levels and Related Global Greenhouse Gas Emission Pathways, in the Context of Strengthening the Global Response to the Threat of Climate Change, Sustainable Development, and Efforts to Eradicate Poverty*, edited by V. Masson-Delmotte, P. Zhai, H.-O. Pörtner, D. Roberts, J. Skea, P. R. Shukla, A. Pirani, W. Moufouma-Okia, C. Péan, R. Pidcock, S. Connors, J. B. R. Matthews, Y. Chen, X. Zhou, M. I. Gomis, E. Lonnoy, T. Maycock, M. Tignor, and T. Waterfield, 175–312. Cambridge University Press, 2018.

Hoke, Jimmy. *Feminism, Queerness, Affect, and Romans: Under God?* SBL Press, 2021.

hooks, bell. *Salvation: Black People and Love*. William Morrow, 2001.

Hope, Elan C. "Rethinking Civic Engagement: How Young Adults Participate in Politics and the Community." Brennan Center for Justice at New York University School of Law, February 16, 2022. https://tinyurl.com/5x75bejd.

Howard, Lisa. "Uncovering the Hidden Life of Soil: Microbes in Soil Are Essential for Life and May Help Mitigate Climate Change." *UC Davis News*, March 2, 2017. https://tinyurl.com/3fsyhz94.

"How to Manage Trauma." National Council for Behavioral Health. Accessed December 9, 2024. https://tinyurl.com/3dkd3wsx.

Hözel, Britta K., James Carmody, Mark Vangel, Christina Congleton, Sita M. Yerramsetti, Tim Gard, and Sara W. Lazar. "Mindfulness Practice Leads to Increases in Regional Brain Gray Matter Density." *Psychiatry*

Research: Neuroimaging 191, no. 1 (January 2011): 36–43. https://doi.org/10.1016/j.pscychresns.2010.08.006.

Hummel, Daniel G. *The Rise and Fall of Dispensationalism: How the Evangelical Battle over the End Times Shaped a Nation.* Eerdmans, 2023.

"Hurricane Ian's Path of Destruction." NOAA, October 4, 2022. https://tinyurl.com/mrfpjjch.

"If All of Earth's Ice Melts and Flows into the Ocean, What Would Happen to the Planet's Rotation?" NASA. Accessed December 9, 2024. https://tinyurl.com/626fec5e.

Isasi-Díaz, Ada María. *En la Lucha / In the Struggle: Elaborating a Mujerista Theology.* Tenth anniversary ed. Fortress, 2004.

Jemisin, N. K. "The Ones Who Stay and Fight." In *How Long 'til Black Future Month?* Little, Brown, 2018.

Jennings, Willie James. *The Christian Imagination: Theology and the Origins of Race.* Yale University Press, 2010.

Kaemingk, Matthew, and Cory B. Willson. *Work and Worship: Reconnecting Our Labor and Liturgy.* Baker Academic, 2020.

Keller, Catherine. *Cloud of the Impossible: Negative Theology and Planetary Entanglement.* Columbia University Press, 2015.

———. *Facing Apocalypse: Climate, Democracy, and Other Last Chances.* Orbis Books, 2021.

———. *Political Theology of the Earth: Our Planetary Emergency and the Struggle for a New Public.* Columbia University Press, 2018.

Kendi, Ibram X. *Stamped from the Beginning: The Definitive History of Racist Ideas in America.* Nation Books, 2016.

Kimmerer, Robin Wall. *Braiding Sweetgrass: Indigenous Wisdom, Scientific Knowledge, and the Teachings of Plants.* Milkweed, 2013.

Kotsko, Adam. *Neoliberalism's Demons: On the Political Theology of Late Capital.* Stanford University Press, 2018.

Latuor, Bruno. *Down to Earth: Politics in the New Climatic Regime.* Translated by Catherine Porter. Polity, 2018.

Law, Eric H. F. *Fear Not: Living Grace and Truth in a Frightened World.* Chalice, 2019.

Lee, Daniel D. *Doing Asian American Theology: A Contextual Framework for Faith and Practice.* InterVarsity Press, 2022.

Bibliography

Levine, Amy-Jill, and Marc Zvi Brettler. *The Jewish Annotated New Testament*. 2nd ed. Oxford University Press, 2017.

Lorde, Audre. *Sister Outsider: Essays and Speeches*. Crossing Press, 1984.

MacIntyre, Alasdair. *After Virtue: A Study in Moral Theory*. Bloomsbury, 2011.

Marsh, Charles. *Evangelical Anxiety: A Memoir*. HarperOne, 2022.

McCabe, Marilyn. *The Paradox of Loss: Toward a Relational Theory of Grief*. Greenwood, 2003.

Meadows, Donella H., and Diana Wright. *Thinking in Systems: A Primer*. Chelsea Green, 2008.

Menakem, Resmaa. *My Grandmother's Hands: Racialized Trauma and the Pathway to Mending Our Hearts and Bodies*. Central Recovery, 2017.

"Mental Health Has Bigger Challenges Than Stigma." Sapien Labs, 2021. https://tinyurl.com/2388hfjj.

Meraji, Shereen Marisol, Natalie Escobar, and Kumari Devarajan. "Is It Time to Say R. I. P. to 'POC'?" *NPR*, September 30, 2020. https://tinyurl.com/4tbr3hpp.

Mignolo, Walter. "Interview—Walter Mignolo/Part 2: Key Concepts." Interviewed by Alvina Hoffmann. *E-International Relations*, January 21, 2017.

"Millennials' Diverse Political Views: A Typology of the Rising Generation." Center for Information & Research on Civic Learning & Engagement, March 2018. https://tinyurl.com/vm7sr6p2.

Moltmann, Jürgen. *Experiences of God*. Translated by Margaret Kohl. Fortress, 1980.

Muñoz, José Esteban. *Cruising Utopia: The Then and There of Queer Futurity*. New York University Press, 2009.

Myers, Jeremy. "The Vocation of the Local Congregation as Public Companion." In *Forming Leaders for the Public Church: Vocation in Twenty-First Century Societies*, edited by Samuel Yonas Deressa and Mary Sue Dreier. Lexington Books; Fortress Academic, 2023.

Neihardt, John G. *Black Elk Speaks*. Bison Books; University of Nebraska Press, 2014.

Newland, Bryan. "Federal Indian Boarding School Initiative Investigative Report." United States Department of the Interior, May 2022. https://tinyurl.com/3zhcbkds.

"(1977) The Combahee River Collective Statement." Black Past. Accessed December 9, 2024. https://tinyurl.com/2672ea9d.

Bibliography

Noisecat, Julian Brave. "How Indigenous Peoples Are Fighting the Apocalypse." *Emergence Magazine*, November 23, 2021.

Oakes, Caroline. *Practice the Pause: Jesus' Contemplative Practice, New Brain Science, and What It Means to Be Fully Human*. Broadleaf Books, 2023.

Osborne, Margaret. "Drying Great Salt Lake Could Expose Millions to Toxic Arsenic-Laced Dust." *Smithsonian Magazine*, January 13, 2023. https://tinyurl.com/3cakkkfc.

Osorio, Emma Kauana, and Emily Hyde. "The Rise of Anxiety and Depression Among Young Adults in the United States." *Ballard Brief*, Winter 2021. https://tinyurl.com/mr3meau3.

"Our Epidemic of Loneliness and Isolation." U.S. Surgeon General's Advisory on the Healing Effects of Social Connection and Community, 2023. https://tinyurl.com/46j626r3.

"Over One Billion People at Threat of Being Displaced by 2050 Due to Environmental Change, Conflict and Civil Unrest." Press release. Institute for Economics & Peace, September 9, 2020. https://tinyurl.com/56a89s7k.

Paintner, Christine Valters. *Breath Prayer: An Ancient Practice for the Everyday Sacred*. Broadleaf Books, 2021.

Palmer, Paula. "The Quaker Indian Boarding Schools: Facing Our History and Ourselves." In *Quakers and Native Americans*, edited by Ignacio Gallup-Diaz and Geoffrey Plank, European Expansion and Indigenous Response, vol. 30. Brill, 2019.

Pemberton, Glenn. *Hurting with God: Learning the Language of Lament*. Abilene Christian University Press, 2012.

Perez, Kristen Glass, and Pamala Silas. "Land Acknowledgement and Invocation." Northwestern University Commencement, June 13, 2022.

Peterman, Amar D. "Adoption Is Sacramental." *Sojourners*, May 11, 2023.

———. "Navigating a White Evangelical World in This Brown, Indian Body." *Sojourners*, June 16, 2021.

Peters, Zachary J., Loredana Santo, Danielle Davis, and Carol J. DeFrances. "Emergency Department Visits Related to Mental Health Disorders Among Adults, by Race and Hispanic Ethnicity: United States, 2018–2020." National Health Statistics Reports, no. 181, March 1, 2023. https://tinyurl.com/tjyarz3p.

Phillips, Anita. "Barna: The State of the Church." Barna Group, May 7, 2021.

"Postcards from a World on Fire." Editorial, *New York Times*, December 13, 2021.

Pui-lan, Kwok. *Postcolonial Imagination and Feminist Theology*. Westminster John Knox, 2005.

Rah, Soong-Chan. *The Next Evangelicalism: Freeing the Church from Western Cultural Captivity*. InterVarsity Press, 2009.

———. *Prophetic Lament: A Call for Justice in Troubled Times*. IVP Books, 2015.

Rainer, Thom S. *Autopsy of a Deceased Church: 12 Ways to Keep Yours Alive*. B&H, 2014.

Rendle, Gil. *Quietly Courageous: Leading the Church in a Changing World*. Rowman & Littlefield, 2019.

Rodkey, Christopher D., and Jordan E. Miller, eds. *The Palgrave Handbook of Radical Theology*. Palgrave Macmillan, 2018.

Rum Ku, Eliana Ah. "A Call for Practicing Hospitality Based on Lament in Preaching for a Wounded Community." *Journal of the Academy of Homiletics* 42, no. 2 (2022): 15–26.

Russell, Letty M. *Church in the Round: Feminist Interpretation of the Church*. Westminster John Knox, 1993.

Said, Edward W. *Orientalism*. Pantheon Books, 1978.

Schmitt, Carl. *Political Theology: Four Chapters on the Concept of Sovereignty*. Translated and introduced by George Schwab. University of Chicago Press, 1985.

Schüssler Fiorenza, Elisabeth. *The Power of the Word: Scripture and the Rhetoric of Empire*. Fortress, 2007.

———. *Rhetoric and Ethic: The Politics of Biblical Interpretation*. Fortress, 1994.

———. *Wisdom Ways: Introducing Feminist Biblical Interpretation*. Westminster John Knox, 2001.

Segovia, Gernando. *The Farewell of the Word: The Johannine Call to Abide*. Fortress, 1991.

"The Seven Generation River: Great Lakes Now." PBS Learning Media. Accessed December 9, 2024. https://tinyurl.com/5n82hm78.

Share, Jeff, Tessa Jolls, and Elizabeth Thoman. *Five Key Questions That Can Change the World*. Center for Media Literacy, 2007.

"Six Reasons Young Christians Leave Church." Barna, September 27, 2011. https://tinyurl.com/26r36d3k.

Slade, Darren M., Adrianna Smell, Elizabeth Wilson, and Rebekah Drumsta. "Percentage of U.S. Adults Suffering from Religious Trauma: A Sociological Study." *Socio-Historical Examination of Religion and Ministry* 5, no. 1 (2023): 1–28.

Smith, James K. A. *How to Inhabit Time: Understanding the Past, Facing the Future, Living Faithfully Now.* Brazos, 2022.

Smith, Mitzi J. *Womanist Sass and Back Talk: Social (In)Justice, Intersectionality, and Biblical Interpretation.* Cascade, 2018.

Smith, Mitzi J., and Yung Suk Kim. *Toward Decentering the New Testament: A Reintroduction.* Cascade, 2018.

Snorton, C. Riley. *Black on Both Sides: A Racial History of Trans Identity.* University of Minnesota Press, 2017.

Taylor, Charles. *A Secular Age.* Harvard University Press, 2018.

Thurman, Howard. *Footprints of a Dream: The Story of the Church for the Fellowship of All Peoples.* Wipf & Stock, 1959, 2009.

Tippett, Krista. "Three Callings for Your Life and for Our Time." Middlebury College Commencement Address, May 26, 2019. https://tinyurl.com/5rfvp3xy.

Tran, Jonathan. *Asian Americans and the Spirit of Racial Capitalism.* Oxford University Press, 2021.

———. "Linguistic Theology: Completing Postliberalism's Linguistic Task." *Modern Theology* 33, no. 1 (January 2017): 47–68.

Tsing, Anna Lowenhaupt. *The Mushroom at the End of the World: On the Possibility of Life in Capitalist Ruins.* Princeton University Press, 2015.

Tyson, Alec, Brian Kennedy, and Cary Funk. "Gen Z, Millennials Stand Out for Climate Change Activism, Social Media Engagement with Issue." Pew Research Center, May 26, 2021. https://tinyurl.com/34vnm75b.

Vince, Gaia. "How to Survive the Coming Century." *New Scientist*, February 25, 2009.

Volf, Miroslav, and Matthew Croasmun. *For the Life of the World: Theology That Makes a Difference.* Baker Books, 2019.

Wallace-Wells, David. *The Uninhabitable Earth: Life After Warming.* Random House, 2019.

Walton, Kate. "Mass Evacuation as Catastrophic Bushfires Worsen in Australia." *Al Jazeera*, January 4, 2020. https://tinyurl.com/yvkswdb7.

Weissbourd, Richard, Milena Batanova, Virginia Lovison, and Eric Torres. "Loneliness in America: How the Pandemic Has Deepened an Epidemic of Loneliness and What We Can Do About It." Making Caring Common

Project, Harvard Graduate School of Education, February, 2021. https://tinyurl.com/yjum6u9s.

Wendel, Alex R. "Trauma-Informed Theology or Theologically Informed Trauma? Traumatic Experiences and Theological Method." *Journal of Reformed Theology* 16, no. 1-2 (April 8, 2022): 3-26.

Westermann, Claus. *Praise and Lament in the Psalms*. John Knox, 1981.

Whitehead, Andrew. *American Idolatry: How Christian Nationalism Betrays the Gospel and Threatens the Church*. Brazos, 2023.

Whitehead, Joshua, ed. *Love After the End: An Anthology of Two-Spirit and Indigiqueer Speculative Fiction*. Arsenal Pulp, 2020.

"Why Remove the Four Lower Snake River Dams?" Save Our Wild Salmon. Accessed December 9, 2024. https://tinyurl.com/22zws32w.

Wingren, Gustaf. *Luther on Vocation*. Wipf & Stock, 2004.

Wirzba, Norman. *This Sacred Life: Humanity's Place in a Wounded World*. Cambridge University Press, 2019.

Wohlleben, Peter. *The Hidden Life of Trees: What They Feel, How They Communicate—Discoveries from a Secret World*. Translated by Jane Billinghurst. Greystone Books, 2016.

Yusoff, Kathryn. *A Billion Black Anthropocenes or None*. University of Minnesota Press, 2018.

Zizioulas, John. *Being as Communion*. St. Vladimir's Seminary Press, 1985.